JAPAN UNESCORTED

JAPAN UNESCORTED

James K. Weatherly

KODANSHA INTERNATIONAL
in cooperation with
JAPAN AIRLINES CO., LTD.

All maps except Shinjuku, Matsuyama, and the subway map
on pp. 214-215 by Business Information Corporation.
Maps of Shinjuku and Matsuyama by T. Sato.
Subway map by M. Hiraoka.
Jacket illustrations by A. Odagiri.
Sketches by H. Doki.

Distributed in the United States by Kodansha International/
USA Ltd., 114 Fifth Avenue, New York, New York 10011. Published by Kodansha International Ltd., 17-14, Otowa
1-chome, Bunkyo-ku, Tokyo 112 and Kodansha Internation-
al/USA Ltd., 114 Fifth Avenue, New York, New York 10011 in
cooperation with Japan Airlines Co., Ltd., Tokyo Bldg., 7-3,
Marunouchi 2-chome, Chiyoda-ku, Tokyo 100. Copyright ©
1990 by Japan Airlines. All rights reserved. Printed in Japan.

First edition, 1986
Second edition, 1990

Library of Congress Cataloging-in-Publication Data

Weatherly, James K.
Japan unescorted/James K. Weatherly—1st rev. ed
p.   cm.
1. Japan-Description and travel—1945—
Guide-books.   1. Title
DS805.2.W43   1990   915.204'48-dc 20 89-77630
ISBN 0-87011-987-7 (U.S. pbk.)
ISBN 4-7700-1487-2 (Japan)

CONTENTS

WHY THIS BOOK?

The visitor to Japan has traditionally been coddled by Japanese tour operators from the moment he/she sets foot on Japanese soil until his/her departure. These operators are still there, of course, and as willing to coddle as ever. But such coddling is expensive anywhere in the world, and generally more so in Japan. For that reason the members of the Japanese travel industry—hotels, restaurants, sightseeing tour companies—who have catered to the Japanese traveler on a tight budget for many years have begun to realize that more and more foreign sojourners would rather travel the way the Japanese do and are starting to throw open their doors to visitors from abroad.

Companies like Japan Airlines (JAL) that are more closely in touch with foreign travelers have helped get the doors ajar. All that's necessary to widen the crack is for the visitor to put his big foot in. For the Japanese travel industry, the attitude toward the individual traveler from overseas is "Wait and see."

The industry's eyes are on you, dear vagabond on your own. This book was designed to help you get your foot in the door and to know how to conduct yourself once inside. No attempt was made to cover every nook and cranny of the country. Some of the weightier volumes in the Helpful Reading section are more comprehensive. Rather, *Japan Unescorted* was designed to put you on the track to locations where you'll gain an understanding of Japanese life as it was—and is.

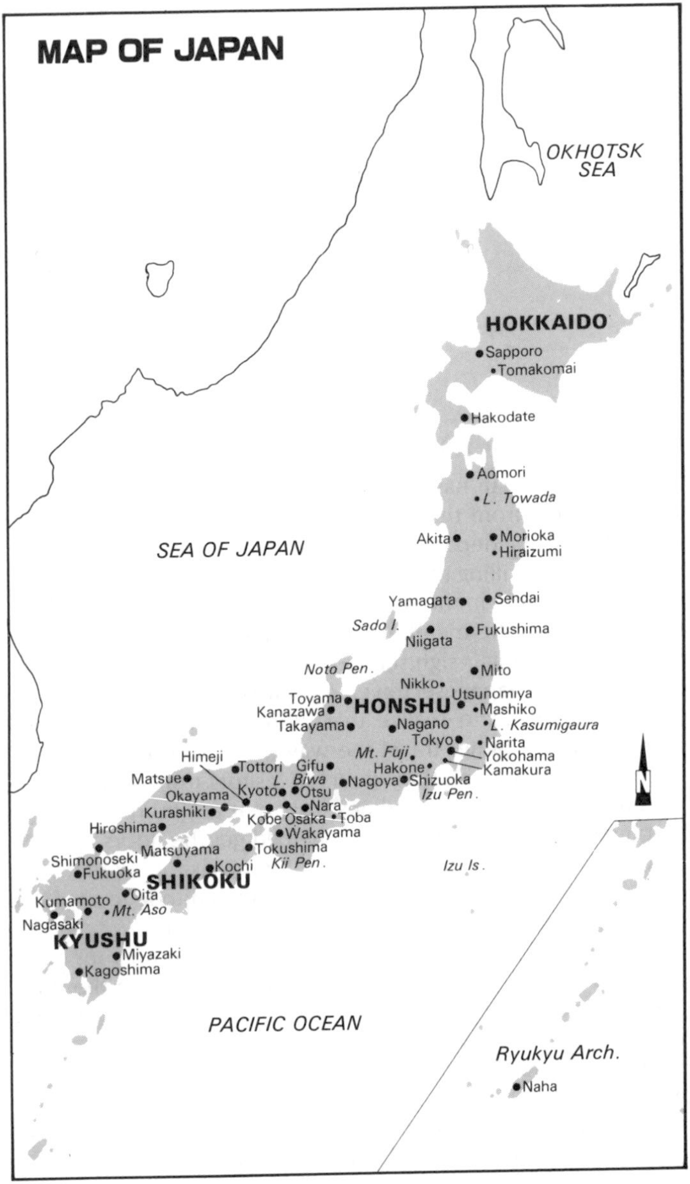

MAP OF JAPAN

OKHOTSK SEA

HOKKAIDO

• Sapporo
• Tomakomai

• Hakodate

• Aomori
• *L. Towada*

SEA OF JAPAN

Akita • • Morioka
• Hiraizumi

Yamagata • • Sendai

Sado I.

• Fukushima
Niigata

• Mito

Noto Pen.

Nikko • Utsunomiya

Toyama • Mashiko
Kanazawa • **HONSHU** • *L. Kasumigaura*
Takayama • Nagano •

Tokyo • • Narita
Mt. Fuji • • Yokohama
Himeji • Tottori • Gifu • Hakone • Kamakura
Matsue • Kyoto • Nagoya • Shizuoka
Okayama • *L. Biwa* • Otsu *Izu Pen.*
Kurashiki • Nara
Kobe Osaka • Toba
Hiroshima • • Wakayama

Shimonoseki • Matsuyama • Tokushima
Fukuoka • Kochi • *Kii Pen.* *Izu Is.*
SHIKOKU
Kumamoto • Oita
Nagasaki • *Mt. Aso*
KYUSHU
• Miyazaki
• Kagoshima

PACIFIC OCEAN

N

Ryukyu Arch.

• Naha

WHAT YOU'RE UP AGAINST

The paradox for the person on his/her own in Nippon is that while there is no country in Asia or perhaps the world whose remote areas are more accessible by public transportation, perhaps no country is more difficult to travel in without a guide. The problem is primarily the language barrier and a general lack of experience among Japanese with other peoples.

Another paradox: If Japanese today study English for an average of six years, why can't more people speak it? It's a question the Ministry of Education is asking, too. But the problem is far from being solved. For starters, the Japanese language—except for the great number of English words which are used today though pronounced with Japanese phonetic sounds—is in no way like English. It grew out of the needs of a very homogeneous people packed together for many centuries on a group of islands far from the rest of the world. Living so close together, the Japanese created a language that, above all else, was designed to promote harmonious relations between people.

Honorifics abound, and an indication of a man's good breeding is the ability to hide his true feelings for the sake of making the other party feel good. One party strokes with a few carefully chosen words, and the other party strokes right back.

The true meaning of what has been said, however, is often not clear. Did he mean that? Or that? You can only really know by playing the same kind of word games from an early age, which is an opportunity few foreigners have.

And still another paradox: In this world full of Sonys, Nissans, and Toyotas where the Japanese have seemingly sold something to even the African Bushman, why don't they feel more comfortable with foreigners?

9

The answer perhaps is because their experience with non-Japanese has largely been on a business level only. This is not the same as swapping stories about the office idiot, the great weekend they had with the family in the country, or their favorite baseball team.

More and more Japanese are traveling abroad and a greater number than ever are being posted to New York or Düsseldorf or Bangkok on overseas assignments. Their experiences with foreigners are beginning to penetrate the Japanese population at large, but, alas, only slowly.

Deeply ingrained in the Japanese psyche is the notion that they are very different from any other people in the world. Traditionally a division has always been made between what's "ours" and what's "theirs." Japanese things are separated from Western things in the department stores. Rarely does a restaurant serving Western food also serve Japanese food.

Among today's Japanese the dichotomy between East and West is less and less clear-cut. They may have dinner in a French restaurant, see a Japanese translation of Shakespeare's *Romeo and Juliet* on stage, then go home and spread out their *futon* sleeping mattress on the *tatami* mat floor. If all this seems a little incongruous to us, it doesn't strike the Japanese that way.

Flirting with Western food and fashion is one thing, but coming face-to-face with a real, live foreigner or, worse, having to say something in comprehensible English is something else entirely.

The Japanese call it *gaijin shokku*, or outsider shock, and the reaction can range from embarrassed giggles to hysterics. Fortunately, the former is far more common. In Tokyo, Kyoto, and Osaka, where foreigners are not quite such an unusual sight, there is general indifference or, at the most, a restrained curiosity. Deep in the country you may be followed for what seems like hours by wide-eyed kids. Be understanding. If a Japanese suddenly showed up on the streets of Possumtrot, Arkansas, the locals would stare too.

By no means should this speechless awe of you be taken as disrespect. The average Japanese has envied the West's technological ability from the time it was introduced. The admiration has extended to the people who created that technology as well. Having now leapt into the sphere of the superpowers, Japan is less in awe. But the memories linger.

The problem remains that few Japanese have had any real experience with a foreigner over an extended period of time. The traveler on his own in Japan can't change this situation overnight. But it's a step in the right direction.

HOW TO COPE

If you're traveling alone in Japan, the easiest way to surmount the language problem and the general Japanese inexperience with Westerners is to get yourself a Japanese friend who can speak English. Since that could take almost as much time as learning the language, however, more practical advice is in order.

The JAL Japanese Jet Age Language Course, a set containing a cassette tape and companion phrase cards, is available in North America for US$12 from the JAL Literature Distribution Center, P.O. Box 7712, Woodside, NY 11377. English–Japanese phrase books also offer some help, provided the user can simulate Japanese pronunciation, which is not difficult. JAL's *Speak a Little Japanese* is available from their overseas sales offices, or in Japan you can pick up one of several other phrase books at English-language bookstores in major cities.

In most situations you'll have to rely on English to get you through, however. Here, a few hints are in order. Speak slowly, using the simplest vocabulary possible. Don't use slang or colloquialisms. Since Japanese words often end in vowel sounds, English words that end in a consonant are frequently given a vowel, usually "o" or "u," at the end.

The word "beer," for example, becomes "*biiru*" in Japanese pronunciation. The letter "l" sounds like "r" to Japanese, so any word with the letter "l" in it will be pronounced with a slight "r" sound. Hotel thus becomes "*hoteru*."

Should the spoken word prove absolutely impossible, write

out your question. Japanese generally understand written English far better than spoken, because it is the written that is emphasized in school.

If you find yourself in some desperate situation outside Tokyo and Kyoto, you can take advantage of the Japan National Tourist Organization's (JNTO) "Travel-Phone" service. Just insert a ten-yen coin in any yellow, blue, or green public telephone and dial 0120-22-2800 for answers to questions on eastern Japan, and 0120-44-4800 for western Japan. You will be connected toll-free to a center in Tokyo or Kyoto where an English-speaking staff will be on hand to help you. The ten-yen coin will be returned on completion of the call. This service is available daily during regular office hours. In Tokyo or Kyoto, dial TIC's local number as listed under these cities' headings in this book.

Depending on your personality, coping with being constantly stared at can make you either the worst introvert in the world or a raving exhibitionist. Your presence alone can sometimes stop traffic, so it goes without saying that you should act with some decorum in public places.

You'll see plenty of loud and boisterous Japanese, especially in the entertainment districts and train stations of the big cities after an evening of bar-hopping. But as is true in practically any country in the world, the foreigner out on the town had better not act that way. Loud talking and laughing, particularly by foreign women, jangles the tight corners of the land like shattering glass.

Exercise patience, even in situations which aggravate you to the point of shouting. Screaming by foreigners will bring a hush over a negotiation with Japanese faster than almost anything. And it will get the foreigner nowhere. For the Japanese, keeping a harmonious front is far more important than standing up for the principle of the matter.

Dress neatly. The Japanese, of course, don't expect you to be wearing the same styles they do. In fact, they rather enjoy eyeballing what you have on, because it's not what they are used to seeing. But they do abhor dirt.

The secret to avoiding the feeling of being a minority is one of attitude. Face it. Hiding is impossible. So just relax and enjoy being the most exciting thing in sight since Marilyn Monroe—or Frankenstein. Allow a little extra time when trying anything for the first time. You'll need it, while the Japanese you encounter recuperate from seeing you.

Is a little cross-cultural communication worth all this commotion? Definitely yes. As the cultural barriers begin to crumble, you'll discover that the Japanese sensitivity toward others can also take a foreigner into its scope. Express a genuine concern for the Japanese you meet, and you'll be richly rewarded.

JAPAN NOW

For most Westerners, the lure of Japan began with some outdated travel posters of young girls in kimono gazing at Mt. Fuji. The fear of the educated Westerner is that neither the kimono— nor Mt. Fuji—is visible anymore. Fear not. Both are still very much on the scene, though the kimono-wearer today is usually a grandma, and Mt. Fuji's visibility from the Tokyo metropolis depends, as it always has, on the weather (more often visible from October through February).

13

Perhaps the most interesting thing about the Japan experience for the foreigner, though, is to observe a society that has moved so rapidly into the twentieth century, and at the same time been able to hang on to its traditional values. Sincerity, honesty, dedication to hard work, a constant striving for doing even the tiniest job well, a willingness to sacrifice individual will for the good of the community—these are the basic beliefs that have kept and to a large extent are still keeping Japanese society together. It's the American Protestant work ethic, without the religious overtones. And in a land where less than 1 percent are Christians!

One of the joys of traveling in Japan is seeing these common beliefs being put into practice. Whether it's the little old lady or man who cleans the public toilet, or the president of the giant trading company—whatever the task at hand, it's done with the enthusiasm of a zealot. Probe deeper, however, and you'll discover few Japanese sit down and analyze exactly why or in what direction they are running. They have so far been spared the American pastime of self-analysis. When a decision must be made as to whether they will do what they really want to do, or do what their family, company, or the society at large expects, it's the group and not the individual that usually wins.

Little signs are apparent everywhere among young people that the perennial self-sacrifice is now being questioned. Privately the young generation will frankly admit that they'd like a life of their own outside the group. Young couples now generally live separately from their parents. More young men are forsaking the company of their male colleagues in the office after working hours to be with their wives and children. A few dream of "dropping out" of the proverbial rat race to raise vegetables in the country. There are even a few willing to forsake their homeland altogether for space and more freedom to "do their own thing" in another land.

14

Attachment to family holds strong, and this will not quickly change, given the potent symbiosis between mother and child. A Japanese mother is expected by her husband, the family, and society to completely devote herself to the little darlings, regardless of her natural inclinations. Even the least observant visitor can't help but notice how Japanese mothers, and often fathers as well, cluck and coo over everything a child does. The dependence created by that kind of smothering relationship is never completely broken.

For the Western visitor all this togetherness is astounding, a harking back to simpler times in our own societies when a sense of community was still a strong force. You'll be asking yourself over and over again how the Japanese have been able to preserve this sense under living conditions in many ways more chaotic than our own. If you arrive at any answers, your trip to Japan will have been worth every minute. As a lone wanderer you have an opportunity to discover what makes Japan Japanese—their unique way of seeing and doing things that makes a visit to this country so special.

HOW JAPAN GOT THIS WAY

The miracle of today's Japan didn't just happen, of course. The energy which hoisted the Japanese economic state into the number-two position behind the United States after World War II has naturally been at work for a long time, expressing itself sometimes peacefully, often not.

At no time in their history have the Japanese just sat around contemplating the universe, for they are by nature a restless people given to doing more than thinking. Their history teaches that they are practical above all. When a conflict arises, they jump to the fore, driven more by gut reaction to the issues than by reasoning. Not being philosophically inclined, they spend little time looking for the principles involved.

During the past century, when Western ideas came into vogue, the nation has often been busy showing the rest of the world that it can compete on equal if not better terms, whether in conquering other nations, as the major world powers were doing through World War II, or building better automobiles.

Prior to the Meiji period (1868–1912), however, power struggles were confined primarily to Japanese shores. Much of the nation's history before the Tokugawa (Edo) period (1603–1867), named after the family of military shoguns who took control of the nation after it had been unified at the beginning of the seventeenth century, centered on feuds between local lords or between militant Buddhist sects.

Until the end of World War II, the Japanese emperor was revered as a god, but outside of his duties as spiritual leader, he seldom held much real power. Throughout recorded history the emperor or empress was constantly being manipulated by power-hungry families, first by regents within the Imperial Court, later by military dictators. Even when the emperor Meiji was restored to power in 1868, the event was less an achievement for the emperor than for an able body of feudal clan leaders.

Foreign influence has washed over the country in waves, first from China—often through Korea—and much more recently from Western nations. In contrast to the Chinese, who traditionally followed their own path and rejected the ways of others, the Japanese saw nothing wrong in discarding their methods when they thought a foreign method was better. But whatever was borrowed from other cultures was eventually tailored and adapted to meet Japanese needs.

With the Meiji Restoration came Japan's craving for things Western. For education, they patterned their system after that of Europe. The Japanese army was modeled on Germany's, the navy on England's. During the American postwar Occupation, it was America's turn. The Japanese constitution was rewritten following American lines and thought processes. For the first time the Japanese were given individual freedoms, although the average Japanese did not know quite what to do with them. The concept is just now beginning to be understood.

The modern craving for things Western stems partly at least from the nearly 250 years of enforced isolation by the Tokugawa shoguns. Except for the port of Nagasaki, where the Dutch were allowed to trade, the nation was sealed off like a sarcophagus from the rest of the world. Guided by neo-Confucian ethics, the Tokugawas divided the society into four classes: samurai, farmers, craftsmen, and merchants, in that order. Each class's life was prescribed, right down to the type of clothes its members could wear. But during the long period of peace it proved an impossible task to keep the classes in line. With no battles to fight, the samurai gradually gave themselves up to sensual pleasures. Not content at the bottom of the social scale, the merchants saw their chance and eventually took the reins. For the first time in Japanese history the common people found ways to gain first wealth and then power. The great cities of Edo (Tokyo) and Osaka flowered, their attractions well documented in the woodblock prints familiar to Westerners.

A MATTRESS FOR THE NIGHT

Since this book is geared for the traveler on his/her own and probably on a limited budget, the large Western hotels are not listed; rather the emphasis is on good value for money in the types of accommodations that the average Japanese would lodge in, particularly when the company isn't paying the bill. In the large cities the emphasis is on business hotels, and in Tokyo and Kyoto, at least a few Japanese inns—*ryokan* or *minshuku*— are included. Outside the large cities, *minshuku* are a bargain for the budget traveler. *Ryokan* and *minshuku* are essentially the same type of accommodation: In both you sleep on a mattress on a *tatami* mat floor and the prices per person usually include a Japanese dinner and breakfast. *Ryokan* are supposed to offer better quality and more service with, of course, higher prices. But deep in the country the difference in standards between the two is often slim. In resort areas, pensions and publicly owned lodgings offer yet another hotel experience for the traveler with an interest in how the Japanese relax.

Business hotels, a rather recent phenomenon, are designed for the traveling businessman less interested in frills than a place to wash up and a clean bed. They are most often "Western-style," meaning you sleep in a bed rather than on a *futon* mattress on a *tatami* mat floor, and the toilet will be designed for sitting rather than squatting. Both room and bath are miniscule, but often bright and cheery. There are not always restaurants in the hotel, but it is always located in a business area where a restaurant is never far away. Of course, these establishments offer privacy that is nonexistent at the *minshuku*. Rates average ¥5,000 per night for a single, higher in Tokyo.

Many business hotels are listed under the cities in this book. The Japan Business Hotel Association, 43 Kanda-Higashi Matsushita-cho, Chiyoda-ku, Tokyo, publishes the **Business Hotel Guide** with names, addresses, telephone numbers, and rates in English, usually available at JNTO. Reservations can be made directly by telephoning the hotels.

If Western hotels suit you better than Japanese-style inns, you might also consider "JAL Room & Rail," a do-it-yourself budget travel kit of Japan Travel Bureau (JTB) Super-Saver Hotel Coupons and the Japan Rail Pass (described under CITY TO CITY). Offered to JAL passengers only, the plan includes a book of coupons good for a period of one or two weeks which entitles the holder to special discounts at hotels in many cities, including most of the cities featured in this book.

The book of coupons is sold for ¥92,000 if you share a twin room, ¥56,500 for a single room, for seven nights; ¥184,000 if you share a twin room, ¥113,000 for a single room, for fourteen nights. JAL Room & Rail is available at JAL offices outside Japan only and the hotel coupons are sold only in conjunction with the Japan Rail Pass.

The budget travel kit must be purchased at least seven days

17

prior to the first night's stay in Japan. Check at your nearest JAL office for details.

Ryokan or *minshuku* are for the independent traveler who wants to go native as much as possible and be in an atmosphere conducive to meeting Japanese. They are often owned by a family, so it's more like being a guest in a private home. But be warned, few inn owners speak more than the bare minimum of English. Again, an understanding attitude works wonders. Some foreign guests leave raving about the experience, even though they were able to communicate only with grunts and gestures.

The *minshuku* range from charming old farmhouses with an *irori* fireplace built into the *tatami* floor, exposed beams, sliding paper doors, and thatched roofs to new, multistory structures whose exteriors are modern and whose interiors are plastic and plywood.

Depending on the place, you may have a room to yourself or share it with others, the latter being a good possibility during the busy summer months. In either case, the toilet, bathing, and dining facilities will be communal.

By the time you've reached a *minshuku* on your own, you'll no doubt have had some experience with Japanese toilets. The chief difference from the ones you use at home is that they are built flush with the floor, and there are no seats. If crouching in a fetal position over the toilet sounds like an impossible feat, remember that far more of the world's people squat than sit, and doctors insist the position is natural.

One of the chief attractions of the toilet at a *minshuku* is that it's probably the only place you'll have a chance to be alone. Each is in its own individual stall, usually with a lock on the door. Locked or not, however, someone will probably give two taps on the door to make sure it's occupied. The custom is to give two taps right back—and you'd best follow the rule or the person outside will tap to eternity.

These toilets are often shared by both men and women, and the men at the urinals in the outer room are supposed to be ignored. The Japanese have learned to pretend that anything offensive, especially regarding bodily functions, is not there.

Then there is the plastic slipper syndrome. The reasoning is that the toilet is, after all, a dirty place. The slippers you put on at the inn's entrance for wearing in the halls, therefore, just won't do in the toilet. So plastic slippers always await you at the door, and in some places there will be yet another pair waiting outside the toilet stall. All this fussing with slippers is questionable from a sanitary standpoint, but it's good exercise.

The *ofuro* (bath) is also shared by both sexes at these places—but almost always separately. If you're not quite sure whether yours or the other sex is inside, take a look at the clothes lying in the plastic baskets in the dressing area before entering. In this unisex age, however, such examinations are not always foolproof.

The *minshuku* guest always carries a small hand towel and soap in his/her kit, as they are seldom provided. Once inside the bath itself, you'll spy a wall of water taps situated at about mid-calf level and a caldron of boiling water, usually set into the floor. Grab a plastic stool and a pail and position yourself in front of a pair of water taps—one for hot and one for cold running water. If you can't find any hot water tap, it means you'll have to ladle the hot water from the tub and temper it with the cold running water. All soaping is done outside the tub. As you'll quickly discover, the Japanese can spend hours gouging at every crevice with a variety of devices to get the dirt and old skin off. This is as much a ritual as a means of getting clean. No foreigner can match them for time consumed in scrubbing without losing his/her epidermis. The soap is carefully rinsed off by pouring buckets of fresh water over yourself.

Then it's soaking time in the caldron. The water temperature can range from tepid to torrid, so beware. If it's too hot, it's quite acceptable to add some cold water. Not all Japanese are fond of being boiled alive either. When you think it's bearable, don't be finicky. Get yourself submerged as quickly as possible. Within minutes the cares of the day will quickly pass, and you'll discover why these few minutes in the water before bed are to the Japanese a natural birthright. It's such a pleasure that many can't wait until before bedtime and have a bath before dinner too. At some *minshuku*, however, you'll be told when to take your bath. Remember not to pull the plug—everyone uses the same water.

You'll spring out of the tub with your skin a rosy red and the steam rising off your body. Better take it easy for a few minutes until you regain your senses. You can dry yourself with the same hand towel you used for washing by constantly wringing out the excess water, or you can carry a bath towel, as many Japanese now do.

The price at *minshuku* includes two meals—dinner and breakfast—which are usually served family-style in one of the large rooms on the main floor of the building. You'll sit on the floor before a low table. Most of the dishes will be spread out before you in a vast array, and no attempt is made at serving in courses. Japanese take no concern about hot dishes being hot and cold dishes being cold. The only things you can depend on being hot are the *miso* soup, rice, and green tea. Beer and saké are always available at dinner, but you'll be charged extra for these.

The food usually consists of a variety of local delicacies—ocean fish and shellfish, if you're near the sea; mountain trout and vegetables in the mountain areas; and the inevitable pickled cabbage, turnips, or radishes, which you flavor with soy sauce. This garnishes the generally bland and sticky rice.

The foreigner who must have his coffee in the morning and wants his eggs done to a turn with bacon on the side will have a problem in a *minshuku*. Except in rare cases where the host or hostess is willing to make special concessions (and this is always trouble for them), you'll have to be content with a piece of salted fish, more *miso* soup, and rice.

The morning custom is to plop a raw egg over the steaming rice in your bowl; stir it up with your chopsticks; add a little soy sauce to taste; then, after dipping a thin piece of dried seaweed into your soy sauce, wrap the seaweed around a bite-size ball of egg and rice with your chopsticks and plunge it into your mouth. The swallowing is sometimes difficult. Forget the taste and think of all that nutrition.

Bedding down in a *minshuku* is also in the traditional Japanese way. You spread a mattress (two, if you like your bed soft) from the closet out on the *tatami* mat floor, tuck the clean sheet provided around it, throw over the lighter *futon* quilt (usually no top sheet), place that small pillow, seemingly filled with steel balls (actually buckwheat chaff), at the head—and you're ready to crawl in for a good night's rest. Remember to put your bedding back in the closet in the morning.

Minshuku guests are reminded that in a land where practically every service is provided, the *minshuku* is not a service establishment. You do practically everything by yourself except make your own food. When not pressed for time, the owners can be expected to be very helpful in offering tips on what to see in the area, but the generally low rates do not allow for paid help to meet your every whim. This should be no sacrifice to the traveler alone in Japan.

JAL, JNTO, and major travel agents can give you the names and addresses of *minshuku* in the areas you plan to visit. The easiest method of making advance reservations is by contacting the **Japan Minshuku Center**, Tokyo Kotsu Kaikan Building, 2-10-1 Yurakucho, Chiyoda-ku, Tokyo 100, Tel. 216-6556. The organization's MINPAK Reservations Desk for a fee of ¥6,000 can book rooms, advise of late arrival, or request a vegetarian meal for you at their member inns keen on serving foreign guests. If you have sufficient time, write to them in advance for an application form. If you're already in Tokyo, stop at their office on the B1 level of the Kotsu Kaikan just east of Yurakucho Station. Minshuku rates average ¥5,500 per person per night, including dinner and breakfast (more often breakfast only in Tokyo, Osaka, and Kyoto).

Although not called *minshuku*, the group of inns belonging to the **Japanese Inn Group** offers the same simple Japanese-style accommodations in about the same price range. The group's members are supposed to offer a few of the amenities that foreigners look for such as locks on the room doors, towels and soap, and English signs explaining the use of the bathroom.

An English-language brochure, published quarterly and listing each inn with current prices and a general description of the place and nearby attractions, is available from either their Tokyo office at 2-3-11 Yanaka, Taito-ku, Tokyo 110, their Kyoto office at 314 Hayaocho, Kaminoguchi-agaru, Ninomiyacho-dori, Shimogyo-ku, Kyoto 600, or JNTO.

Also similar in style to *minshuku*, except usually government-run, are the **Kokumin Shukusha**, or public lodgings in scenic spots or national parks (average ¥4,800 per person per night, with dinner and breakfast). There are also the **Kokumin Kyuka Mura**, or vacation villages with recreational facilities included (average ¥6,500 per person per night with dinner and breakfast). Write to the **Kokumin Kyuka Mura Service Center** for reservations at Tokyo Kotsu Kaikan, 2-10-1 Yurakucho, Chiyoda-ku, Tokyo (Tel. 216-2085). Reservations for either of these types of accommodations should be made at least six months in advance, as they are popular.

Usually located in resort areas, especially the ski areas, are pensions, where prices are a bit higher (average ¥7,500 per person with two meals), but facilities are usually better. Like *minshuku*, the pensions are owned by families, often young couples who have fled the big cities for the great outdoors. Reservations can be made through travel agents or the **Pension Reservations Center**, Takahashi Bldg., 3F, 1-4-4 Kudanshita, Chiyoda-ku, Tokyo (Tel. 295-6333).

Rock-bottom prices are offered by **Japan Youth Hostels, Inc. (JYH)**, a private company operating almost 500 hostels throughout the country, and the more than 75 hostels operated by the national or regional governments. Rates average ¥1,100 to ¥2,100 per night for a bed only, the government-operated spots being cheaper. Meals cost from ¥350 to ¥1,100, or you can cook for yourself in the central kitchen facilities. These are essentially dormitory operations, with strict check-in (between 3 and 8 P.M.) and checkout (not later than 10 A.M.) times (closed between 10 A.M. and 3 P.M.). Curfew time is 9 P.M. (10 P.M. in Tokyo). Lights out at 10 P.M., which may be a bit early for Tokyo.

If JYH appeals to you and your first stop is Tokyo, visit their office at the Hoken Kaikan Building, 3F, 1-2 Sadoharacho, Ichigaya, Shinjuku-ku, Tokyo 162 (Tel. 269-5831/3), a five-minute walk from the JR Ichigaya Station (Sobu Line). If you're not already a member of the International Youth Hostel Federation, you can buy an International Guest Card here (¥2,200; bring a passport-type photo) as well as pick up copies of the JYH Handbook with handy maps of the hostels and their English-language pamphlet for foreign visitors (the latter also available at JNTO's Tokyo and Kyoto Tourist Information Centers).

EATING THE JAPANESE WAY

Japanese food is becoming increasingly familiar to Westerners with a proliferation of restaurants the world over. No matter how much you've eaten Japanese cuisine at home, however, you'll discover infinitely more taste possibilities in Japan itself. The essential idea is to enhance the natural taste of the food, not camouflage it with rich sauces. Freshness borders on fanaticism, and where could the ingredients be more fresh than from the land where this cuisine originated? Rice is the staple, boiled until sticky and not until dry, and, indeed, the word for meal in Japanese (*gohan*) means rice.

Meats are chopped into bite-size pieces or thin slices that can easily be picked up with your chopsticks. These are most often dipped into a tiny dish of sauce, usually with a soy sauce base and a few fresh ingredients such as ginger, onions, or grated radish.

Vegetables range from all the familiar things such as carrots and cucumbers to wild plants from the mountains, and may be served fresh, boiled, pickled, or deep-fried.

All meals will be accompanied with a bowl of hot soup, either made from soybean paste (*miso*) or a clear fish stock, and pickled cucumbers, cabbage, *daikon* radishes, etc. The pickles are usually eaten with the rice at the end of the meal.

Like so many things Japanese, the food is subtle. At first it is seemingly tasteless. Bite by bite, it grows on you, and in time you start believing that little twig, root, or flower really did taste a bit different from the one you had during the last meal. But this takes time.

Regardless of what you think about the taste, you will inevitably be intrigued with the way it's served. With no attempt to match colors or sizes, plates and bowls are selected to suit the food's color and texture, often with only a few morsels in a sizable dish.

Kaiseki, which originated in Japan's Zen temples, where meat was shunned, is the ultimate Japanese eating experience—at least for a Japanese obsessed with form and beauty rather than content. At the best *kaiseki* spots, each course is served in gorgeous lacquerware or china. The average Westerner more interested in volume than aesthetics, however, will be shocked at the infinitesimally tiny portions—and probably the taste. Further, genuine *kaiseki* is a luxury that has been priced beyond the means of the average mortal, Japanese or Western, more in fact than you will pay for a French dinner in Tokyo. Nevertheless some *kaiseki* spots have been listed, again with an eye to good value for money. The experience should be tried by a visitor to Japan at least once.

Many Westerners will probably pale at the thought of rice, noodles, and a bit of fish every day. For that reason, when available, some foreign restaurants where the taste is close to authentic will be recommended under the restaurant listings in cities.

THE DRINKING HABIT

As you'll quickly discover if you're out after dark in any Japanese big city or hamlet, there is scarcely a Japanese man in the land who draws a sober breath past 9 P.M. The chances are good, however, that he didn't get high the way you do.

It's a rare gentleman here who drinks anything but beer, saké (*Nihonshu*), *shochu*, or scotch whiskey. If you like any of the above, you'll have absolutely no trouble in a Japanese watering hole.

Japanese beer is famous throughout the world. It's served ice cold in the American way and is especially popular during the warm summer months when the rooftops of big department stores and office buildings turn into outdoor beer gardens.

There are literally hundreds of saké breweries, and each area of Japan produces a local version which the area inhabitants swear by, besides the brands sold nationally. It's usually served at body temperature after being heated in hand-sized bottles. In some places it's sold straight from the barrel (*taruzake*).

Shochu, made from various grains and vegetables, most commonly rice, barley, and potatoes, is surely the rawest-tasting of authentic Japanese spirits. After a long period of decline in popularity, it's seen a comeback. It's cheap, and it mixes well with fruit juices for exotic cocktails. Old folks prefer a rougher version mixed with hot water.

Suntory and Nikka whiskey need no introduction. They're most usually drunk with water over ice in Japan—the ubiquitous *mizuwari*.

Now you understand what they drink, the next hurdle for the foreigner is figuring out what type of Japanese bar to go to. Those frequented by laborers and office workers fall into two broad categories: the *nomiya* (literally, "drinking shop") and *sunakku* (from the English word "snack"). Both types are essentially after-work hangouts for men, but women are welcome, and in most cases these gals are office colleagues who have come along to giggle at the guys' jokes and pour their drinks, not participate in any sort of serious conversation—at least not if the ladies are still searching for the man of their dreams.

Nomiya are the more festive—and noisy—of the two. Generally, the lights are brighter and there are more people scurrying around behind the counter, not only to prepare drinks, but also to make various kinds of thirst-stirring dishes to go with the alcohol. Although the purpose is to drink, a person can also make a well-balanced meal out of the fish, meat, vegetable, and seaweed dishes, all served in small portions. The food and drinks are usually Japanese-style.

Sunakku tend to be much smaller—most often nothing but a counter and a few stools in a narrow room—and offer far more intimacy, with a lower decibel level—providing one of the customers isn't singing with amplified background music (known as *karaoke*). The decor, food, and drinks are usually Western-style, though not what you would expect of a bar back home. In an unamplified snack bar, it might just be possible to have a conversation. The customers often know the master or "mama-san" by first name, and these people are generally genial busybodies willing to listen to the joys and sorrows of those on the other side of the counter. Although a few snacks are usually available in these places, the emphasis is primarily on drinking, and you'd best not go before you've filled your stomach.

It's usually possible to order whiskey by the glass in either a *nomiya* or *sunakku*. Japanese customers usually buy their whiskey by the bottle and leave what's not drunk on a shelf in the bar for the next time (the "bottle-keep" system). In this way the owner keeps those patrons coming back for more. As a foreigner, you'll be expected to pay cash on the line. The regulars are trusted, and pay when the owner gets around to making out a bill.

An annoying habit to foreigners is the instant appearance of *chaamu* (charm)—an often obnoxious tidbit to go with your drink, and for which you pay extra. It will do no good to grumble. This is part of the routine.

If you're a man looking for female companionship, neither of the aforementioned bars is what you're looking for. Your goal is one of the hostess bars, which range from swanky elegance in Tokyo's Ginza district to absolute dives. In either a dazzler or a dump you'll pay no small fee for having your drinks poured and smiles (you'll get more only in dives). Your chances of being ripped off in hostess bars are better than anywhere else in Japan. Ignore the touts in any tourist-frequented areas like the Ginza and Akasaka in Tokyo.

Should a foreigner wander into a *nomiya* or *sunakku* alone? There will surely be the usual language problem, but if you can pronounce any of the above drinks, and are prepared to pay a little extra for *chaamu*, there should be no problem. In most of the *nomiya*, the snacks (*otsumami*) are posted on the wall, but unless you can read Japanese, this won't help at all. If your neighbor is eating something that looks tasty, simply point and ask for the same.

You're apt to attract the least attention in a *nomiya*, which is usually a bit larger, with more people coming and going. The *sunakku* are often like private clubs for all those bottle keepers.

Everyone seems to know everyone else, and even an unintroduced Japanese is initially an outsider. You'll definitely be more comfortable in these little bars when in the company of a Japanese friend.

For those addicted to martinis and whiskey sours, forget these typical Japanese drinking spots. Your best bet is either the bars in the big Western-style hotels, or the new and trendy "café bars" that are popping up in every major Japanese city. If you're over thirty, you may feel like a fool in these places. But the decor is usually interesting, and it can be fun to watch the kids cavorting.

CITY TO CITY

The traveler will depend for the most part on the country's extensive railway network, principally the six companies within the **Japan Railways Group (JR)**. Although the old national railways has been divided up among these companies, the change has no effect on foreign visitors traveling around the country. Private railways in big cities and resort areas supplement JR.

The Japan Travel Bureau publishes the monthly *JTB's Mini-Timetable*, with listings of JR's and the major private railways' express trains (as well as expressway buses, long-distance ferries, and domestic airline schedules). Written in both Japanese and English, the pocket-size booklet is available for ¥310 where Japanese magazines are sold. (In Japanese, ask for the *Supiido jikokuhyo*.) A *Railway Timetable* printed in English for foreign visitors with schedules of the express trains of both JR and the major private companies, plus a good explanation of how to use the rail networks, is available from JR Travel Service Centers or JNTO.

A larger, more complete monthly *Jikokuhyo* is printed in Japanese. Both the catalog-sized and condensed version are available at Japanese magazine stands. The foreign traveler alone will need help with reading this, however. Copies are available in every hotel and inn. Explain your destination for the next leg of your journey, and someone at your hotel will tell you the departure times. Complete schedules are also available in the train stations. Except at the Travel Service Centers and the smallest stations, however, the railway employees are likely to be too busy to help you beyond your next destination. Work out complete, detailed itineraries in more relaxed surroundings before going to the station.

JR offers ordinary or "Green" (deluxe) classes of service on most of its inter-city trains and a number of different types of trains: the famous high-speed **Shinkansen** (Bullet Trains); limited express (*tokkyu*), which stop only at major stations; express (*kyuko*), with more stops; rapid (*kaisoku*) between big cities and the suburbs; and regular (*futsu*), which make all stops. The Shinkansen, limited express, and express trains have surcharges above the normal fares. Seats on these trains may be reserved at the "Green Windows" (*midori no madoguchi*) of JR stations or travel agents as early as one month in advance. No-smoking cars are available on all trains.

The foreign visitor planning to stay in Japan at least a week can save himself both a lot of time in figuring out the complicated system and also money by purchasing a **Japan Rail Pass** good for 7, 14, or 21 days on all JR lines. The passes are available at JAL offices or from authorized travel agents outside Japan. Both "Ordinary" and "Green" passes are available, the latter entitling the holder to a seat in the first-class, spacious Green Cars. Seven-day passes are ¥27,800 ("Ordinary"), ¥37,000 ("Green"); 14-day passes are ¥44,200 ("Ordinary"), ¥60,000 ("Green"); and 21-day passes are ¥56,600 ("Ordinary"), ¥78,000 ("Green").

After full payment, the JAL office or travel agent will issue an exchange order which you exchange for the actual pass either at the JR Information and Ticket Office at the New Tokyo International Airport at Narita (7 A.M.–11 P.M.), or at one of the JR Travel Service Centers (10 A.M.–6 P.M.). Japan Rail Passes cannot be purchased in Japan. The passes can be used on JR trains and some JR buses. Sleeping accommodations, however, are charged for at the regular rates.

Japan's famous **Bullet Trains** (*Shinkansen*) need no explanation. They are among the world's fastest, making the country's rugged terrain seem easy to get around, over, and—by tunnel—through.

Three different lines are now in operation: the Tokaido Sanyo Shinkansen between Tokyo and Hakata (Fukuoka) on Kyushu island; the Tohoku Shinkansen between Tokyo's Ueno Station and Morioka on northern Honshu island; and the Joetsu Shinkansen between Ueno and Niigata on the Japan Sea.

Two types of Shinkansen run on each line—an express that makes only limited stops and is called by different romantic-sounding names for each line (*Hikari* for the Tokaido Line, *Yamabiko* for the Tohoku Line, and *Asahi* for the Joetsu Line) and a regular express with a few more stops (called *Kodama* on the Tokaido Line, *Aoba* on the Tohoku Line, and *Toki* on the Joetsu Line).

Individual JAL passengers can make Shinkansen reservations before leaving home through JAL's computerized reservations system. After confirmation, a Seat Reservation Slip is issued through the JAL office. On arrival in Japan the slip is exchanged for the real ticket at any of JR's Travel Service Centers. Reservations can be made from three to forty-five days prior to actual departure time of the train in Japan.

Train passengers are reminded to hang on to all of their tickets throughout their journey. The tickets will be collected when you exit at your final destination.

Japan's private railways are often convenient in and around the big cities and in resort areas, and are usually cheaper than JR. Certain lines will be recommended under destination headings.

JR also operates "**highway buses**" between major cities such as Tokyo, Nagoya, Kyoto, and Osaka at fares lower than the trains. Special nonstop "Dream" buses depart from Tokyo Station every night for Nagoya (¥6,180), Kyoto (¥8,030), and Osaka (8,450), arriving the following morning. (There are also nightly departures from Osaka, Kyoto, and Nagoya to Tokyo). All seats are reserved, and reservations should be made well in advance.

In really remote areas of Japan, local buses reach spots the trains won't. Departures are usually scheduled for easy connections from railways. Fares vary on these buses, but the usual system is to collect a tab on entry which shows the zone where you boarded. When you exit, you match the zone number on your tab with that on the fare board at the front of the bus and read the corresponding fare. On some buses there is a conductor who collects fares while roaming up and down the aisle. You simply state your destination and the conductor will tell you the fare.

Finally, you might consider one of the **intercoastal steamships** which, of course, take longer than the train but offer more scenic possibilities, especially through the Inland Sea between Osaka or Kobe to Beppu (Kyushu). This overnight trip offered by Kansai Steamship Co. takes thirteen hours from Osaka, with fares from ¥5,870.

From Tokyo and nearby Kawasaki there are car ferries to ports on other islands. These are time-consuming but cheap (Tokyo to Tomakomai in Hokkaido, ¥11,840; Tokyo to Tokushima in Shikoku, ¥8,200; Kawasaki to Hyuga, near Miyazaki, Kyushu, ¥17,710).

If time is a problem, and money is not, Japan's three major airlines—JAL, All Nippon Airways (ANA), and Japan Air System (JAS)—link the two major air hubs of Tokyo and Osaka with practically all of Japan's prefectures—and each other. Remember, Japan domestic flights out of Tokyo operate from close-in Haneda Airport, not Narita.

MEETING THE JAPANESE

This is a formal society. No one walks up, grabs your hand, and says, "Hello. My name's Yukio. What's yours?" The Japanese prefer introductions through others. So the wise traveler who really wants to meet Japanese had better lay the groundwork well before his/her departure from home.

If you know a Japanese, show your interest and explain that you're going to Japan. The chances are good the Japanese will make an effort to put you in touch with friends or relatives on your arrival.

The foreigner on the street in Japan generally attracts only the Japanese eager to speak English. The rest are perhaps curious, but too shy to initiate a conversation. Being thought of as an instant English-speaking machine is not especially flattering. But never mind—if you have anything in common after the English break, let it develop.

There are organizations in Tokyo and other large cities geared especially to bring the foreigner and the Japanese together. Again, the prime motivation for the Japanese is a chance to practice English. But it's a start. The English-language press is your best source of information for learning about the activities of these organizations. Most of the publications carry regular listings.

Another possibility is to take advantage of the "**Home Visit System**" under the sponsorship of JNTO and the governments of most of the major cities. By applying to either the JNTO Tourist Information Center in Tokyo or the city government offices elsewhere, foreign visitors can arrange to visit a Japanese family in their home for an hour or so. The JNTO and city offices are closed on Saturday afternoons and on Sundays and holidays. Allow at least a day to make the arrangements. JNTO publishes a Home Visit System brochure listing the offices where you can apply and explaining what you can expect from the experience.

As is true anywhere, a real friend is often better discovered by chance than calculation. As a traveler alone, your opportunities for contact are far better than for the person following the well-trodden tourist trail.

WHEN TO VISIT JAPAN

There are two major considerations: One is the weather; the other, trying to travel when the Japanese don't. Japan has four distinct seasons with a climate not unlike that of the American mid-Atlantic states. Winters are cool, but bright and sunny, along the Pacific Coast; frigid and usually snow-covered along the Japan Sea and on Hokkaido island. Spring is mild, and you really will be able to see cherry trees in full bloom, but you can expect rain and mist along with the flowers. June is the so-called "rainy" month, but you can easily see more rain in April or

May. July and August seem hotter than on the equator, with humidity matching that of a South American jungle. Wear your coolest clothes and carry a big fan. Fall is easily the most reliable season for bright, blue skies, plus the lure of the fall foliage, which starts in Hokkaido in late September and moves down the archipelago, reaching Tokyo and Kyoto in early November and southern Kyushu a bit later.

During Japanese holidays, and especially the holidays that follow each other almost consecutively, be prepared for all public transportation to be packed to the ceilings and windows—literally. The New Year's holidays begin a few days before January 1 and continue throughout the first week of the year. During this period and again in late July or mid-August the big-city dwellers return to their home villages in the country en masse, making a last-minute reserved seat on anything virtually impossible.

Another period to be avoided at all costs is "Golden Week," which begins with Nature Day on April 29 and continues through Children's Day on May 5. This is the time for many Japanese to discover their own country, or for some to take trips overseas. It's virtually impossible again to get a reserved seat or a hotel room unless you plan well ahead. School vacation begins in mid-July and continues through August. While perhaps not quite as crowded as the periods mentioned above, these two months are still the favorite for Japanese travelers, especially for families with children. If you're coming to Japan at that time, again, make reservations well in advance.

While the Japanese are roaming the countryside, however, their big cities are relatively quiet and empty. Japanese vacation periods are generally good times for a foreigner to discover Tokyo under less crowded conditions.

USEFUL TIPS

The following will add to your comfort or pleasure, and maybe save you embarrassment.

Carry **pocket-size tissue**, because public restrooms rarely provide toilet paper; also a **handkerchief** to dry your hands in these places, because paper towels are a relatively unknown commodity; a **can opener** and **bottle opener**, if you're expecting to picnic; and a small **flashlight**, for a better look at works of art that are often displayed in near or total darkness.

Wear **soft-soled shoes**, preferably loafers or slip-ons. The gravel and stone paths of the temples and shrines and public parks are murder on a good pair of shoes and your feet, though Japan's fashion-conscious young ladies sprint over them in spike heels.

Slip-ons are the most practical, because you'll be constantly taking your shoes off and putting them on when entering *minshuku*, temples, homes, and sometimes even museums and shops. Don't forget that taking off your shoes and your slippers is a hard and fast rule when you are entering a *tatami* room. The number of places you'll be forsaking shoes for plastic slippers will amaze you. Plan accordingly.

Don't tip. Foreign visitors from countries where tipping is an established custom find it hard to break the habit. Some taxi drivers and restaurant and hotel personnel may accept a tip, often because they don't know how to refuse in English. But no one expects it, and more often it creates embarrassment. Small gifts in return for some kindness are something else. They are appreciated, often cherished. Any sort of trinket or doll from your own hometown, something typical of the area from which you come, is best.

ARRIVAL IN JAPAN

Practically all international flights from North America and Europe land at the New Tokyo International Airport, Narita, a distance of 66 kilometers from the city center. Once in the arrivals lobby, a decision must be made as to how to make the long trip to Tokyo. Most convenient is the "limousine bus" just outside the lobby which departs at frequent intervals for the **Tokyo City Air Terminal** (TCAT), from where you can take a taxi or walk to one of two nearby subway stations (Kayabacho or Ningyocho on the Hibiya Line) to reach your final destination. Buses depart from Narita at less frequent intervals to the major Tokyo hotels. It takes about seventy minutes to TCAT, and more to the hotels, especially those in Shinjuku. The fare is ¥2,500, and you purchase your ticket from a well-marked booth in front of the customs-area exit.

A cheaper—and because of crowded traffic conditions sometimes quicker—way is the Keisei Line Skyliner express train, which departs from the Keisei Airport Station, a short bus ride from Narita airport, for Ueno Station, not far from the city center. The fare is ¥1,750 including the bus trip from the airport to the station. The trains depart about every half hour, and the trip takes just over an hour. Tickets can be purchased at a booth in the arrivals lobby, or at the Keisei Airport Station.

PRICES

All prices listed in this book were accurate in 1989. In this inflationary world, however, kindly plan to pay a little more than what is listed, and be pleased if the figures quoted are close to accurate. Under a **consumption tax**, restaurants and hotels may charge an additional 3 percent above the cost up to ¥2,500 for meals and ¥5,000 for accommodations. There is an additional special 3 percent tax on top of the regular 3 percent tax on meals costing ¥5,000 or over and hotel rooms costing ¥10,000 or over. In addition to the tax, service charges are often added to the amount of 10 percent at better restaurants and hotels. No tipping necessary, of course. Prices listed do not include taxes and service charges unless otherwise noted.

TOKYO

THROBBING NERVE CENTER

At first glance Tokyo looks like a great, gray blob of concrete, steel, glass, stucco, and flimsy wood. Then the little things begin to come into focus: a finely pruned pine tree gracefully draped over a stone wall; some petite, well-dressed bar hostess on her way to work in the Ginza; a piece of rustic pottery filled with only a wheat stalk in a shop window; a winding lane full of bobbing red paper lanterns; a sumo wrestler in Japanese dress, his hair in a topknot, making a telephone call on a street corner. Little thing by little thing, Tokyo envelops even the casual, short-time visitor with its charms.

This is Japan's "Big Apple," the ultimate destination for the overachievers in a land where overachieving is a mania. The nation's top businessmen, politicians, artists, writers, actors, intellectuals—all those talented people that make any great city great—converge here to give Tokyo a throbbing life matched by few other urban areas in the world. In population, area, wealth, abundance of artistic objects, and its role in world affairs, Tokyo stands right up there with New York, London, or Paris. Beyond that, comparisons fail.

Big-city sophistication abounds, but the overall impression of the man in the street is that he still has one foot back in the rice paddy of his home village. The jaded ways of the West are becoming more tempting to Mr. Yamamoto, but he hasn't yet been able to shake off his wide-eyed innocence. For the hard-boiled New Yorker or Parisian, this makes Tokyo nothing short of refreshing.

36

TOKYO

Higashi–Nakano

Okubo

Shin-Okubo

SHINJUKU

To Kichijoji

To Hakone

Keio Line

Odakyu Line

KOSHU KAIDO

OME KAIDO

YAMATE DORI

● Sword Museum

● Yoyogi

Inabaso Ryokan 18

Sendagaya

Inokashira Line

● Japan Folk Crafts Museum

● Yoyogi Park
● Meiji Shrine

Chuo Main Line

Shinano-machi

SHIBUYA-KU

Harajuku

11 Harajuku Trimm.

Shin-Tamagawa Line

KANNANA DORI

Hillport Hotel 9

SHIBUYA
AOYAMA DORI
The President Hotel 13
Nezu Art Museum ●

Akasaka Palace ●

Asia Cent of Japa

● Aoyama 6
Cemetery

Akasaka

To Yokohama Toyoko Line

MEGURO DORI

Yamanote Line

Ebisu

Roppongi

MEGURO-KU

Hotel Watson
3
Meguro
12 Gajoen Kanko Hotel

● National Park for Nature Study

Hotel Toranomon Pastora

DORI

Tokyo Tower

● Zojoji Temple

MINATO-KU

SAKURADA DORI

HIBIYA DORI

Mekama Line

Ikegami Line

SHINAGAWA-KU

Gotanda

Osaki

Hotel Tokyo
15

Tamachi

Hamamatsu-cho

● Sengakuji Temple

8 Shinagawa Prince Hotel

Shinagawa

Hinode Pier

To Shin-Osaka Shinkansen

Oimachi

Keihin Kyuko Line

KAIGAN DORI

To Tokyo (Haneda) Airport

To Kamata

TOKYO PORT

Omori

Numbers refer to accommodations listed on pages 80-82.

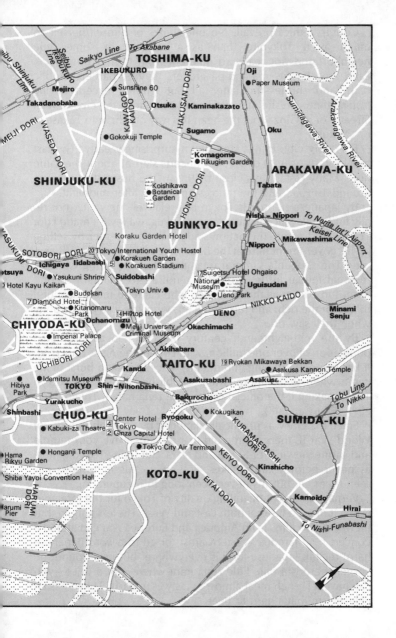

TOSHIMA-KU

Saikyo Line   To Akabane

Seibu Ikebukuro Line
Seibu Shinjuku Line

IKEBUKURO

Oji
● Paper Museum

● Sunshine 60

Mejiro

Otsuka   Kaminakazato

Takadanobaba

KAWAGOE KAIDO

HAKUSAN DORI

Sumidagawa River

Arakawagawa River

MEIJI DORI

WASEDA DORI

Sugamo

Oku

● Gokokuji Temple

Komagome
● Rikugien Garden

ARAKAWA-KU

SHINJUKU-KU

Koishikawa
● Botanical
Garden

HONGO DORI

Tabata

BUNKYO-KU

Nishi – Nippori   To Narita Int'l Airport
Keisei Line

Koraku Garden Hotel

YASUKUNI DORI

SOTOBORI DORI   20 Tokyo/International Youth Hostel
● Korakuen Garden
Ichigaya   Iidabashi   5 ● Korakuen Stadium

Nippori   Mikawashima

tsuya   ● Yasukuni Shrine   Suidobashi

Hotel Kayu Kaikan

17 Suigetsu Hotel Ohgaiso
National ●■■■■ ● Uguisudani
Museum

● Budokan

Tokyo Univ.●

● Ueno Park   NIKKO KAIDO

7 Diamond Hotel
● Kitanomaru
Park   14 Hilltop Hotel

UENO

Minami
Senju

CHIYODA-KU   Ochanomizu
● Meiji University
Criminal Museum   Okachimachi

● Imperial Palace

UCHIBORI DORI

Akihabara

Kanda   TAITO-KU   19 Ryokan Mikawaya Bekkan
● Asakusa Kannon Temple

● Idemitsu Museum   Asakusabashi   Asakusa

Hibiya
Park   TOKYO   Shin –Nihonbashi

Shinbashi   Yurakucho   Bakurocho

Tobu Line
To Nikko

CHUO-KU   Center Hotel   ● Kokugikan
4 Tokyo   Ryogoku
2 Ginza Capital Hotel

● Kabuki-za Theatre

SUMIDA-KU

KURAMAEBASHI DORI

● Hama
Rikyu Garden   ● Honganji Temple   ● Tokyo City Air Terminal

Shiba Yayoi Convention Hall

KEIYO DORO

Kinshicho

KOTO-KU   EITAI DORI

HARUMI DORI

Kameido

Harumi
Pier   Hirai

To Nishi-Funabashi

Country ethics prevail. No one thinks of himself/herself so much as a Tokyoite than as a resident of some little neighborhood not really so different from his/her birthplace. Each area has its ma-and-pa grocers, tailors, barbers, public bath, and shrine—the latter all but ignored except during festival time. He/she may work in Marunouchi, the city's "Wall Street," or in Ginza, but the heart lies way out there in Takasago or Ogikubo.

For a big city, things shut down surprisingly early. The last movie starts at 6:30 or 7 P.M. Concerts start at about the same time. Many restaurants close by 9 P.M. The buses stop running around 10 P.M., and the trains stop shortly after midnight.

By Japanese standards Tokyo is a relatively new city, not really finding its place in history until Tokugawa Ieyasu made Edo, Tokyo's old name, the nation's administrative center by setting up his government here at the beginning of the seventeenth century. The shogun's samurai retainers followed, along with the regional feudal lords who were required to maintain second homes in Edo, plus the craftsmen who came to make beautiful things for the rich, and the merchants who knew an opportunity when they saw one.

By the mid-eighteenth century the city had an estimated population of over one million, with London being its only rival. It has stopped growing infrequently since. An extra burst of life came when the emperor Meiji established himself in Edo in 1868, making it the official capital and renaming it Tokyo (literally, "East Capital").

Since the city was practically flattened by the firebombings of World War II, there is little old that remains: Save your temple and shrine viewing for Kyoto and Nara. But today Tokyo glitters as never before. Earthquakes, fires, war—this metropolis has seen them all, but it's never been long in recuperating.

Perhaps the most beguiling quality of Tokyo for the foreigner is that it offers a taste of both East and West. There's Kabuki, but there are also films from America and Europe. You can attend a concert by a famous Western artist, or go to a *koto* (Japanese harp) recital. Japanese food is everywhere, but just around the corner there is a chic little restaurant where—for a price—you can have a French meal almost as tasty as in Paris. Tokyo has an eclecticism that's hard to beat.

GETTING YOUR BEARINGS

The problem is sorting out what suits you from the rich abundance, then finding it. Start by stopping at JNTO's **Tourist Information Center (TIC)** located near Yurakucho Station, Hibiya, in the Kotani Building, 6-6, Yurakucho 1-chome, Chiyoda-ku (Tel. 502-1461). The staff can speak several foreign languages and are eager to help you search out whatever fascinates you. First ask for their **Tourist Map of Tokyo**, with close-up pictograph maps of the major neighborhoods, and including a map of the JR commuter lines and subways on which the traveler will mostly rely. Then pick up a copy of the weekly **Tour Companion** tabloid designed especially for the independent, bargain-seeking traveler and featuring whatever special events are happening in Tokyo that week, plus listings of movies, concerts, Kabuki, restaurants, nightspots, art exhibitions, etc. **Tokyo Journal**, a monthly magazine designed for foreign residents, features more offbeat listings—good for the visitor with more time to spend. (¥500 at bookstores, kiosks, and major hotels.) TIC is open from 9 A.M. to 5 P.M. on weekdays, 9 A.M. to noon on Saturdays, and is closed on Sundays and holidays.

   JAL Plaza across the street from TIC is an alternative. Unlike TIC, it's open every day of the year from 10 A.M. to 6:30 P.M., including Japanese holidays and Sundays. The Tokyo Metropolitan Government operates an **Information Bureau** from inside the Travel Plaza JR reservations area on the Yaesu side of big Tokyo Station. It's especially helpful with English information on the city's extensive sports and recreation facilities.

Covering some 800 square miles, Tokyo sprawls to infinity. With time and patience, you might begin to understand just where Ginza is in relation to Shinjuku, or Asakusa to Shibuya, in a year. No visitor has that much time. The best way to explore is by taking walks in the various sections of the city, a feat made easier by the neighborhood guides and maps in this book. We've tried to explain what gives each particular area its character, but Japanese and Western, new and old, rich and poor, overlap constantly. Don't expect the startling contrasts of Harlem and East Side New York. Along with the points of interest, we've recommended shops and restaurants in each area.

A ride up the elevator to some of the city's high spots might help you sort out just what is where. **Tokyo Tower** (¥720, plus ¥500 for the upper deck; 9 A.M.–8 P.M.; Nov.–Mar., 9 A.M.–6 P.M.) offers the best view of the bay and harbor. The observation floor of the **Kasumigaseki Building** (no charge) in the government office district offers the supreme view down into the Imperial Palace compound, about as close as you can get to these highly secluded grounds. **Sunshine 60** (¥600; 10 A.M.–5 P.M.), now the city's tallest at sixty stories in Ikebukuro, offers a good view of the Tanzawa Mountains and Mt. Fuji beyond to the west.

For what it's worth, like most of the numerous Japanese castle towns, Tokyo grew out in concentric circles from the castle which was first the shogun's residence and later the emperor's. The moat closest to the castle walls remains, and you can make a complete circle around the great stone walls in about an hour on foot. This is a favorite course for the city's joggers. The next in the former concentric circles of moats is still visible at Akasaka-Mitsuke below the New Otani Hotel and from Yotsuya past Ichigaya to Iidabashi, a path lined with cherry blossoms in April.

The favored picture-taking spot at the Imperial Palace is **Nijubashi Bridge**, which has a turret from the former Fushimi Castle in Kyoto perched on the wall above it. With your back to the bridge, follow busy Uchibori Dori to your left until you come to Otemon Gate, through which you can enter the **East Garden**, site of the main buildings of the old castle, between 9 A.M. and 4 P.M. (enter by 3 P.M.) every day except Mondays and Fridays. You can leave the East Garden through the **Kita Hanebashimon**

Gate, across the street from which you'll find **Kitanomaru Park**, home of three fine museums, plus **Nippon Budokan**, a modern arena for Japanese martial arts as well as rock concerts. The **Tokyo National Museum of Modern Art** (¥360; 10 A.M.–5 P.M.; closed Mon.) has a permanent collection of Japanese art of the last century and usually a special exhibition of some twentieth-century Western artist lodged on its main floor. This museum also has a separate **Crafts Gallery** (¥360; 10 A.M.–5 P.M.; closed Mon.) devoted to modern Japanese crafts and housed in what was the home of the Imperial Palace guards in the nineteenth century, up the hill and inside the park from the main museum. This is a good starting place for studying Japan's rich tradition in folk art. Also inside the park is the **Science and Technology Museum** (¥515; 9:30 A.M.–4:50 P.M.; closed Mon. and December 25–January 1), no threat to the great science museums in Chicago or Munich, but adequate for science enthusiasts.

Across the moat to the west of Kitanomaru Park is **Chidorigafuchi Park**, famous for its cherry blossoms in spring. And just north of Chidorigafuchi is **Yasukuni Shrine**, devoted to Japan's war dead, noted for its sixty-six-foot-high bronze gateway at the main entrance. This shrine is tremendously popular among the Japanese for visits during the New Year's holidays.

East of the Imperial Palace compound lie the **Ginza** and **Marunouchi** districts, which together form the closest thing to a center this city has. Almost all of the subway (*chikatetsu*) system's ten lines pass through or near these areas, like spokes on a hub. The subway, along with the JR Yamanote and Sobu lines which connect with the subway at various points, will be your prime means of getting around, and a word on how to use the system will be helpful.

Tickets for both the subway and JR lines are purchased from vending machines outside the stations' wickets. The fares are based on distance traveled, so you'll have to refer to the map above the machines to find out the fare to your particular destination. At stations frequented by foreigners, there is usually a small map with the stations written in roman letters posted somewhere. If not, you can match your map in roman letters with the one in Japanese above the machines.

In any case, if you didn't pay enough, the man who takes your ticket at your destination will tell you what the difference is. If you paid too much, however, the loss is yours. Currently fares on the subway are somewhat cheaper than on the JR lines.

If you're using the subway at least five or six times in a single day, pick up a "One Day Free Ticket" at a subway station for ¥600. It entitles you to "free" use of all lines except the Asakusa, Mita, and Shinjuku lines for the date stamped on the ticket. For another ¥650, you can pick up a "Toei One-Day Economy Pass," which entitles you to use the other three lines, plus the buses and street cars operated by the Metropolitan Government. It's available at station ticket counters and on the buses and trains.

JR's Yamanote Line makes a wide loop through the Ginza and Marunouchi districts at Shinbashi, Yurakucho, and Tokyo stations, and on around through the major transfer terminals of Ueno, Ikebukuro, Shinjuku, Shibuya, and Shinagawa where commuters switch to other lines for the suburbs. The Sobu Line is convenient for reaching points in central Tokyo between Akihabara and Shinjuku.

Tokyo's buses generally run between the subway lines and sometimes will take you much closer to your destination than the trains. The buses all have numbers, but the signs on the buses and at most bus stops are not in roman letters. If you must use a bus, get your directions clearly from a Japanese before you leave. The fare is ¥160, regardless of distance. A machine at the bus entrance will give you change for ¥200 or ¥500 in coins. No bills.

Finally, there are taxis everywhere, and the drivers are eager to stop at the wave of your hand. Fares start at ¥480 for the first two kilometers, however, and a trip between the Ginza and Roppongi areas, for example, can easily push the meter up to ¥1,000. Handy though they are, a few taxi rides can easily wreck a small travel budget. The drivers rarely speak English and, unlike those in most other cities, seldom know any but the most common destinations. The passenger must often guide them block by block, no easy task if you can't speak Japanese. Always allow for more time than you think you need, and don't tip.

GINZA AND NIHONBASHI

Contrary to foreign understanding, Ginza is not a street but a whole district distinguished by day, along with the nearby Nihonbashi district, as the capital's and the nation's chief center of high fashion and luxury goods and including the greatest concentration of art galleries; and by night for what is perhaps the most expensive nightlife in the world.

For the city's old-rich, never as distinguishable as their counterparts in the West, and new-rich, as flashy as anywhere, the Ginza is simply IT. Class-consciousness is discreet in Japan. The majority think of themselves as middle-class, and by American and European standards they are. But tycoons and old aristocrats, if not obvious, are still on the scene, and the Ginza is where you're most likely to find them.

The best introduction is a leisurely stroll at dusk when the sky is lavender and those famed neon signs begin flashing their commercial messages—veritable dreams for color fans and typographers. This is Tokyo's best hour, when the millions of office workers begin pouring out of their companies, through the streets, and into the thousands of bars, many no bigger than walk-in closets.

Tokyo's nightlife and bar scene comes in many forms. The Ginza variety includes some big-name nightclubs with floor shows similar to those of any city in the world; some *nomiya*, the Japanese-style drinking places where the junior staff gather for booze and tidbits; and a great number of hostess bars, the modern-day version of the geisha houses of old.

There are hostess bars all over Tokyo, of course, but none quite so classy as those in the Ginza, and none so much aspired to by the ladies of the profession. Quite simply, this is where the big money is spent, most of it from the lavish expense accounts of major companies. With few exceptions, the girls are in the business for money first and foremost, along with the common dream among Japanese women of finding someone to take care of them. For the bar hostess, this means playing mistress to some company top executive and maybe one day having her own bar.

The Ginza bars close around midnight, and the late-night rush hour is a sight unmatched anywhere. Those black limousines with the white seat covers and the thousands of taxis, each waiting for some bleary-eyed executive to come lumbering out into the street, make the streets impassable. The mama-sans follow their customers right out and bow them away with a gush of thank-yous.

The following two suggested walking tours wind from Hibiya Park to Tsukiji, and from the main Ginza intersection to Mitsukoshi department store's headquarters in Nihonbashi. Both can be done in half a day, if you're a fast mover. But a full day offers a more leisurely pace. Ginza shops are open from 11 A.M. to 8 P.M., department stores from 10 A.M. to 7 P.M.

Hibiya Park was the city's first Western-style public park and, like so many parks and gardens in Tokyo, was formerly the site of a feudal lord's mansion. It's a popular picnic lunch spot for office workers on weekdays and, since it's one of the few parks without a wall around it and a late-afternoon closing time, one of the more active parks after dark.

Across the street is the **Imperial Hotel**, Tokyo's grand-daddy of Western hotels made especially famous among foreigners when the site was occupied by a Mayan monolith designed by American architect Frank Lloyd Wright. Today its new buildings would be at home in any Western city. The shopping arcades both in the basement of the main building and on the first four floors of the new Tower in the rear are smart—and expensive—but great for window-shoppers.

Exit at the side entrance and turn right. Across the street is the **Takarazuka Theater**, Tokyo home for the all-girl revue popularized by James Michener in his novel *Sayonara*. For reasons understood only by students of Japanese psychology, these revues are frequented not by men but by teen-age girls in bobby sox, who have been known to wait in line all night to get the best seats to see their favorite stars. Ticket prices range from ¥1,000 to ¥4,500 and the show is recommended for spectacular costumes and staging. Curtain times are 1:00 and 5:30 P.M. on weekdays, with matinees on Mondays and Fridays only; 11 A.M. and 3:30 P.M. on Sundays and holidays. Takarazuka performances alternate with other stage productions.

Further down the street flanking the Imperial Hotel is the **Sakai Kokodo Gallery**, a favorite for woodblock prints. Originals are scarce, but the shop is one of the best in town for reproductions of the popular prints. Under the railroad tracks on both sides of the street is the **International Arcade**, also fun for tourists. **Hayashi Kimono** on the right is recommended for old kimono and *obi* sashes, often used by foreign women for dressing gowns and table center runners respectively.

On the other side of the tracks and on the right is the New Riccar Building where you'll find the **Riccar Art Museum** (¥300; 11 A.M.–6 P.M., closed Mon.) specializing in *ukiyo-e*, old Japanese woodblock prints. At the next corner is the **Gallery Center Building** with seven floors of art galleries. It's a convenient place to survey the Tokyo art scene.

Turn left at the next big intersection onto Sotobori Dori, marked with a sign in roman letters. This street is commonly known as Dentsu Dori, because it holds some of the offices of Dentsu, Japan's gigantic advertising agency. One block to the left at the intersection with Harumi Dori is one of the city's

more awesome displays of neon. The **Sony Building** is a landmark and favorite rendezvous point. It serves as a showroom for Sony products, and the upper floors, as well as the basements, hold boutiques and restaurants—the most famous of which is the Tokyo branch of Maxim's of Paris.

Now walk from the Sony Building along Harumi Dori back toward Hibiya Park. Squeezed between the overhead expressway and the railway tracks on the right hand side is the **Mullion Building** (Yurakucho Center Building), Ginza's new showplace holding two major department stores, with six movie theaters on top. **Yurakucho Seibu** (closed Thurs.) has all that's good about the Ikebukuro flagship store, arguably Tokyo's trendiest department store, with the latest in both Japanese and foreign design displayed with eye-catching flair. Neighboring **Hankyu** (closed Thurs.) is one of the Tokyo branches of a more traditional Osaka department store.

Every hour on the hour crowds gather out in front of the complex to watch gold cherubs dash out from behind the Seiko clock to announce the time with a burst of chimes. Old Japan hands will remember this is where the famous Nichigeki Theater used to be.

Exiting from the rear of the Yurakucho Center Building, take a short walk to the right back to Sotobori Dori, where to the left you'll find another newcomer–Ginza **Printemps** (closed Wed.), connected with the famous Parisian store. Geared primarily for

The Imperial Palace moat

The Bullet Train

young women, it has many fashion boutiques and restaurants, and the annex connected by a bridge across the street features both Western and Japanese household wares. Foreign travelers will enjoy the fourth-floor corner devoted to quality Japanese crafts.

Retrace your steps along Sotobori Dori toward Shinbashi Station. The avenue is lined with art galleries. Four blocks ahead on the left is **Takumi Craft Shop**, a good introduction to Japan's flourishing folk art industry, with rustic pottery, paper-covered boxes, papier-mâché toys, fabrics, and furniture. Just ahead is the Nikko Hotel from where you take a left onto a narrow street. Straight ahead on Namiki Dori is **S. Watanabe**, one of several galleries in Tokyo specializing in modern woodblock prints and graphic arts, great favorites of the city's foreign community and tourists.

Adjacent to S. Watanabe on the second floor above the Victoria Coffee Shop is the **Tokyo Gallery**, which specializes in avant-garde and modern art. Namiki Dori is one of Ginza's most fashionable avenues. As you stroll along this narrow, tree-lined street back toward the Sony Building, you'll pass more art galleries, dozens of smart fashion boutiques, including the Tokyo branches of Gucci, Louis Vuitton, and A.C. Bang, furriers. **Ketel** offers German dishes. On the right, close to busy Harumi Dori, is the **Yoseido Gallery**, a pioneer establishment in the world of modern Japanese woodblock prints.

Walk back along Namiki Dori to the next intersection and take a left on Miyuki Dori, another attractive Ginza-area thoroughfare paved with brick and lined with trees, to Ginza Fifth street. Turn left, and on the right is the Tokyo branch of Kyoto's famous **Tachikichi** ceramics shop (closed Sun.), featuring both traditional and modern styles at reasonable prices. Continue on Miyuki Dori to what's known as Ginza Street but is officially called Chuo Dori. Across the street on the right is **Matsuzakaya** (closed Wed.), a Nagoya-based department store.

Follow Ginza Street (Chuo Dori) back toward Harumi Dori, and on your left, just before you reach the distinctive glass, silo-like Sanai Building at the intersection, you'll spot **Kyukyodo**, famous for stationery and writing materials, which in Japan means handmade paper, fine brushes—not pens—and incense.

Back on Harumi Dori again, turn right and walk for about five minutes across the next main intersection. On the left is the ornate **Kabukiza Theater**, rebuilt almost to its former splendor after burning down in World War II. If you're even slightly serious about live theater, don't miss seeing one act of Kabuki.

Performances are normally scheduled twice each day throughout the year, except for a few days toward the end of each month. Curtain times are by tradition scheduled at 11:30 A.M. and 4:30 P.M. and programs usually include something old, something more modern, and a dance act, with a different program at each curtain time. Check the English press to see what's playing. Seats range in price from ¥2,000 to ¥13,000. English

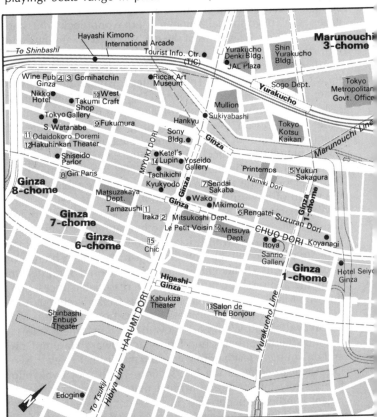

programs and earphone guides are available for an extra fee. If a full program is too long, buy a special ticket for a top balcony seat at a cheaper price for the act of your choice from a special box office on the far left beside the main entrance. You can make reservations by phoning 541-3131.

Continuing east on Harumi Dori another ten or fifteen minutes will bring you to **Tsukiji**, the city's burgeoning fish market, which is at its busiest around 5 A.M., and a number of excellent fish restaurants where freshness is guaranteed. Some 70,000 dealers handle 2,500 tons of seafood per day here. If you're in the neighborhood at lunch- or dinnertime, stop by the

GINZA & NIHONBASHI

Marunouchi Bldg.

Tokyo

Tokyo

Mitsubishi Bank

Tokyo Central Post Office

To Shinjuku, Ueno

okyo Bldg.

Tokyo Station

Tozai Line

Nippon Bldg.

Bank of Japan

• Daimaru Dept.

SOTOBORI DORI

Kokusai Kanko Kaikan

Daini Tekko Bldg.

• Yaesu Book Center

Yaesu 2-chome

YAESU DORI

Yaesu 1-chome

EITAI DORI

Mitsukoshi Dept.

To Kanda

Mitsukoshi-mae

• Meijiya

Ginza Line

• Maruzen

Kyobashi

Bridgestone • Museum of Art

Nihonbashi

• Mayuyama

Takashimaya Dept.

Tokyu Dept.

Nihonbashi 3-chome

Nihonbashi 2-chome

Nihonbashi 1-chome

akaracho

Toei Asakusa Line

SHOWA DORI

Edobashi

main shop of **Edogin** (11 A.M.–9:30 P.M.; closed Sun.), a traditional sushi shop low on looks and price but high on taste. If it's still wiggling, you know it's fresh. Ten pieces of raw fish over vinegared rice balls (*nigirizushi*) plus beer or saké will cost around ¥4,000.

The second walk in the Ginza and Nihonbashi districts takes you from Mitsukoshi to Mitsukoshi, that is, from the Ginza main intersection branch of what is perhaps Japan's most famous department store to the main store at Nihonbashi.

Skip the Ginza branch of Mitsukoshi and save your energy for the big mother store at the end of this tour. **Wako** (closed Sun.) across the street specializes in imported fashions, jewelry, and accessories—most with prices that will make your eyeballs roll. A neighbor just up the street is the **Mikimoto** store, the showcase for Japan's famous cultured pearls of the same name.

Matsuya Ginza (closed Tues.) dominates the next block on the right. Continuing up the street on the right is **Itoya** with nine floors of novelties for the office or graphic design studio. Next door **Sanrio**, the toy manufacturer, operates a glittering toy gallery reached by escalator from the main floor—the closest thing to Disneyland in the city center.

A good place to examine Japanese everyday ceramic housewares is **Koyanagi**, which has been in operation for over a hundred years, on the next block on the left. Here you can pick up some original and inexpensive gifts, such as tiny chopstick rests for a few hundred yen.

If you're searching for authentic oriental antiques, particularly ceramics, sculptures, and paintings, drop into **Mayuyama**, which with over a seventy-five-year history, is the city's oldest antique shop. You'll find it tucked into a street lined with galleries. Continue on Chuo Dori under the expressway to the Kyobashi intersection, then take a right and continue to the next stoplight. It's just around the corner on the left. Tokyo boasts some of the top oriental ceramics dealers in the world today, befitting the Japanese love for fine porcelains and stoneware.

Continue on this narrow street past other galleries and small shops to Yaesu Dori, the next wide boulevard, and turn left. At the end of this avenue you'll spot the modern side of busy **Tokyo Station**, where an average of 3,000 trains depart each day (compared with about 500 at New York's Grand Central).

Just before you reach the next big intersection, in the headquarters of the Bridgestone Tire Co., is the **Bridgestone Museum of Art** (¥500; 10 A.M.–5:30 P.M.; closed Mon.), famous in Tokyo for its French impressionist collection, but more interesting to foreigners for works by Japanese artists who were influenced by the impressionists.

Take a right at the big intersection, and you're back on Chuo Dori, just a few short blocks from **Takashimaya** (closed Wed.), which the Japanese claim is the best department store for Western goods and which foreign residents like because its style of merchandising is similar to that of department stores back home. Especially interesting are the cavernous food halls in the basement, and in the rear on the same floor are a series of small shops featuring oriental curios and antiques. A floor-by-floor guide in English is available from the girls at the information counters, who are smartly dressed, as are the elevator operators, to suit the season.

Across the street is **Maruzen** (closed Sun.), another department store but noted chiefly for its foreign-language book section on the second floor, the largest and most convenient in this part of the city. On the fourth floor don't miss **Craft Center Japan**, a corner devoted to good modern Japanese crafts.

Continue on Chuo Dori to **Nihonbashi Bridge**, which was the hub from which all distances in Japan were measured during the Edo era. The current bridge dates from 1912 and is more Victorian than Japanese.

Just over the bridge and one more block to the left is the **Mi-**

tsukoshi mother store (closed Mon.), its distinctive fuchsia and white wrapping paper a long-time sign of class. The main floor is dominated by a giant sculpture of the Goddess of Sincerity, assuring customers they'll get a fair deal. The store features boutiques of many shops from back home, including Cartier and Tiffany. High tea is served in the late afternoon in an authentic replica of London's Fortnum & Mason Tea Room on the third floor.

This completes your look at Ginza and Nihonbashi, Tokyo's sparkling retail heart, an enticing combination of traditional Japanese good taste and the latest fashions from the West.

GINZA EATS, DRINKS, AND MUSIC

[1] **Tsukiji Tamazushi** 築地 玉寿司 銀座5–8 銀座コアビル ☎573-0057
This Ginza branch of a 50-year-old Tsukiji *sushi* shop packs them in for low-cost, tasty raw fish. Squeeze in at the counter and start pointing. B2 of the Ginza Core Building near the main Ginza crossing. ¥2,000–¥2,500; 11 A.M.–10 P.M.

[2] **Iraka** 甍 銀座5–8 銀座コアビル ☎572-8465
Kansai-style (Osaka area) goodies, easy to select from pictures of set courses outside. B2 of the Ginza Core Building. ¥3,000–¥3,500; 11 A.M.–10 P.M.

[3] **Gomihatchin** 五味八珍 銀座8-2-16 ☎571-2486
The specialty is *kushiage*—meat and seasonal vegetables dipped in a batter and deep-fried—and the atmosphere is Japanese rustic with a bevy of old lamps, china, and glass, plus Christian emblems used by Kyushu feudal lords. No menu. Ask for the *teishoku*, a set course of several skewers with rice, or say "*moriawase kudasai*" and they'll give you a variety of whatever is available. Shout *sutoppu* (stop) when you've had enough, or the bill will keep climbing. Average ¥5,000; 4–10 P.M.; closed Sun., holidays.

[4] **Wine Pub Ginza** ワインパブ・ギンザ 銀座8-2-15 ☎574-1937
A little bit of the Left Bank on the left side of the railroad tracks, this little bistro is popular with Japan's growing number of wine drinkers, mostly under thirty. Casual, and a bargain, compared to the prices at one of Ginza's nearby fancy hotels: wine by the decanter for ¥1,800 up and a snack menu with favorites like fish and chips, pizza, sausage, or spare ribs. 5–11 P.M.; closed Sun., holidays. There's a big-sister establishment named Wine Bar Ginza with higher prices down the street.

[5] **Yukun Sakagura** 有薫酒蔵 銀座2-2 ☎561-6672
Kyushu country food inside a folk-style basement room resembling a saké brewery by stage-designer Kisaku Ito. Yukun *teishoku*, ¥1,200;

onigiri (rice balls wrapped in seaweed) or *udon* (thick noodles) at ¥700; from 11:30 A.M. to 1:30 P.M. Around ¥3,000 from 5 to 10 P.M. No English sign outside. Entrance next to Ginza 1-chome Station across from Yuraku Food Center. Closed Sun., holidays, and the first, second, and third Sat. of each month.

6 **Rengatei** 煉瓦亭 銀座3-5-16 ☎561-7515
This is a Ginza old-timer serving the Japanese idea of Western food, and popular with shoppers and businessmen. The jumbo pork cutlet at ¥1,600 is perhaps the tastiest. 11:15 A.M.–3:15 P.M., 4:40–8:15 P.M.; closed Sun.

7 **Sendai Sakaba** 仙台酒場 銀座4-4-13 ☎564-2082
Northern Honshu cuisine, with fish stews as the specialties in the winter months, amid the Tohoku region's *kokeshi* dolls. The English sign says "Japanese Public Bar Sendai," and this basement room is just off Harumi Dori on the right side of the street leading from Tenshodo jewelers. 4:30–10:30 P.M.; closed Sun., holidays.

8 **Gin Paris** 銀巴里 銀座7-9-11 ☎571-0085
Japan's up-and-coming *chanson* singers draw steady crowds to this theater-style basement room. Pay ¥1,800 for coffee or ¥2,000 for booze at the door and you can sit here forever dreaming of Paris. Just off the Ginza main street across from the Shiseido Boutique Building. Weekdays, 5:30–10 P.M.; Sat., 1:30–10 P.M.; Sun. and holidays, 1:30–9 P.M.

9 **Fukumura** 富久むら 銀座7-6 ☎571-0437
Oden, a vegetable dumpling stew, is a great wintertime warmer-upper. Point to what you want over the counter. A favorite with painters and writers. On Ginza Fifth Street. 11:30 A.M.–1:30 P.M., 4:30–10 P.M.; closed Sun.

10 **West** ウェスト 銀座7-3-6 ☎571-2989
Perhaps the classiest tearoom in all the Ginza. White linen, fresh flowers, and classical music. Popular with shoppers by day, bar hostesses by night. On Dentsu Dori and easy to spot, because the shop's baked goods are sold from the front window. Also branches in Aoyama, Meguro, and Harajuku. 9 A.M.–1 A.M.; Sat., 9 A.M.–11 P.M.; Sun., noon–9 P.M.

11 **Odaidokoro Doremi** お台所どれ味 銀座8-7-10 ☎574-6776
A counter laden with this shop's own dishes of the day makes it easy to order here, and the homemade taste comes cheaply with most dishes below the ¥1,000 mark. They serve a lunch set for ¥850. 11:30 A.M.–2 P.M.; 6 P.M.–1 A.M., closed Sat., Sun., holidays.

12 **Hakuhinkan Theater** 博品館 銀座8-8-11 ☎571-1003
This small theater on the eighth floor of the Hakuhinkan Building on the main Ginza street beside the expressway offers shades of off Broadway far from New York but at Broadway prices, from ¥3,000–¥5,000.

The drama and musical reviews are always changing. The language is Japanese. Ask a Japanese friend to call and find out what's playing.

13 **Salon de Thé Bonjour** サロン・ド・テ・ボンジュール 銀座3-11-15 ☎545-3787

Sleek little Art Nouveau coffee shop offering French coffee and tasty cakes as well as quiche, salads, and cocktails on busy Showa Dori around the corner from the Kabukiza Theater. Coffee and cakes, or a light lunch for less than ¥1,000. 10 A.M.–10:30 P.M.; Sun., holidays, 11 A.M.–9 P.M..

14 **Lupin** ルパン 銀座5-5-11 ☎571-0750

In the alley behind Ketel's German restaurant, this bar dating from 1928 is a gathering place for the intelligentsia and attracts some of the most serious-looking faces in town. 5–11 P.M.; closed Sun., holidays.

15 **Chic** シック 第一銀座ビルB1 銀座5-10-6 ☎289-0474

54

This is a stylish disco for adults, popular with young businessmen and women who work in the area. No jeans allowed; dress should be up-market. A cocktail lounge is available. Most drinks and snacks are under ¥1,000, and on weekends ¥4,000 will buy tickets for all the drinks and food you can handle. 6 P.M.–1 A.M., till 12 midnight Sun., holidays.

16 **Le Petit Voisin** プティ・ボワザン 銀座3-6-1 松屋8F ☎567-1375

The portions are minuscule but the taste is great at this cozy French bistro on the eighth floor Restaurant City of Matsuya. A branch of a popular French restaurant at Kudanshita. ¥1,400 to ¥5,000 for special lunches; from ¥3,600 in the evening. 11:30 A.M.–9:30 P.M.; closed Tues. Special entrance on main Ginza street after 6 P.M. Matsuya closing hour.

ASAKUSA

If the spirit of old Japan survives anywhere in Tokyo, you'll find it in *shitamachi*, Tokyo's "downtown" neighborhoods, meaning down by the several wide rivers—the Sumida, Arakawa, and Edogawa—that flow into Tokyo Bay.

This is where the *Edokko*, or true Tokyoites of at least three generations, still live, and here are preserved two qualities the Japanese still hold dear—*giri* (a sense of obligation to others) and *ninjo* (empathy).

The spiritual heart of *shitamachi* is Asakusa, and especially around **Sensoji Temple**, more popularly known as **Asakusa Kannon** from the Kannon, or Goddess of Mercy, enshrined there. This neighborhood bursts with life at any time, but during the many festivals held here it's especially spirited.

At the **Sanja Festival** on the third Saturday and Sunday in May, for example, the area residents, mostly laborers, bound through the narrow streets carrying one-ton portable shrines. Each group jostles the other with hearty insults, all meant in fun. Japanese macho is in great display—tattooed men looking tough and wearing nothing but their loincloths. The geisha strut around in high wooden clogs with their heads crowned with twenty-five-pound wigs. This is what Japan used to be, and still is, where Westernization hasn't completely obliterated it.

This neighborhood looks, well, almost old—at least compared with the flashier uptown sections. The folks here still take pride in their wooden houses, despite the cost of maintenance these days. Sensoji was rebuilt after being damaged in the last world war, but it looks not so different from before. And the raucous entertainment district full of vaudeville shows, third-rate striptease, X-rated movies, and bath houses with women attendants appeals to the earthy tastes of the area residents just as it always has.

This just may be the Tokyo neighborhood you remember best, because it's nothing like your own hometown.

Asakusa Station is the last stop on the Ginza subway line. A more interesting way to get there is by the Tokyo-to Kanko Kisen water taxis which ply the Sumidagawa River about every forty to sixty minutes between 9:50 A.M. and dusk daily from either Hinode Pier (ten minutes by foot east from the south exit of Hamamatsucho Station) or the Hama Rikyu Park boat landing (ten or fifteen minutes east of Shinbashi Station) to Azuma Bridge, Asakusa (you can also return from Azuma Bridge). It's a forty-minute trip from the pier and costs ¥480. The teahouses which once lined the river have long ago been replaced with a concrete embankment, but the minicruise still has its moments, especially for bridge and engineering lovers.

From Asakusa boat landing or the station, follow the wide avenue west away from the river. Across the street from the Tobu Station is the **Kamiya Bar**, which claims to be Tokyo's first "Western" bar. The Victorian atmosphere has vanished, but its homemade specialty known as "Electric Brandy" is still guzzled. Just down the street is the big gateway **Kaminarimon**, across the street from which the Taito ward office operates an information booth. Flanked by the gods of wind and thunder who protect the goddess enshrined in the **Asakusa Kannon Temple**, the gate leads to the main hall down a colorful alley lined with open-front shops, some with the usual tourist junk, but some with true specialties including fans and tortoiseshell hair ornaments for geishas' wigs—or for you, if your hair is thick enough to hold them.

Through Hozomon Gate, decorated with giant straw sandals, lies the main building which holds a tiny gold image of the Buddhist goddess. Out front is a copper incense burner, the smoke from which is supposed to keep you healthy and free from accidents.

Follow the wide path, usually lined with outdoor stalls selling clothing, to the left as you face the temple. This will lead you to the heart of the "gay" quarter, in the old-fashioned and somehow very appropriate sense of the word. You'll soon come to

a wide cross-street full of second-run feature films and X-rated flicks at prices cheaper than uptown.

For ¥1,800 you can see the Japanese version of a vaudeville show—mostly stand-up comedians, singers, and storytellers—at the **Asakusa Engei Hall**, which has an entrance on the same pedestrian mall.

The Asakusa neighborhood is undergoing a general refurbishing. The old Kokusai Theater, home to a high-kicking dance troupe à la the Rockettes for years, has been replaced with the high-rise Asakusa View Hotel. The beloved striptease house Rockza has moved upstairs above a glittering *pachinko* parlor. Pedestrian walkways are being paved in tiles reminiscent of Rio. The best improvement is **Sumida Park** beside the Sumidagawa River, running north from Azuma Bridge. It's one of the few places in the city where views of the river aren't blocked by warehouses and factories. In early April the park, which spans both sides of the river, is pink with blossoming cherry trees.

ASAKUSA EATS AND DRINKS

1 **Kuremutsu** 暮六つ 浅草2-2-13 ☎842-0906
In an alley just east of Hozomon Gate, entrance to Sensoji Temple. Drinking country-style around the hearth. The walls are decorated with folk art from all over Japan. Drinks (saké or beer), plus a fresh fish from the tank for about ¥5,000. 4–10 P.M.; closed Thurs.

2 **Nakasei** 中清 浅草1-39-13 ☎841-7401
At the end of another alley, this one just off the next wide street west of the Nakamise Dori. A favorite with tempura connoisseurs, including the late writer Kafu Nagai, with the tempura *teishoku* (tempura lunch of the day) from ¥2,500 at tables, ¥7,000 in a *tatami* room, it is as pleasant for its teahouse atmosphere as for the deep-fried seafood and vegetables. Noon–8 P.M.; closed Tues.

3 **Yonekyu** 米久 浅草2-17-10 ☎841-6416
In the covered street arcade which leads north from the theater promenade. Sukiyaki for from ¥2,400, served at low tables in a large *tatami* room. This old restaurant is easily distinguished by the red porch outside. Uses prized Omi beef. 12 A.M.–9 P.M.

4 **Tatsumiya** 東南屋 浅草1-33-5 ☎842-7373
Reasonably priced set menus at ¥2,300 or ¥3,800, depending on quantity and variety, of home-style Japanese dishes in an old house brought from Gifu Prefecture and filled with antiques. Prices cheaper at lunchtime. Try their *gyu rosu bento*, thin slices of tender beef over rice, for

¥800. Noon–2 P.M., 5–9 P.M.; closed Mon.

5 **Otafuku** 大多福 千束1-6-2 ☎871-2521

Asakusa's oldest *oden* palace, with over forty varieties of vegetable and fish-cake dumplings to pick from. ¥1,500 average; 5–11 P.M.; Sun., holidays, 3–10 P.M.; closed Mon.

6 **Ichimon** 一文 浅草3-12-6 ☎875-6800

Saké is the feature—forty-five different types—served in an old Japanese farmhouse. Average ¥3,000; 5–11 P.M.; closed Sun., holidays.

7 **Namiki** 並木 雷門2-11-9 ☎841-1340

The area's most famous noodle restaurant, easily found by the bamboo trees at the entrance. Tempura *soba* (buckwheat noodles with tempura on top) is a favorite. ¥1,400; 11:30 A.M.–8 P.M.; closed Thurs.

58

MORE ASAKUSA ENTERTAINMENT

8 **Mokubakan** 木馬館 浅草2-7-5 ☎842-0709

Japanese storytelling guaranteed to make you cry on the first floor, small-time drama performances on the second. You may not understand the Japanese, but you'll enjoy watching the neighborhood grandmas wiping their eyes and sniffling. ¥900 upstairs; ¥1,200 downstairs.

9 **Rockza** ロック座 浅草2-10-12 ☎844-0693

Striptease to make you scream, "Put it on, put it on!" ¥3,700.

10 **Furansuza** フランス座 浅草1-43 ☎844-7013

More of the same. ¥3,000.

ASAKUSA SHOPPING

Along Nakamise Dori, try **Matsuzakaya** for hair ornaments priced from ¥350; **Kaneso** (just off Nakamise Dori) for Japanese cutlery from ¥1,000; and **Sukeroku** (near Hozomon Gate) for miniature dolls, scenes of old Edo, from ¥500 up.

Yonoya, to the left on the last wide street off Nakamise Dori before reaching Hozomon, specializes in handmade combs of boxwood and camellia wood, all works of art and great for giving hair a luster.

It's fun to explore the covered arcades between the temple and Kokusai Dori. Asakusa is no Western fashion center, as you'll quickly discern. Last year's styles fill the shops.

Japan's **plastic food**, pure kitsch to the foreigner, is on display in a wide variety, along with other restaurant equipment, in the restaurant wholesale district along Kappabashi Dori, the next wide street parallel and to the west of Kokusai Dori. Prices begin around ¥3,000 for a bowl of sweet red beans, a popular dessert. Many of the shops sell retail.

UENO AND NIPPORI

Near Asakusa is this park full of high-brow cultural attractions, plus an adjacent neighborhood reminiscent of the Edo of old.

Ueno Park is a meeting ground for both the cultural cognoscenti, who flock to concerts at the **Tokyo Metropolitan Festival Hall** and art exhibits at three major museums, and a far greater number of citizens seeking the earthier pleasures of the zoo with its panda pair and the honky-tonk spots at the south end of the park.

Although one of the city's largest public green spots, it's the zoo and museums that are the draw, and not the lawns, which are practically nonexistent. It has neither Central Park's views of the skyscrapers through the trees nor the primness of Hyde Park.

Emerging from the north exit of Ueno Station, you'll walk right into the Festival Hall. Across from the hall is the **National Museum of Western Art** (¥360; 9:30 A.M.–4:30 P.M.; closed Mon.), more interesting to the foreigner for its building designed by Le Corbusier than for the European paintings inside. Unless you've had few chances to see European art back home, save your feet for the Japanese and Far Eastern collection at the nearby **Tokyo National Museum** (¥360; 9 A.M.–4:30 P.M.; closed Mon.).

This museum, in a compound with two other buildings, houses the greatest collection of Japanese art in the world. It includes Buddhist sculpture, textiles, woodblock prints, lacquer- and metalware, pottery, and paintings on scrolls and screens. The riches are in such great abundance that not all can be shown at one time. Another building houses Japanese prehistoric artifacts, and the third building a small collection of art from other Asian countries.

Outside the museum gate, take the road to the right and follow it past Tokyo University of the Arts to the second stoplight. Across the street at the right of the intersection a tiny tea-house-like shop named **Torindo** sells sugar-coated vegetables done up in lovely shapes, ideal for gifts for friends back home, and perhaps a nice treat for a Japanese friend, or you can tarry here to take green tea and a Japanese sweet in a set for around ¥500, depending on the cake you choose.

Outside Torindo, take a right and follow the road to the next corner. Then turn right, taking a deep breath as you pass one of the many traditional restaurants in this area—this one serving grilled eel—before the next traffic light.

Across the street on the left is Ichiyoji, the first of many Buddhist temples you'll pass on the paths ahead which follow the

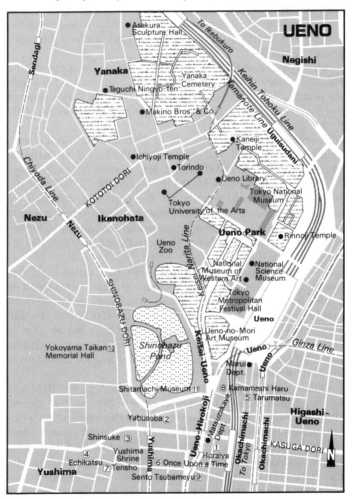

top of a ridge. *Teramachi*, or temple towns, are common in many Japanese cities, though the reason the temples group together in a particular part of town is not very clear. Some old Edo hands say many of the temples in this neighborhood moved out here into what was once the outskirts to avoid the frequent fires in the city proper. Since the houses and temples were made of wood, paper, and straw, and heating and cooking were done with open fires, conflagrations were an everyday occurrence. Sometimes they destroyed large areas of the city.

Whatever the reason, the temples and what goes with them— wooden memorial tablets to dead ancestors, gravestones, flowers, and the heady smell of incense—lend a certain solemnity and dignity that is rare in modern Tokyo.

This temple road takes a bend to the left, then to the right again around a gravestone shop. Notice the old wooden houses on the side street to the left as you pass, and on your route again on the right before you reach the next traffic light.

Take a right at the intersection, and a few steps ahead the road widens, then veers to the right. Shortly past the bend in the road on the right is **Makino Brothers & Co.**, a wholesaler of carvings, where for as little as ¥2,000 you can pick up a simple *netsuke*, the toggle used to secure the medicine or money purses over the belt worn with the kimono in the old days. Such carving is a dying craft in Japan, with only some 200 carvers still at work. Unlike other Asian countries, it's still done by hand here and Makino acts as a middleman between the carvers and retailers.

Follow the road back past the intersection where you turned right. A few steps to your right is **Taguchi Ningyo-ten**, makers of doll heads in an amazing variety. Taguchi-san takes orders from all over the country.

The first road on the right past Taguchi—quite long and narrow—leads past more temples with well-maintained gates and stone gardens. At the far end you'll spot the small weather-worn vermilion gate of another temple, and just to the right of the gate is a fine old wall made of mud, topped with gray roof tiles.

Turn left facing the red gate and follow the narrow path around the temple to the right. At this point the road becomes a footpath too narrow for cars. Below the hill on the left you'll spot the Yanaka Community Center, a long, modern building.

Follow the path on down the hill and around to the left. Just
before you reach the next main road you'll see on the left a narrow lane of old wooden houses with potted plants at the doors
and the family bedding hanging out to dry.

Take a right onto the wide road ahead. This was the main
street of the neighborhood in the old days. Go past a children's
playground on the right, and you'll soon come to a fork in the
road. Take a left, and within seconds you'll come to the entrance of **Yanaka Ginza**, this old neighborhood's equivalent of
the more famous Ginza. The name aside, there is absolutely no
resemblance. Enjoy what is a typical residential area shopping
street full of the things ordinary people buy.

Back up a flight of steps, past a pet shop on the right, and onto
the wide street leading to Nippori Station, you'll come to
another gravestone shop on the right. Turn right onto this street,
and not far on your left, set back off the street through a gate,
you'll spot a sizable concrete building. This is the **Asakura
Sculpture Hall**, (¥300; daily, except Mon. and Fri., 9:30 A.M.–
4:30 P.M.), named after a well-known modern Japanese sculptor
named Fumio Asakura. After seeing some of his works in the
high-ceilinged studio on the main floor, be sure to climb the narrow steps from the second floor onto the roof garden, which affords a fine view of the paths you've trodden, plus the sizable
Yanaka Cemetery, which is parallel to the railroad tracks between Nippori and Uguisudani stations.

UENO EATS AND DRINKS

1 **Horaiya** 蓬莱屋 上野3-28-5 ☎831-5783
A good *tonkatsu* (deep-fried pork cutlet) lunch for ¥2,700; 11:30 A.M.–
1:30 P.M., 4:30–7 P.M.; closed Mon.

2 **Yabusoba** 藪蕎麦 湯島3-44-7 ☎831-8977
An old shop in a new but charming Japanese building serving
buckwheat noodles nothing like your mother made. Considered one of
Tokyo's three best Edo-style noodle shops. Try their *zarusoba*, cold
noodles you dip in a soy-based sauce, during the summer months.
Around ¥1,200–¥1,500; 11:30 A.M.–2 P.M., 4:30–8 P.M.; closed Wed.

3 **Shinsuke** シンスケ 湯島3-31-5 ☎832-0469
The quintessential neighborhood *nomiya* where the area business types
drop in after work for saké, fresh from the barrel in the winter months,
and light snacks, mostly fish-and-seaweed-oriented. If you can pronounce saké (*taruzaké*, if you want it from the barrel) or *biiru* (beer),

you shouldn't feel intimidated here. Average ¥3,000 for beer or saké and a snack; 5–10 P.M.; closed Sun., holidays.

4 **Echikatsu** 江知勝 湯島2-31 ☎811-5293

Sukiyaki in a walled-in private house and garden. This place was once frequented by Meiji-period writers Natsume Soseki and Mori Ogai. ¥5,000; 5–10 P.M.; closed Sun., holidays.

5 **Tarumatsu** たる松 上野6-8-10 ☎835-1755

The drinking man's favorites—seafood and pickled veggies—are the specialty of this Ueno hangout, especially popular with saké lovers since they serve fifteen different kinds here, some of it fresh from the barrel. Behind Marui. ¥3,000–¥4,000 average; 4–11 P.M.; Sun., holidays, 3–10 P.M.

6 **Once Upon a Time** 上野1-3-3 ☎836-3799

Booze, coffee, and snacks—all a bargain by Tokyo standards—in a tiny red-brick 100-year-old saké brewery cluttered with knickknacks. Shades of a Greenwich Village coffeehouse. Drinks, ¥500–¥600; snacks, ¥600–¥800; 6–12 P.M.; closed Sun., holidays.

7 **Tensho** 天庄 湯島2-26-9 ☎831-6571

Some of the best tempura in town is offered in this small restaurant on the street just behind Yushima Tenjin Shrine—and at prices you can afford: ¥1,000 for the special lunch (*teishoku*) (except Sun.) and ¥2,000, ¥2,500, and ¥3,000 for dinner (*teishoku*). Noon–2 P.M., 5–10 P.M.; closed Tues.

8 **Kamameshi Haru** 釜めし春 上野4-9-2 ☎835-0401

If you can't eat plain rice like the Japanese do, try *kamameshi*, a steamed rice casserole flecked with your choice of chicken, vegetables, crab, or shrimp. This restaurant, with a branch in Asakusa, is one of Tokyo's most famous *kamameshi* spots, with tables or tatami mats. ¥850, or you can order set courses with raw fish and soup for ¥3,500 on up; 11:30 A.M.–9:30 P.M.; Sat., Sun., holidays, 11 A.M.–9:30 P.M.

OFFBEAT UENO ATTRACTIONS

9 **Sento Tsubameyu** 銭湯燕湯 上野3-14-5

Tokyo's only all-day public bath open from 6 A.M. to midnight, closed Mondays. A morning bathers' association from the area gathers here for the opening each day. ¥290.

10 **Yokoyama Taikan Memorial Hall** 横山大観記念館 池の端1-4-24 ☎821-1017

This spacious home was once occupied by the late Yokoyama Taikan, one of Japan's most celebrated early-twentieth-century artists, and it offers the best opportunity in the city to see how celebrities used to live, as well as a few of the artist's works. ¥500; 10 A.M.–4 P.M.; closed Mon., Tues., Wed.

Children's sumo match

11 **Shitamachi Museum** 下町風俗資料館 上野公園2-1 ☎823-7461
Here's your chance to see the combination shops/homes of Tokyo's
downtown merchants before the Great Earthquake in 1923 and the fire
bombings in 1945—a re-created street lined with a sweet shop, a cop-
persmith's shop, and many more. The handsome new building faces
the south end of Shinobazu Pond. ¥200; 9:30 A.M.–4:30 P.M.; closed
Mon.

SHINJUKU

The main gateway to Tokyo's ever-growing western suburbs,
Shinjuku forever grows along with the sprawl—a hodgepodge of
urban life that was a few years back made the subject of a New
York Museum of Modern Art exhibit. It's a nightmare for those
who like their urban landscapes well ordered, but proof of the
"No planning is best" concept that chaos can be exciting.

If you can find your way out of **Shinjuku Station**—Japan's
busiest—through which pass more than 1.5 million passengers
per day, you are halfway to capturing the frenzied atmosphere.
Take the west exit, and you're funneled into an underground
plaza which leads to the Odakyu and Keio private railway lines,
each with its own department store. Surface, and you're in
Japan's only skyscraper complex—no match for Manhattan, but

on its way. **Yodobashi Camera Shop**'s store near the south exit usually offers the best prices in Tokyo for cameras and photo equipment. Otherwise the west side is a wasteland for tourists— an urban landscape common to cities everywhere. Kenzo Tange's **Tokyo Metropolitan Government** skyscraper is the most architecturally interesting. The Keio Plaza, Century Hyatt, and Hilton International hotels are in the area.

Of more interest to the visitor is the shopping and entertainment area on the east side of the tracks. Perhaps more than any other section in Tokyo, Shinjuku exudes a feeling of youth. It's the favorite haunt for Tokyo's over a million students, many of whom pour in here after dark to sample the myriad cheap restaurants, bars, and coffee shops.

The blaze of bright lights just outside the east entrance of the station rivals the Ginza for blinding splendor. The animated advertising on the **Studio Alta Building** is a special treat and a traffic stopper. Follow this wide street known as Shinjuku Dori to the right, away from the tracks. This is the area's main shopping drag. The **Takano Fruit Parlor** was once a simple fruit stand; now it's a building full of a lot more than fruit. The **World Restaurant** on the sixth floor offers reasonably priced Scandinavian, German, Indian, Mexican, and Italian food, each in its own little corner. Down the street on your left is **Kinokuniya**, also full of boutiques, but most famous for books, with a large selection of foreign-language books and periodicals on the sixth floor. Along with Takano, this is a favorite get-together point for Shinjuku frequenters. Kinokuniya also shows second-run art films, one of several places in the area specializing in movie revivals.

Farther down the street on the left is **Isetan** department store (closed Wed.), very smart, very popular with the young for the latest fashions from Europe and America. Isetan is one of the city's trendiest stores.

The side street next to Isetan holds a number of movie theaters. Follow it to the left when exiting from Isetan's side entrance to the next big street, Yasukuni Dori.

Across the street and to the left is **Kabukicho**, which stretches from here to the railroad tracks. Packed full of cinemas, restaurants, coffee shops, bars, and discos, it's one of the liveliest night quarters in Tokyo. No special route is recommended. Just wander and let your good judgment be your guide. If you think you're lost, tag along behind any swarm of humanity. Inevitably, they'll eventually lead you back to Shinjuku Station.

SHINJUKU EATS, DRINKS, AND MUSIC

[1] **Tamagawa-zushi** 玉川寿司 新宿3-35-10 ☎352-0331

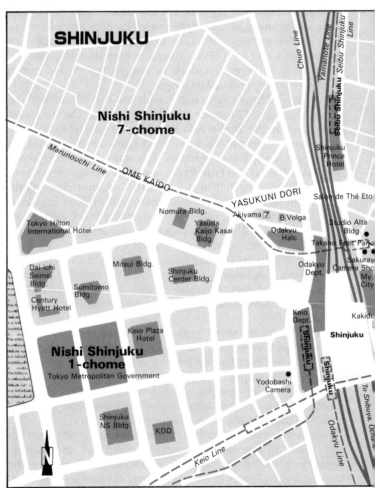

Reliable and reasonably priced sushi in an old building constructed
hastily after World War II. An assortment (*moriawase*) of sushi ranges
from ¥1,200–¥2,000. Their *chirashizushi* is a hit at ¥1,700. 11 A.M.–
11:30 P.M., closed Mon.

2 **Kakiden** 柿傳 新宿3-37-11 安与ビル ☎352-5121

Kyoto's *Kaiseki*-style food—tiny delicacies beautifully served and
guaranteed to leave room for a Big Mac—is the specialty of this

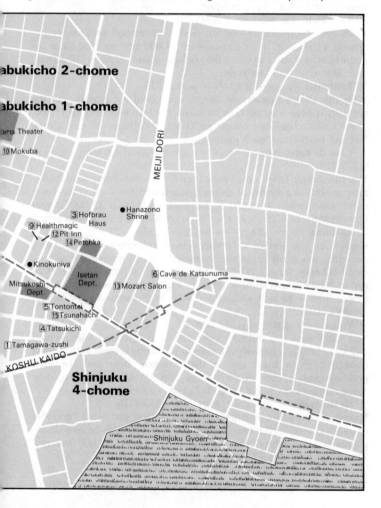

Japanese restaurant on the eighth and ninth floors of the building just behind My City on the east side of Shinjuku Station 11 A.M.–9 P.M.

③ **Hofbräu Haus** ホフブロイ ハウス 歌舞伎町1-1-17 明治生命新宿東ビルB1 ☎207-7591

A branch of the Munich original in beer-loving Tokyo—complete with an oompah-pah band and sausages. A giant mug of draft beer is sold at around ¥1,500; an assortment of sausages for ¥1,500. 5:30–11 P.M.; from 3 P.M. on Sat., Sun., holidays.

④ **Tatsukichi** 立吉 新宿3-34-16 ☎341-9322

Kushi-age—deep-fried vegetables, meat, and seafood on skewers—for around ¥150 each, or in a course for ¥4,000 and up. You sit at the counter, where you can watch the cooks in action. 12 noon–10:30 P.M., to 9:30 P.M. on Sun., holidays.

⑤ **Tontontei** とんとん亭 新宿3-35-10 ☎352-2825

With this shop's homemade sauces you could eat erasers, but the specialty is deep-fried pork, or *tonkatsu*. The lean fillet sells for ¥1,300. There's also a beef-stew course for ¥1,600. 11:30 A.M.–10 P.M.; closed first and third Thurs. each month.

⑥ **Cave de Katsunuma** カーヴ・ドゥ・カツヌマ 新宿3-11-25 飛栄三光町ビルB1 ☎225-4101

You can sample Japan's own wine from Katsunuma, Yamanashi Prefecture, as well as a variety of dishes flavored with the wine in this basement wine cellar. A bottle of the wine costs from ¥2,000; dinner courses from ¥3,500. 11:30 A.M.–2 P.M.; 5:30–9:30 P.M., closed Sun.

⑦ **Akiyama** アキヤマ 西新宿1-4-9 新宿西ビル ☎346-2429

Owned by the son of a famous female columnist named Chieko Akiyama, this small basement restaurant features homemade stews—oxtail (¥2,600), tongue (¥1,800), beef (¥1,700), shrimp (¥1,150), Hungarian (¥1,250). Special stew lunch for ¥580 between noon and 3 P.M.; dinner from 4:30 to 9 P.M.; closed Sun. In the second alley behind Odakyu Halc.

⑧ **Volga** ボルガ 西新宿1-4 ☎342-4996

You can't miss this intimate beer hall in the second alley behind Odakyu Halc. Just follow your nose to the *banyaki* shish kebab being cooked over an open grill at the entrance. Beer and skewered goodies—and a bare room full of film directors and would-be revolutionaries. ¥1,500–¥2,000; 5–11 P.M.; closed Sun., holidays.

⑨ **Healthmagic** ヘルスマジック 新宿3-16-4 ☎350-5736

Soups, pita bread sandwiches, omelettes, salads, and some "gourmet entrees" geared for the health-conscious. Try their high-protein shake, guaranteed to bolster your energy level. ¥1,000–¥2,000 average; 11 A.M.–11 P.M. Also a branch in Harajuku.

⑩ **Mokuba** 木馬 歌舞伎町1-14-7 林ビルB2 ☎200-6484

Ear-blasting recorded modern jazz amid old clocks and gramophones in the second basement of a building facing the side of Koma Theater. Coffee and cocktails in the ¥600–¥800 area; 6 P.M.–12 P.M.; Sun., holidays, from 2 P.M.

11 **Salon de Thé Etoile** サロン・ド・テ・エトワール 新宿アルタ裏 三峰青銅館 ☎354-2255

This place must be seen to be believed. Buried in the bowels of Shinjuku is a replica of the Versailles Palace, complete with crystal chandeliers and cherubs and naked ladies à la Boucher scampering across the walls. Japanese kitsch at its best. Coffee, tea, desserts. Less than ¥1,000; 10 A.M.–10:30 P.M.

12 **Pit Inn** ピットイン 新宿3-16-4 ☎354-2024

A live-jazz enthusiasts' hangout. Performances usually between 11:30 A.M. and 2 P.M., 2:30 and 6 P.M., and 7:30 and 11 P.M. In the alley leading west from the west side of Isetan. ¥1,300 afternoon cover charge, including one drink; evenings, ¥2,500; special events, ¥2,000 and up.

13 **Mozart Salon** モーツアルトサロン 新宿3-5-4 ☎356-6580

The schedules are sporadic, but when classical music performances are held here, it's a casual way to be highbrow—an intimate cabaret-style room on the sixth floor above the Scalaza Theater beside Isetan. Prices vary, depending on performers. Call ahead to be sure if something's playing—and to check the price.

14 **Petchka** ペチカ 新宿3-15-17 伊勢丹会館 ☎352-3554

Russian food is the specialty, although a Russian is not likely to recognize it. The *borscht* soup, *piroshiki*, and Russian tea set lunch is a bargain at ¥800. Also Stroganoff, chicken Kiev, and *shashlik*. On the second floor of the Isetan Kaikan, behind and to the left of Isetan's main store. 11 A.M.–10 P.M.; closed Wed.

Sakuraya Camera Shop

Volga

15 **Tsunahachi** つな八 新宿3-31-8 ☎352-1012

The best tempura in Shinjuku in a local landmark building with a counter, tables, and *tatami* mats. Ask for their *teishoku* at around ¥1,000—several pieces of deep-fried fish and vegetables, rice, soup, and pickles. On the street leading from the east end of Mitsukoshi. 11:30 A.M.–10 P.M.

HARAJUKU, OMOTESANDO, AND SHIBUYA

Like Shinjuku, the Harajuku—Omotesando—Shibuya area is young and trendy. But surrounded by expensive residential areas where the Japanese elite and foreign diplomats rub elbows, it's quite probably the most international nook in all of Tokyo. This is where the boys and girls come to show off and especially on Sunday, when the wide Omotesando Avenue adjacent to Harajuku Station is closed to traffic through Yoyogi Park and on the tree-lined stretch leading from the station all the way down to the Omotesando intersection.

Groups of young teenagers from all over the city flock to **Yoyogi Park** on Sundays to dance their well-practiced routines to recorded music. The majority are considered dropouts and would rather play than adhere to the country's rigid educational system. They leave their middle-class homes in regular rags, then later slip into satin pajama outfits or crinolines kept during the week in train station lockers.

Adjacent **Meiji Shrine**, one of Tokyo's most serene corners, stands in dramatic contrast to the fracas. The vast forest of trees and wide gravel paths there are dedicated to the memory of the emperor Meiji. The shrine buildings are imposing for their stark simplicity. Especially stunning are the iris beds in June, set apart in a separate garden.

Strolling down **Omotesando**, which Tokyoites call their "Champs-Elysées," you'll notice a narrow lane veering slightly uphill on the left side of the street behind the Laforet Building of boutiques before you reach the next main intersection. A few steps up the lane sits the **Ohta Memorial Museum of Art** (¥500; 10:30 A.M.–5:30 P.M.; closed Mon. and the last week of each month), featuring old woodblock prints.

Back on Omotesando, cross the busy intersection and continue down this wide avenue, allowing your fancies to run free in the very up-to-date shops and coffee parlors. On the right is **Kiddy Land**, which, as the names implies, is for kiddies—including some pretty sizable ones. On weekends you can barely move through the aisles of novelties and toys.

Farther down Omotesando, distinguished by its red shrine-like facade, is the **Oriental Bazaar**, another shop popular with foreign residents for a large selection of Imari ware, screens, old chests, lamp bases, plus the usual oriental trinkets foreigners buy.

Just before the Omotesando intersection on the right you'll see a futuristic, mirrored palace dedicated to Japan's famous international dress designer **Hanae Mori**. The first floor offers her boutique items, with haute couture on the third, and a basement full of both oriental and Western antiques.

The wide boulevard ends at Omotesando intersection, but the smart shops don't. Fashion, art, and antique enthusiasts will want to continue into the narrow street on the other side of Aoyama Dori and straight ahead from Omotesando. A five-minute walk will bring you to perhaps the most sleekly elegant

Tokyo flea market

Takeshita Dori, Harajuku

coffee shop in a city famous for such, known as **Yoku Moku**. There's an outdoor terrace for summertime sipping.

Japan's biggest names in fashion design—as well as big-name designers from Europe—have their best-stocked boutiques along this street. **Issey Miyake**'s men's shop is just above Omotesando Station. His women's shop is located down the

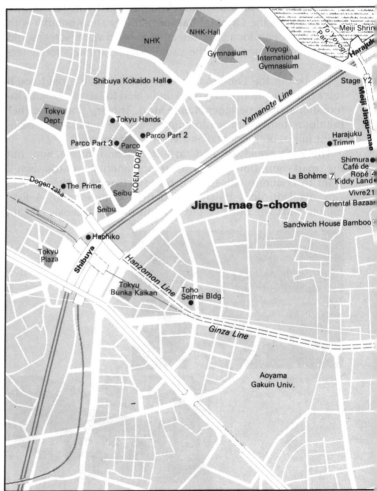

street in the From First Bldg. In between you'll find **Rei Kawakubo**'s Commes des Garçons label, **Georgio Armani**, **Sonia Rykiel** and **Yohji Yamamoto**, to name a few.

Continue along the street and just ahead on the other side of the next traffic signal you'll come to the **Nezu Art Museum** (¥500: 9:30 A.M.–4:30 P.M.; closed Mon., Aug.), a private collec-

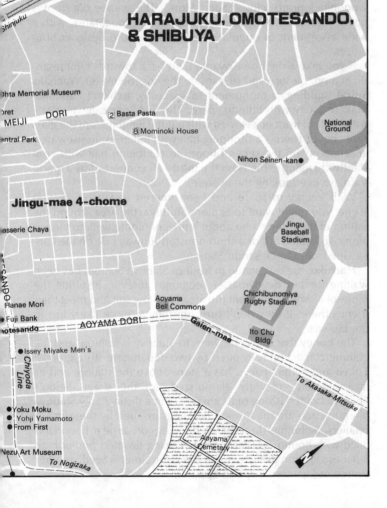

HARAJUKU, OMOTESANDO, & SHIBUYA

Shinjuku

Ohta Memorial Museum

MEIJI DORI

oret

entral Park

2 Basta Pasta

8 Mominoki House

National Ground

Nihon Seinen-kan●

Jingu-mae 4-chome

asserie Chaya

Jingu Baseball Stadium

Hanae Mori

Fuji Bank

notesando

AOYAMA DORI

Aoyama Bell Commons

Gaien-mae

Chichibunomiya Rugby Stadium

Ito Chu Bldg.

To Akasaka-Mitsuke

●Issey Miyake Men's

Chiyoda Line

●Yoku Moku

● Yohji Yamamoto

● From First

Nezu Art Museum

To Nogizaka

Aoyama Cemetery

tion of oriental art, especially renowned for its Chinese bronzes and pottery and paintings connected with the tea ceremony. Don't miss the garden either. Tea ceremony instructions are given in the two teahouses.

Back at the traffic light outside the Nezu entrance gate, turn left and walk to the next traffic light. On the left corner is **Matsushita & Associates**, with a small but good selection of woodblock prints (closed Sun., Mon.). The avenue out front is one of the city's best window-shopping thoroughfares, with a wide assortment of oriental ceramics and more designer boutiques.

If you take a right on Aoyama Dori back towards Omotesando Station, be sure and step inside the lingerie maker Wacoal's **Spiral Building**, a monument to space by architect Fumihiko Maki in a city with little to spare. The first-floor café (11 A.M.– 8 P.M.) sits in front of a garden with natural lighting from the glass roof above. There's a shopping hall with toiletries, housewares, and notions on the second floor; an exhibition hall with constantly changing exhibits on the third—all connected by a grand staircase overlooking the avenue.

With energy to spare and keen interest in Japan's fashion scene, you might want to explore **Shibuya**, the area around the station of the same name about a fifteen-minute walk to the left along Aoyama Dori, or a short nonstop subway ride on the Ginza Line from Omotesando Station.

Hachiko, the dog statue in front of Shibuya Station, has been waiting for her dead master seemingly forever, inspiring the mobs of kids who frequent the area to follow suit and meet their friends there. If they don't turn up, they're more likely lost in the crowds.

The honey that draws the bees to Shibuya is fashion, and the commercial action is inspired by two department store groups, **Tokyu** and **Seibu**. Tokyu has a store above the station, and its flagship store, recently glamorized, up the street. Seibu's Shibuya branch is one of its glitziest. But a distinctively Shibuya phenomenon are the fashion buildings inspired by these major retailers. Seibu has three **Parco** buildings on or near Koen Dori filled with boutiques, **Parco Part II** being devoted primarily to Japanese fashion designers. On the same street is **Seed**, another source of Japanese-inspired apparel.

And now Tokyu and Seibu have moved beyond fashion to fashionable leisure activities. **Tokyu Hands** and Seibu's **Loft** are devoted to do-it-yourselfers who want to make their own household items or crafts. Seibu's **The Prime** on Dogenzaka is filled with restaurants and an American-style cafeteria on the second floor with cuisines from around the world—plus two movie theaters on top.

The increasing number of Japanese youngsters flailing from inside the cocoon of conformity are searching for secondhand clothes in the tiny shops beneath the railroad tracks on the road that leads to Yoyogi Park and Meiji Shrine. Still another celebrated haunt catering to youthful tastes is **Spain Dori**, a narrow lane tumbling downhill from the entrance to **Parco Part III** with a "Spanish" patio and fountain.

HARAJUKU EATS AND DRINKS

1 **Stage Y2** ステージ ワイトゥー 神宮前1-13-12 ☎478-1031
A sleek cafe filled with natural light from the floor-to-ceiling doors that open out onto a terrace for warm-weather sipping and snacking. Popular with the neighborhood's fashion-conscious. Full bar and snacks. A small restaurant is located on the second floor. Drinks less than ¥1,000. Café, 9 A.M.–12 midnight; restaurant, 11 A.M.–10:45 P.M.

2 **Basta Pasta** バスタ バスタ 神宮前2-32-5 フェイスビルB1 ☎478-3022
A great barn of an informal basement room—from every table you can watch the chefs preparing good Italian cuisine in an open kitchen in the center. The seafood is especially good. A la carte menu, but if you choose wisely, you can manage dinner with a glass of wine for ¥5,000 to ¥7,000. Noon–2 P.M., 5:30–10 P.M.

3 **Central Park** セントラルパーク 神宮前4-30-6 ☎478-6200
Drinks and snacks in a neon-ridden central courtyard of an apartment building. Pity the tenants. Open roof in the summer and palm trees the year round give it a New Orleans flavor. Always jammed with teenyboppers. Less than ¥1,000; 11:30 A.M.–9 P.M.

4 **Café de Ropé** カフェ・ド・ロペ 神宮前6-1-9 ☎406-6845
Sidewalk sipping and gawking. Drinks and snacks for less than ¥1,000. You'll almost think you're in Paris. 10 A.M.–11 P.M.

5 **Brasserie Chaya** ブラッセリー茶屋 神宮前5-7-4 ☎486-2695
Authentic French nouvelle cuisine in an unpretentious, well-designed room on the second floor overlooking Omotesando's zelkova trees. There's a daily lunch in the ¥2,000 area; dinner will run from ¥5,000; 11 A.M.–11 P.M., closed Mon.

[6] **Sandwich House Bamboo** バンブー 神宮前5-8-8 ☎407-8427
Tucked behind the Jubilee Plaza Building, this American-style cafeteria serves a variety of sandwiches and salads for under ¥1,000. 11 A.M.–9 P.M.

[7] **La Bohème** ラ・ボエーム 神宮前6-7-18 ☎400-3406
Exotic spaghettis, coffee, and cocktails in an attic-like setting filled with antiques. A great place for late-night noshing. Reached by the alley beside Café de Ropé. 11:30 A.M.–5 A.M.

[8] **Mominoki House** もみの木House 神宮前2-18-5 Youビル1F ☎405-9144
Macrobiotic cooking for the brown-rice crowd, using fresh ingredients untainted by chemical fertilizers. Most dishes, such as a gruel made with brown rice and fermented soybean paste, or grated white radish with ham, are less than ¥1,000. They also serve wine by the glass. 11 A.M.–11 P.M., closed Sun.

ROPPONGI AND AKASAKA

When you're tired of going native—and even the hardiest Japanophile reaches that point occasionally—you have a choice of two swinging nightlife areas full of bars, clubs, and restaurants more like the ones back home. The neighborhoods are Roppongi and Akasaka, and both are just a ten-minute subway ride from the Ginza. Although essentially a pub-crawling district, Roppongi has two new additions which make it worth seeking out by daylight. The **Axis Building** (most shops open 11 A.M.–7 P.M.; closed Mon.), down the street toward Tokyo Tower from Roppongi Station, is an interior designers' fantasy world: furniture, fabrics, accessories, much of it original Japanese design. And **Seibu Wave** (11 A.M.–9 P.M.), just outside the south exit of Roppongi Station, is Seibu's contribution to the scene with four floors of audio-video items, including Tokyo's best record selection, displayed with the very latest video equipment; English-language art books on the fourth floor; and an art-film theater, **Ciné Vivant**, with late-night shows in the basement.

ROPPONGI EATS, DRINKS, AND MUSIC

[1] **Hard Rock Café** ハードロックカフェ 六本木5-4-20 ☎408-7018
Those who know the London original will discover the sophisticates have been replaced here with Japanese youngsters trying hard to look

hip. But there are some reliable American standards like burgers and salads from ¥1,300, and a list of cocktails a mile long. Don't expect to have a conversation, however. Video equipment blaring pop music demands your attention. 11:30 A.M.–2 A.M.; Thurs.–Sat., till 4 A.M., Sun. till 11:30 P.M.

2 **Tong Fu** トンフー 六本木6-7-11 ☎403-3527

Exotic cocktails and American-style Chinese food in a charming house done up in a prewar, decadent Shanghai atmosphere. Better for drinks than food. Drinks from ¥700; dinner averages ¥7,000; 11:30 A.M.–4 A.M.

3 **Mr. Stamp's** ミスター・スタンプス 六本木4-4-2 ☎479-1390

American Al Stamp serves steaks (6 oz for¥2,300 up to 1 lb for ¥5,250) and offers French and American wine from the biggest cellar in Tokyo in an intimate room overlooking the Self-Defense Force headquarters. 5–11 P.M.; closed Sun., holidays.

4 **Cipango** シパンゴ 六本木3-8-15 ☎478-0039

A popular disco done up with orientalia that draws a young crowd. Movies are also shown on a large-screen video. The admission fee of ¥4,000 for men or ¥3,500 for women includes tickets for food items. ¥500 surcharge on weekends. 5 P.M. until the wee hours.

5 **Café Bar 5/6** カフェバー5/6 六本木5-16-52 フォーラム六本木ビル ☎584-5689

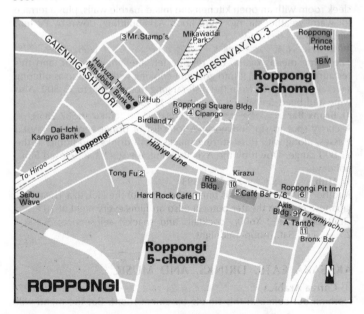

Art Deco and early-thirties flourishes with all your favorite cocktails plus coffee, cakes, and snacks make this a handy place for a rendez-vous. In new Forum Roppongi Building with panthers prancing in the "forum" outside. Drinks from ¥800; noon–1 A.M.; Fri., Sat., noon–2 A.M.

6 **Roppongi Pit Inn** 六本木 ピットイン 六本木3-17-7 ☎585-1063

Rock and jazz, and sometimes the big names turn up here. The performers change almost daily, so it's better to call and find out what's happening. ¥2,500 cover charge with drinks; 7:30–11 P.M.

7 **Birdland** バードランド 六本木3-10-3 ☎478-3456

One of Tokyo's top jazz spots, and it's the performers who are the draw, not the food or ambience. In the sub-basement of the Roppongi Square Building. ¥2,500 cover charge; drinks from ¥750; shows at 7, 8:45, and 10:30; 8:30, 10:15, and midnight on Fri. and Sat.

8 **Roppongi Square Building** 六本木スクエアビル 六本木3-10

Not a single disco, but a building with several. The names and popularity of these places change regularly, so it's best to just step inside each and discover the action for yourself. Roppongi discos average from ¥3,000 to ¥5,000 per person.

9 **A Tantôt** ア・タント 六本木5-7-1 アクシスビル3F ☎586-4431

Good French food, with bargain set lunches at ¥2,300 to ¥3,300 in a sleek room with an open kitchen and inlaid marble walls, plus a terrace for warm-weather dining. Third floor, Axis Building, down by Pit Inn. Noon–3 P.M., 6–10 P.M.

10 **Kirazu** 雪花菜 六本木5-16-5 インペリアルフォーラム2F ☎582-4469

The name means *okara*, the residue left after making tofu, and this restaurant has turned it into gourmet cooking with set courses offering several dishes made from the dish ranging from ¥3,500 to ¥5,500. Also wine and beer. 5 P.M.–5 A.M.; Sun., 5–11 P.M.

11 **Bronx Bar** ブロンクス・バー 六本木5-18-1 ピュア六本木6F ☎587-2850

A classy spot to sip and nosh. A long list of drinks served in crystal glasses, along with thirst-stirring snacks. Both drinks and tidbits in the ¥1,000 range. Down by the Axis Building. 6 P.M.–2 A.M.; closed Sun., holidays.

12 **Hub** ハブ 六本木4-9-2 ☎478-0393

Another "British pub," this one in the lobby of the Haiyuza Theater, a Japanese modern theater outpost (also art films every night at 10 P.M.). Draft beer (¥400–¥600), cocktails and snacks; self-service; 5 P.M.–2 A.M.; Fri., Sat., noon–midnight.

AKASAKA EATS, DRINKS, AND MUSIC

1 **Coffea Arabica** コヒア アラビカ 赤坂3-18-2 第一三州ビルB1 ☎582-1827

Nothing but coffee in this simple basement room. But the menu will bring tears to the eyes of the sophisticated coffee sipper. They can also put a little hard stuff in it for a nightcap. 10 A.M.–midnight.

2 Kaisenkobachi Udon-no-u 海鮮小鉢 うどんのう 赤坂3-14-7 ユニ赤坂ビル B1 ☎584-7461

Homemade *udon* noodles served in a variety of ways are the draw to this convenient spot across from TBS Hall. Their special lunch includes rice, a side dish, and pickles. At dinner, be sure and ask for their *kaiseki bento* served in a lacquered box for ¥1,900. Beer and wine for ¥500 and up. 11:30 A.M.–11:30 P.M.; closed Sun., holidays.

3 Torisei 鳥勢 赤坂2-13-13 アキ赤坂ビル1F ☎585-3268

Yakitori grilled chicken on skewers draws loyal fans to this homey place. Set menus with seven or nine items are a reasonable ¥1,200 or ¥1,800, and in winter their *nikomi* stew made from white fermented bean paste for ¥800 is recommended. 5:30–11 P.M. (to 9 P.M. on Sat.), closed Sun., holidays.

4 Henry Africa ヘンリー・アフリカ 赤坂3-13-14 石田ビル2F ☎585-0149

Cocktails and snacks, or a light lunch, in this casual second-floor aerie with a good view of the street action below. Right in front of the TBS Building. Also in Ginza, Roppongi, and Shinjuku. Average less than ¥1,000; 11:30 A.M.–11:30 P.M.

5 Anna Miller's アンナ・ミラーズ 赤坂3-5-2 ☎586-7369

''Kissin' wears out, cookin' don't'' says the sign—and what could be more Japanese than that? American-style sandwiches, chili, quiche, good salads—and the best pies in Tokyo in the Tokyo version of a

79

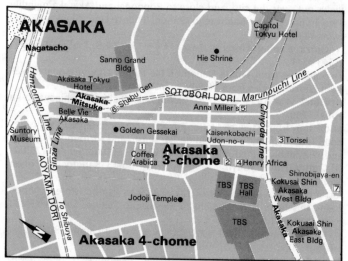

California-based chain of Pennsylvania Dutch coffee shops. 7:30 A.M.–10 P.M. Also on Aoyama Dori, in Meguro, Jiyugaoka, Komazawa, Hiroo, Shibuya, Takanawa, Asakusa.

6 **Shabu Gen** しゃぶ玄 赤坂3-8-1 ☎586-4054

Inexpensive *shabu shabu*—meat, fish, and vegetables you boil yourself—on the fifth floor of the Aruto Building just beside Akasaka-Mitsuke Station. A "Shabu-Gen Dinner" for ¥3,200, or "Special Dinner" for ¥4,200; 11:30 A.M.–2:30 P.M., 5–11 P.M.; dinner only on Sun., holidays.

7 **Shinobijaya-en** しのび茶屋婉 赤坂2-15-10 花柳ビルB1 ☎582-2270

The much-touted Kyoto cuisine right in Tokyo, and at reasonable prices for the genre. The *omakase* set menu with 10 dishes goes for ¥5,000. 11:30 A.M.–2 P.M.; 5:30 P.M.–12 midnight; closed Sun., holidays.

80

TOKYO SLEEPING

BUSINESS HOTELS

The following list was compiled with an eye to convenience and ambience. (Please refer to the map on pages 36–37.)

1 **Hotel Toranomon Pastoral** ホテル虎ノ門パストラル 1-1-1 Toranomon, Minato-ku, ☎432-7261.

Two hundred new rooms on top of a famous wedding hall with fine views out over the city, and close to Roppongi and Akasaka nightlife. Two minutes from Kamiyacho Station, Hibiya Line. Singles ¥7,500, twins ¥11,800.

2 **Ginza Capital Hotel** 銀座キャピタルホテル 3-1-5 Tsukiji, Chuo-ku ☎543-8211.

Two minutes from Tsukiji Station on the Hibiya Line, reasonable walk from Ginza. Singles from ¥6,800, twins from ¥11,800.

3 **Hotel Watson** ホテルワトソン Kamiosaki 2-chome, Shinagawa-ku, ☎490-5566.

Just a hop from Meguro Station on the Yamanote Line, this business hotel is a notch above most in design sense, and surrounded by good and reasonably priced restaurants. Singles ¥7,000 up, twins ¥12,000.

4 **Center Hotel Tokyo** センターホテル東京 15-13 Kabutocho, Nihonbashi, Chuo-ku, ☎667-2711.

Just a couple of blocks east of Takashimaya's flagship store in Nihonbashi, this hotel is convenient to Kayabacho Station. Singles ¥7,200, twins from ¥11,600.

5 **Koraku Garden Hotel** 後楽賓館ホテル Koraku 1-chome, Bunkyo-ku, ☎816-6130.

Tucked quietly between the Toyota headquarters and pretty

Koishikawa Korakuen garden near Iidabashi Station, this business hotel is part of a Chinese culture complex, popular with mainland Chinese. Singles ¥6,500, twins ¥11,000.

6 **Asia Center of Japan** アジアセンター Akasaka 8-chome, Minato-ku, ☎402-6111.

Six minutes from Aoyama 1-chome Station on the Ginza Line subway. Convenient to Aoyama Dori, Akasaka, and Roppongi. Singles from ¥5,000, twins from ¥8,610.

7 **Diamond Hotel** ダイヤモンドホテル 25 Ichibancho, Chiyoda-ku, ☎263-2211.

Five minutes from Kojimachi Station on the Yurakucho Line, by which it's a ten-minute ride to the Ginza, twenty minutes to Ikebukuro. In a quiet residential area behind the British Embassy and near the Imperial Palace. Singles from ¥8,837, twins from ¥15,862, including tax and service.

8 **Shinagawa Prince Hotel** 品川プリンスホテル 4-10-30 Takanawa, Minato-ku, ☎440-1111.

Across the street from Shinagawa Station on the Yamanote Line, this big (1,020-room) hotel sits on top of a complete sports complex. Singles from ¥8,724, twins ¥14,162, including tax and service. A budget member of a big chain.

9 **Hillport Hotel** ヒルポートホテル 23-19 Sakuragaokacho, Shibuya-ku, ☎462-5171.

Streamlined, functional little hotel with updated Art Deco lobby and restaurant, perfect for the visitor interested in Tokyo's fashion scene. Five minutes from south exit, Shibuya Station, and close to Daikanyama's fine boutiques. Singles from ¥9,400, twins from ¥15,000, including tax and service.

10 **Hotel Kayu Kaikan** ホテル霞友会館 8-1 Sanbancho, Chiyoda-ku, ☎230-1111.

Ten minutes from Kudanshita Station, near Chidorigafuchi Park. The Hotel Okura's fine food and service at about half the cost. In a quiet residential area, and good value for the money. Singles ¥10,000, doubles ¥13,000, twins from ¥16,500, including tax and service.

11 **Harajuku Trimm** 原宿トリム 6-28-6 Jingu-mae, Shibuya-ku, ☎498-2101.

Near Harajuku Station on the Yamanote Line; Meiji Jingu-mae Station on the Chiyoda Line. Trendy Harajuku area. Great for jocks, as they can use in-house club facilities. Singles ¥7,200, twins ¥11,400, including tax and service.

12 **Gajoen Kanko Hotel** 雅叙園観光ホテル 1-8-1 Shimo Meguro, Meguro-ku, ☎491-0111.

Five minutes from Meguro Station on the Yamanote Line, from which it's a fifteen-minute ride to Shinjuku, twenty minutes to Tokyo Station.

The perfect spot for Japanese Art Nouveau lovers. Don't let the lobby fool you. Behind it is a treasure of pre–World War II interior detail. In a quiet residential area. Singles ¥9,000, twins ¥15,000.

13 **President Hotel** プレジデントホテル 2-2-3 Minami Aoyama, Minato-ku, ☎497-0111.

In a top location beside Aoyama 1-chome Station on the Ginza Line, near smart shops and restaurants. Lobby offers hints of Europe, though in plastic replica. Singles from ¥9,500, twins from ¥12,500, including tax and service.

14 **Hilltop Hotel** (Yamanoue Hotel) 山の上ホテル 1-1 Surugadai, Kanda, Chiyoda-ku, ☎293-2311.

Pricey in comparison with the others in this listing, but a good buy for the money, if you like well-restored old buildings and a quiet location. Five minutes from Ochanomizu Station on the Chuo and Sobu lines, close to Kanda's bookstores and universities. Nice restaurants and a summertime outdoor beer garden sheltered by trees. Singles from ¥11,000, twins from ¥18,500, including tax and service.

15 **Hotel Tokyo** ホテル東京 2-17-8 Takanawa, Minato-ku, ☎447-5771.

Quiet, family-style hotel featuring Western rooms with Japanese touches such as a tatami area and wooden baths. Just above Sengakuji Station on the Toei Asakusa Line. Singles ¥12,626, twins from ¥13,596.

16 **Shiba Yayoi Convention Hall** 芝弥生会館 10-27, Kaigan 1-chome, Minato-ku, ☎434-6841.

Great views from Takeshiba Pier location over the harbor and Hama Rikyu Park. Seven minutes from Hamamatsucho Station on the Yamanote Line. Singles ¥5,665, twins ¥9,664, including tax and service.

JAPANESE INNS

The following *minshuku* and *ryokan* offer a taste of Japanese life in big-city surroundings.

17 **Suigetsu Hotel Ohgaiso** 水月ホテル鴎外荘 3-3-21 Ikenohata, Taito-ku, ☎822-4611, 828-3181.

¥5,000 for Japanese-style, ¥5,500 for Western-style rooms in a quiet pocket of Tokyo near Ueno Park Zoo and the Yanaka district. Three minutes from Nezu Station, Chiyoda subway line.

18 **Inabaso Ryokan** 稲葉荘旅館 5-6-13 Shinjuku, Shinjuku-ku, ☎341-9581.

Cozy Japanese inn handy to Shinjuku shopping, nightlife, plus pretty Shinjuku Gyoen garden. Three minutes from Shinjuku Gyoen-mae Station, Marunouchi subway line. ¥4,400 per person; Japanese breakfast ¥600, American breakfast ¥300.

19 **Ryokan Mikawaya Bekkan** 旅館三河屋別館 1-3-111 Asakusa, Taito-ku, ☎843-2345.

Japanese inn popular with foreigners, and a stone's throw from the Asakusa Kannon Temple in an old neighborhood. Five minutes from Asakusa Station, Ginza subway line. ¥4,800 per person; Japanese breakfast ¥700, American breakfast ¥700.

YOUTH HOSTEL

20 **Tokyo International Youth Hostel** 東京国際ユースホステル 18th Fl., Central Plaza, 21-1 Kagurakashi, Shinjuku-ku, ☎235-1107. Something different in the youth hostel category—a skyscraper penthouse above Iidabashi Station with nice views over the city. ¥3,850 with two meals; closed Dec. 29–Jan. 3.

SHOPPING OFF THE TOURIST TRAIL

Akihabara, just two stops north of Tokyo Station on the Yamanote Line, is a must for stereo, video, and electronics gadget freaks. Prices are 20 to 30 percent less than the rest of the city, and the big stores have tax-free sections where the equipment is made for the volts and cycles back home.

Ameya Yokocho beside Okachimachi Station, one stop north of Akihabara on the JR Yamanote Line, is for imported jewelry, handbags, lighters, and pens, all piled high in the many tiny shops beneath the tracks. The well-traveled insist that prices for these types of luxury goods are cheaper here than even Hong Kong, and that the dealers are more reliable.

Flea markets are held once a week at various locations: **Arai Yakushi Temple** (Arai Yakushi-mae Station, Seibu Shinjuku Line) and **Togo Shrine** (Harajuku Station, JR Yamanote Line; or Meiji Jingu-mae Station, Chiyoda Line) on the first Sunday of every month; **Nogi Shrine** (Nogizaka Station, Chiyoda Line) on the second Sunday; **Hanazono Shrine** (Shinjuku 3-chome Station, Marunouchi and Toei Shinjuku lines) on the second and third Sundays; **Roi Building** front steps in Roppongi (Roppongi Station, Hibiya Line) on the fourth Thursday and Friday; and again at **Togo Shrine** on the fourth Sunday. Good places to pick up old fabrics, a secondhand abacus, china, chests.

Kanda around Jimbocho Station (Mita Line, Shinjuku Line, Hanzomon Line) is packed with tiny bookshops, many of them specializing in particular subjects and practically all of them with at least a few English-language books. **Kitazawa** and **Isseido** are especially good for used books on Japan and Asia. **Yamada**, across the street from Isseido, has a nice selection of both old and modern prints. Farther up the street is **Ohya Shobo** with a large selection of old prints, books, and maps.

Kokusai Kanko Kaikan, just outside the north entrance of Tokyo Station on the Yaesu side, houses the Tokyo promotional offices of the prefectural governments, each with its own products for sale, mostly handicrafts and food items.

TOKYO DISNEYLAND

By now the whole world knows that Disneyland has come to Japan. It may not be your prime reason for traveling all the way there, but the Tokyo version—practically a copy of the California prototype with a Japanese accent—is certainly worth a day. It offers a nice break from Tokyo's general confusion.

Of course, there is still the confusion of getting there. The easiest means of transportation are the buses operated by JR and Airport Transport Service Co., which leave at ten-minute intervals every day from 9:20 A.M. (from 8 A.M. in summer) from the *very* far north exit of Tokyo Station's Yaesu side (just behind the Daini Tekko Building, where JAL has a ticket office).

The one-way fare is ¥600, and tickets are purchased at the gate. Tokyo Disneyland Ticket Center just inside the Yaesu North Exit of Tokyo Station next to Daimaru Department Store offers admission tickets to the park, or you can wait until you arrive. The trip normally takes about thirty-five minutes. The return buses depart about every fifteen minutes, and the trip usually takes fifty minutes back to town.

The ¥4,400 "Passport" ticket entitles the user to enter all the park's attractions on weekdays; "Big Ten" ticket at ¥4,100 offers ten attractions on weekdays.

Tokyo Disneyland's operating hours vary with the season—shorter in the winter, longer in the summer—and it closes one or two days each week. Call 366-5600 to make sure it's open.

You can also get there by subway. Take the Tozai Line east to Urayasu Station (fifteen minutes from Nihonbashi Station), then hop on the special shuttle bus to the gates. The subway fare varies depending on where you board the train. The one-way bus fare is ¥200, and the trip from Urayasu Station takes about twenty minutes. An alternative is the Yurakucho Line east to Shin Kiba Station, transferring to the JR Keiyo Line direct to Maihama in front of Disneyland, or the Keiyo Line direct from Tokyo Station.

MUSEUMS FOR THE SPECIALIST

Japan Folk Crafts Museum 日本民芸館 (Komaba Todai-mae Station, Inokashira Line—just two stops from Shibuya). A must for the Japanese folk-craft enthusiast. This was once the home of Soetsu Yanagi, the man who got the Japanese back on the folk-art trail, and the building alone is a treasure. ¥700; 10 A.M.–5 P.M.; closed Mon., August.

Paper Museum 紙の博物館 (Oji Station, JR Keihin Line). This is the world's largest museum of paper, with a special section on the manufacture of traditional Japanese *washi*. ¥200; 9:30 A.M.–4:30 P.M.; closed Mon., holidays.

Idemitsu Art Gallery 出光美術館 (Yurakucho Station, JR Yamanote Line). Located on the ninth floor of the Kokusai Building, Marunouchi, this museum is a must for ceramics fans. Also oriental bronzes, calligraphy, and paintings. ¥500; 10 A.M.–5 P.M.; closed Mon., holidays.

Sword Museum 刀剣博物館 (Sangubashi Station, Odakyu Line). A good introduction to Japan's fine art of swordmaking, with thirty "National Treasures." ¥500; 9 A.M.–5 P.M.; closed Mon.

Museum of Maritime Science 船の科学館 (reached by ferry, ¥520, from Hinode Pier, near Hamamatsucho Station, JR Yamanote Line). Replicas and visuals from the shipping industry in a concrete building shaped like a steamship out in Tokyo Bay. ¥500; 10 A.M.–5 P.M. daily.

Meiji University Criminal Museum 明治大学刑事博物館 (Ochanomizu Station, JR Chuo or Sobu lines). On the third floor, Ogawamachi School Building. Criminal-capturing tools from the Edo period, plus old documents. No charge; 10 A.M.–4:30 P.M.; closed Sat. afternoon, Sun., all day Sat. from August 1 to September 31, one week in mid-August.

Fukagawa Edo Museum 深川江戸資料館 (Monzen Nakacho Station,

Tozai Line, then #33 bus to Kiyosumi Teien bus stop). A stage set out of watery old Edo which you can wander through at will, sniffing the life of the city's common folk. ¥300. 10 A.M.–5 P.M.; closed December 28–January 5.

TOKYO DAY TRIPS

Tokyo is smack in the middle of a host of scenic and historic sights which can be reached within a few hours. Possibilities include:

Kamakura, administrative center of the military government in the twelfth and thirteenth centuries, still has enough old temples and shrines, as well as classic Japanese homes with thatched-roofed gates, to make you forget the present. Highly recommended is a walk behind **Kenchoji Temple** (Kita Kamakura Station, Yokosuka Line, ¥880 from Tokyo Station) through a small valley and up the steps to another small temple, from where you catch a trail over the tree-studded hills and

Toshogu Shrine, Nikko

The Great Buddha, Kamakura

down the other side into a residential street that leads to
Kamakura Shrine. The hike takes about one hour. Have a
Japanese-style taco at the coffee shop Bon across the street.
Then stroll back through the residential lanes to **Tsurugaoka
Hachiman Shrine**, dedicated to the war god that no doubt
helped put the town's military Minamoto clan in the driver's
seat. You can stroll to Kamakura Station through the park in the
center of the wide boulevard leading to the shrine, or on a narrow shopping street paralleling the main road to the right. Three
stops from Kamakura Station on the old-fashioned Enoshima-
Kamakura Kanko Line is Hase Station, from where it's a ten-
minute walk to the famous **Great Buddha**, which sits outside in
the open air.

Hakone, in the mountains between the city and Mt. Fuji, is a
spectacularly scenic resort area with many hot springs, hiking
trails, small museums, and views of the famous mountain. Take
the Odakyu "Romance Car" from Shinjuku to Hakone-Yumoto
at the foot of the mountains (¥1,200, 1 hour 50 minutes). At
Yumoto, switch to the Hakone Tozan Railway, a cute little two-
car tram that zigzags up the mountains all the way to Gora
(¥300, 45 minutes), from where you can take a cable car to
Sounzan (¥290) and then a ropeway to Togendai (¥1,180) on
the north shore of Lake Ashi. Before Gora you can stop off at
Chokoku-no-mori to see the **Hakone Open Air Museum** of
sculpture, or one stop before at Kowakidani for a ten-minute
hike to **Chisuji-no-taki** waterfall, then on to a hiking trail which
will bring you back down to the next town below, Miyanoshita
(allow about 2 hours). From Miyanoshita, you can catch the
train back down to Hakone-Yumoto.

Nikko is both a shrine dedicated to the first Tokugawa shogun, Ieyasu, and a scenic wonderland of mountains and lakes.
The foliage is especially beautiful in mid-October. **Toshogu
Shrine**, plastered with gold and polychrome, is less a reflection
of traditional Japanese taste than of the megalomania of the
Tokugawas. But feast your eyes on the very ancient cedar trees
that surround it and, if possible, take a hike up into those forests, right on par with those in the film *Rashomon*. From the
Nishi Sando bus stop near the shrine it's about a 50-minute ride
by Tobu Bus (¥930) to **Lake Chuzenji** and nearby **Kegon Waterfall**. You can reach Nikko town by the private Tobu Line "Ro-

mance Car" from Asakusa Station (¥2,280, 1 hour 45 minutes).

Chichibu is both a town and a national park (Chichibu-Tama) northwest of Tokyo, and about as close to the wilderness as you can get in the city environs. Half the fun of this unspoiled area is getting there. First you take the Seibu-Ikebukuro Line's "Red Arrow" from Ikebukuro to Chichibu (¥1,200). Outside Chichibu Seibu Station, take a left, follow the footpath along the tracks, cross the tracks, and take a right to Ohanabatake Station. Catch the next train on the Chichibu Line bound for Mitsumine Guchi (¥310), the last stop. Then hop on a waiting Seibu Bus to Chichibuko Station (¥380). There, take a waiting yellow microbus up the mountain two stops to Hayashidaira. Just below the bus stop is **Kobushi Minshuku** (☎[04945]5-0457), an old former farmhouse where you can hibernate far from the madding crowd. A path leads down the hill and across the river on a rickety footbridge to **Fudotaki Waterfall**, so pristine you'll think you're in Borneo, not Japan. Allow about four hours from Ikebukuro.

Mt. Fuji, the granddaddy of Japanese peaks at 12,388 feet, can be climbed from July 1 to August 31. But don't expect to have the trail to yourself. You'll be eating the dust of the person ahead of you all the way. There are five climbing trails to choose from, with Kawaguchiko being the most popular and accessible from Tokyo. Buses are available from Tokyo's Hamamatsucho Station (¥2,340) and Shinjuku Station (¥2,160) direct to the fifth stage of the trail daily from July 10 to August 31, and on Sundays only from the third Sunday in April to the third Sunday in November. Allow about 2 hours and 30 minutes. From the fifth stage it's about a five-hour climb to the summit. Some start climbing in the early afternoon and reach the eighth stage before dark to lodge in a hut. Then they climb the rest of the way in the morning. Others prefer starting in late afternoon and climbing all night to see the sunrise from the summit. The descent is usually made on the Subashiri Trail, leaving the summit in the morning and arriving at the fifth stage in late afternoon. From the fifth stage, take a bus to Gotemba (¥930), then a direct JR "Asagiri" train to Shinjuku (¥1,790). You can make a reservation on the direct bus to the Kawaguchiko fifth stage through a travel agent or with Fuji Kyuko (☎374-2221).

KYOTO

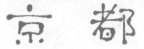

TRADITIONAL JAPANESE TASTE

As in Tokyo, your first stop should be the JNTO TIC office, right across the street from Kyoto Station in the Kyoto Tower Building, ☎(075)371-5649. TIC is open from 9 A.M. to 5 P.M. on weekdays, 9 A.M. to noon on Saturdays, and closed on Sundays and holidays. The staff will give you good maps of the city with bus routes and help you find a place to stay.

Around the station you're apt to think Kyoto is just one more big city. To get a feeling for the old capital, quiet strolls either alone or with a thoughtful friend are recommended, especially in the areas where we've outlined walks. Other spots where you can tune in on this city's special mood will be listed separately.

Kyoto was home to the Japanese emperors, their retinue of courtiers, and Buddhist monks from its founding in A.D. 794, when Tang Dynasty influence from China was strong, until 1868, when Emperor Meiji settled in Tokyo.

The Buddhist monks remained, and Kyoto is still headquarters for many of the major Japanese Buddhist sects. Their presence gives an unmistakable solemnity to the city. It makes you want to walk on tiptoe and speak in whispers.

There is no better place to contemplate true Japanese taste: both its spare aspects influenced by Zen Buddhism and the tea ceremony, and its love for gorgeous decoration. Like few other cities in the world, there is something to stir the mind and heart around every corner.

That so much remains from the past is due partly to the fact

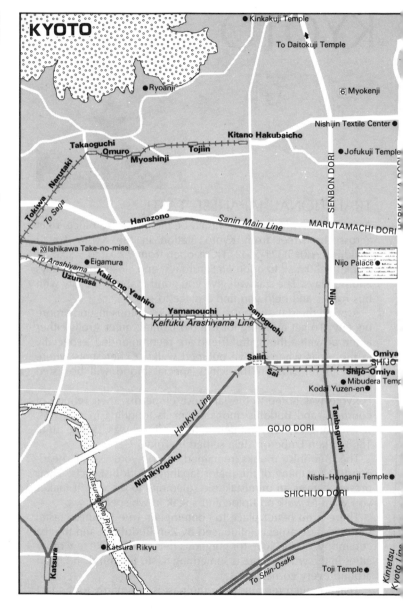

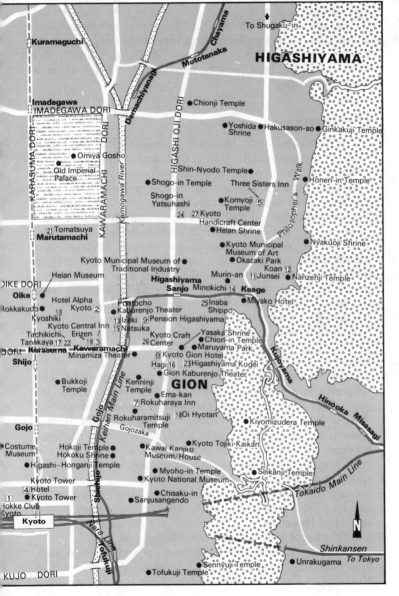

that, unlike Tokyo people, Kyoto people take pride in old things, and partly to the fact that Kyoto was not damaged in World War II. The temple buildings may not be the originals, for this city has, after all, had a long and often violent history. But even if not, they have been painstakingly re-created, some of them many times.

HIGASHIYAMA

The Higashiyama ("East Mountain") area offers all that makes Kyoto truly extraordinary. Start at **Ginkakuji** ("Silver Pavilion"), a fifteen-minute bus or taxi ride from the center of the city. Now a Buddhist temple, this was once the country villa of Ashikaga Yoshimasa, the eighth Ashikaga shogun, who retired here in 1473. It was patterned after the more famous **Kinkakuji** ("Gold Pavilion") on the other side of town, which was built by Yoshimasa's grandfather, Yoshimitsu, though Kinkakuji is a replica, since the original was burned down by an arsonist in the 1950s. Ginkakuji survives as the only original structure from the period. It was never covered in silver leaf as intended, but it is a fine example of the kind of reserved elegance enjoyed by the wealthy of the time. The garden is equally famous for its combination of fine rocks and varieties of moss, and you can almost imagine Yoshimasa ambling down the paths in a silk kimono.

From Ginkakuji, stroll back down the street lined with souvenir shops to a canal bordered by cherry trees and turn left to meander along the gravel "**Philosopher's Walk**," over which Ikutaro Nishida (1870–1945), one of Japan's most famous modern-day philosophers, took his daily constitutional. Since his death the path has taken on a romantic air in the Japanese mind and become popular with young lovers, especially in the spring under the canopy of pink blossoms.

About ten minutes down the path, take a short detour to the left, back up the mountain to the next parallel streets, where you'll find **Honen-in**, a veritable jewel of a Zen garden featuring a thatched-roof gate and two mounds of raked sand.

Back down the hill and on Philosopher's Walk again, continue south past some of the city's finest homes, then pause at **Nyakuoji**, a charming coffee shop where you can admire a garden and European antiques while you drink. The canal and path come to an end not far from the coffee shop. Turn right and walk down the hill to the first wide street, then left for a short walk to **Nanzenji**. It is one of the city's most famous temples, and is noted for its two gateways with sweeping roofs and the dramatic painting over gold leaf of tigers prowling through a bamboo grove, which is on the sliding doors of a room in the superior's quarters. This is a great example of the kind of decorative art popular with the lords of the early seventeenth century. Also, within the quarters is a famous Zen landscape garden.

KIYOMIZU AND GION

Kiyomizudera, perched on the mountainside southeast of the business district, is everybody's favorite temple. What makes it so pleasant are the way the wooden buildings blend with the natural surroundings—the cherry trees in the spring and the maples in the fall—and the wide view of Kyoto from the terrace.

Walk down the steep, narrow street that leads to the temple with shops featuring Kyoto's own Kiyomizu pottery. At a fork in the road a flight of stone steps leads down to the right. From here the granite-paved, narrow streets and alleyways wind past small shops, mud and straw walls, and thatched gateways—all right out of a samurai movie.

You can amble through this area all the way to **Maruyama Park**, another spot famous for its cherry blossoms, and the adjacent **Chion-in**, headquarters for the popular Jodo sect of Buddhism. The temple's gate is considered the most imposing in all Japan, and the gigantic bell in the belfry is one of several which officially ring in the New Year.

Below Maruyama Park and across Higashiyama Dori lies **Gion**, Japan's ultimate geisha quarter, where some of the country's most celebrated geisha still entertain those who can afford it. The quarter is especially noted for its *maiko*, or apprentice geisha, distinguished by their youth and the longer length of their kimono sleeves.

A stroll through Gion, especially after dark, can be rewarding. It's low on neon and high on soft light filtering through paper-covered *shoji* windows, and if you're lucky, a *maiko* may just slip out from a sliding door and pass you on her way to work. With a high wig and her face painted white, she's living proof that this old tradition hasn't been completely abandoned for the women in Tokyo's Ginza.

Song and dance performances by Gion geisha for foreigners are held twice daily at the Gion Corner **Yasaka Kaikan Hall**, a section of the Gion Kaburenjo Theater, March through November, 7:40 and 8:40 P.M. (¥2,100). Perhaps even more enchanting than Gion is Pontocho, a narrow alley lined with places where geisha entertain, parallel to the Kamogawa River along the west bank between Shijo and Sanjo streets.

ARASHIYAMA

This area west of Kyoto, where the Oi-gawa River flows out of the mountains, has been a favorite spot for an outing since the beginning of Kyoto's history. The chief attraction is the scenery—gentle hills covered with cherry, maple, and bamboo—and the river itself. There are buses from the city, but the fastest way is to catch the Keifuku Electric Railway from Shijo-Omiya Station to the terminal at Arashiyama (¥190), or the Hankyu Line from Kawaramachi Station to the Hankyu Arashiyama Station (¥180), changing trains at Katsura Station. From either station it's a short walk to the river, where you can hire a boat for a lazy cruise. Then walk back past the Keifuku Electric Railway station and to the left to **Tenryuji**, another villa turned into a temple, this one once belonging to an emperor. If it's lunchtime, treat yourself to a rare experience at **Sagano**, a restaurant specializing in simmered tofu (*yudofu*), just south of the temple's main entrance. The ¥3,000 lunch is served in a bamboo grove.

Stick to the paths closest to the hills and walk north from Tenryuji. You'll pass a number of Buddhist temples and Shinto shrines which blend into their surroundings so well that it's easy to miss them. Never mind. The lush bamboo forests alone are worth the trip.

PALACES AND ZEN GARDENS

In addition to the special areas already described, Kyoto boasts a variety of sights scattered across the wide plain between the mountains which surround the city on all sides but the south. The attractions fall into two broad types—palaces and castles or more temples, famous either for their Zen gardens or some gorgeously decorated room, often brought intact from a former palace.

Two musts for rock-garden enthusiasts are Ryoanji and Daitokuji. **Ryoanji** is the one you've seen pictures of—just fifteen rocks of various shapes and sizes strategically placed in a long rectangle of raked gravel. Get here no later than 8 A.M., before the tour buses arrive, or forget it. Zen students have been pondering the meaning of this garden since its completion in the early part of the sixteenth century. The pond below, which reflects the verdant hills around, dates from quite early in the city's history and was once part of a villa.

Daitokuji, east of the hills where Ryoanji and Kinkakuji lie, is not a single temple but a collection of subtemples, about a half dozen of which feature famous Zen gardens: Those in Daisen-in, Koto-in, and Ryogen-in are especially nice. These small subtemples were built during the sixteenth century by prominent lords who favored the place. Also notice the gates, especially the big red Chinese gate, brought here from the sixteenth-century warlord Toyotomi Hideyoshi's fabulous Fushimi Castle (parts of which are all over Kyoto), and the two-story gate, attributed to Sen-no-Rikyu, who popularized the tea ceremony in Japan.

Geisha at a tea ceremony

Zuiho-in, Daitokuji Temple

Among the castles and palaces, everyone wants to see **Nijo Palace** (¥200; 8:45 A.M.–4 P.M.), originally the Kyoto home of the first Tokugawa shogun, Ieyasu. It was taken over by the Imperial Household after the Meiji Restoration and has been altered considerably over the years. The Tokugawa crest has been replaced by the Imperial crest wherever possible. There are greater works of art at other palaces, but Nijo gives an overall view of life in a Kyoto palace, complete with wooden corridor floors that creak at the lightest footfall—a way to warn the shogun of impending danger.

At **Nishi-Honganji Temple** near Kyoto Station, you can see a few of the rooms from Hideyoshi's Fushimi Castle. This is probably the finest place in the city to see how the rooms of the rich looked during the Momoyama period (1573–1615), noted for its color and decoration. There are no English tours, but you can join one of the Japanese tours which are scheduled throughout the day. Although somewhat faded, the paintings over gold on the sliding doors and ceilings, plus two Noh stages, offer touches of gilded genius.

For admission to the **Old Imperial Palace** and the two Imperial villas, **Katsura Rikyu** and **Shugaku-in**, you must get permission from the Imperial Household Agency at the Old Imperial Palace. Visits to the two villas require reservations. For details, phone (075)211-1215. Don't forget your passport. At the Old Imperial Palace you can join an escorted morning tour every day except Sundays and holidays by registering at least twenty minutes in advance. Passport necessary. Katsura Villa is most reflective of classic Japanese taste and should be your choice if time is limited. All three are closed Saturday afternoon, Sunday, and holidays.

JUST PLAIN FOLKS

Visits to Kyoto, filled as it is with art treasures created for Japan's religious or highborn elite, are best tempered with breaks at spots with less rarefied atmospheres. The following suggestions are all private homes from not so very long ago which offer glimpses into more modern Japanese life. Each is near some famous Kyoto attraction and, combined with a temple as contrast, gives a chance to get your feet back on the ground.

The **Kawai Kanjiro House**, home to the late famous potter, provides an opportunity to see a country cottage full of folk art, even if not many are works by Kawai (¥700; 10 A.M.–5 P.M.; closed Mon., Aug. 10–20). It's located in the pottery-making neighborhood of Gojozaka and can easily be seen in conjunction with Kiyomizu.

Near Ginkakuji and Philosopher's Walk is **Hakushason-so**, home to the painter Kansetsu Hashimoto (1883–1945), with a nice garden to which Higashiyama's leafy slopes form a backdrop (¥600; 10 A.M.–5 P.M.). At the other end of the walk, near Nanzenji, is **Murin-an**, with another fine garden, this one reflecting the taste of Meiji-era politician and statesman Aritomo Yamagata (1837–1922) (¥200; 9 A.M.–4:30 P.M.).

Although highly commercialized, sorely lacking in adequate English signs, and incessantly buzzing with schoolchildren on outings, **Toei Movieland** in Uzumasa (ask for Eigamura—"Movie Village") has been known to please foreign guests with its samurai movie sets, sometimes peopled by live actors (¥1,550; 9 A.M.–5 P.M., 9:30 A.M.–4 P.M. November 16–March 15, closed Dec. 21–Jan. 1.; Uzumasa Station, Keifuku Electric Railway, Arashiyama Line).

For the experience of seeing how Kyoto folks relax in their spare time, you might visit **Shozan**, a recreation complex with a

Japanese restaurant (10:30 A.M.–9 P.M.) and spacious garden, plus an art gallery (¥300; 9 A.M.–5:30 P.M.), bowling center, and swimming pool, located north of Kinkakuji (Bus No. 6, Doten-jocho stop).

And like practically every Japanese city, Kyoto, too, has its tower—Kyoto Tower, the observation platform jammed with country people knocking each other down to see the down-town rooftops below (¥600; 9 A.M.–9 P.M., Kyoto Station).

DO–IT–YOURSELF CULTURE

Kyoto's traditional cultural institutions open their doors to in-terested foreigners who want to try their hand at some Japanese experience, although don't suppose that these pastimes occupy the modern Japanese mind with abiding passion.

Before choosing a craft, visit the **Museum of Traditional Industry** at Okazaki Park (no charge; 9 A.M.–4:30 P.M.; closed Mon.) to see samples of Kyoto's craft industries, including weav-ing, dyeing, pottery, damascene work, lacquerware, and dolls.

Possibilities for doing-it-yourself include:

Stencil dying on silk (Kyo-yuzen) (call Kodai Yuzen-en, [075] 821-8101; ¥500, 9 A.M.–5 P.M.).

Inspecting a pottery kiln (Kiyomizu-yaki) (call Unraku-gama, [075]591-1506; no charge, open every day, 9 A.M.–5 P.M.).

Woodblock print making (call Gallery Gado, [075]464-1655; ¥1,000; first and third Wed. each month, 1:30–3:30 P.M.; English instruction).

Tea ceremony demonstration (Urasenke School) (call [075]431-3111; ¥1,000; Thurs. only, except Jan., Aug., Dec., holidays, 1:30 or 3 P.M.; English explanation; reservations required).

Zen meditation (Sosenji Temple) (call Mr. Okumura [0774] 88-4103; no charge; first and third Mon. each month, from 6 A.M.; guidance in English).

GETTING AROUND

The tourist on a budget quickly learns the city's bus routes. The JNTO Kyoto map shows where they operate. The fare is ¥170. A single subway line from Kyoto Station north as far as Kitaoji runs under Karasuma Dori, but rarely passes places foreign visitors frequent. Fares begin at ¥160. A one-day ticket for ¥900 entitles you to use the bus and subway line as much as you want on that day. Taxi fares start at ¥480, with ¥80 for each 0.5 kilometer after the initial distance. You can reach most of the major landmarks from the city center for around ¥1,000. Kyoto taxi drivers are more patient with non-Japanese than their Tokyo counterparts. Simply point to your destination on your tourist map.

KYOTO SLEEPING

1 **Hokke Club Kyoto** 法華クラブ京都 Kyoto Eki-mae, Shimogyo-ku, ☎(075)361-1251. Just outside the Karasuma exit of Kyoto Station. Japanese and western rooms, big Japanese bath under a skylight. Singles from ¥6,200, twins from ¥5,300 per person.

2 **Hotel Alpha Kyoto** ホテルアルファ京都 Sanjo-Agaru, Kawaramachi Dori, Nakagyo-ku, ☎(075)241-2000. New business hotel in heart of shopping area and convenient to all attractions. Singles from ¥6,790, twins from ¥11,490.

3 **Kyoto Central Inn** 京都セントラルイン Shiji-Kawaramachi Nishi, Shimogyo-ku, ☎(075)211-8494. Recently renovated. Conveniently located near shopping center and not too far from surrounding attractions. Singles from ¥5,500, twins from ¥9,350.

4 **Kyoto Tower Hotel** 京都タワーホテル Kyoto Eki-mae, Shimogyo-ku, ☎(075)361-3211. Handy location right in front of Kyoto Station. Singles from ¥6,000, twins from ¥11,000.

5 **Three Sisters Inn (Rakuto-so)** 洛東荘 Okazakimichi, Kurodani-mae, Sakyo-ku, ☎(075)761-6336. Japanese rooms, to the joy of the predominantly foreign clientele. English-speaking staff can help you find your way around the city. Nearby annex has a bath in every room. Singles from ¥7,800 without bath, twins from ¥9,800 with breakfast, served family-style around a U-shaped counter.

6 **Myokenji** 妙顕寺 Horikawa-Teranouchi, Kamigyo-ku, ☎(075)414-0808. A Buddhist temple *minshuku* convenient to Daitokuji and Ryoanji. ¥4,000 with breakfast.

7 **Rokuharaya Inn** 六波羅屋 147 Takemuracho, Higashiyama-ku, ☎(075)531-2776. Old-style inn in charming Gion quarter, handy to Kiyomizudera and Higashiyama attractions. Singles ¥5,000 per person with two meals, ¥4,500 with breakfast only, ¥3,500 with no meals.

8 **Kyoto Gion Hotel** 京都祇園ホテル Gion Minamigawa 555, Higashiyama-ku, ☎(075)551-2111. Cozy business hotel in convenient location right on the Shijo Dori shopping street and handy to Kiyomizu, Gion, and Higashiyama. Singles from ¥8,100, twins from ¥13,800.

[9] **Pension Higashiyama Gion** ペンション東山 Sanjo-sagaru, Shirakawa-suji, Higashiyama-ku, ☎(075)882-1181. Brand new, tiny inn with just thirteen rooms on pretty Shirakawa River near all Higashiyama attractions. Singles ¥3,600, twins ¥7,200; American breakfast ¥800, Japanese dinner ¥1,800.

KYOTO EATS AND DRINKS

[10] **Kyoshiki** 京四季 中京区麩屋町三条上ル ☎(075)221-4840, 4866
This old house and garden, made into a restaurant, was a favorite of the late writer Yasunari Kawabata and was also a must stop for sculptor Isamu Noguchi when he visited. The name means ''four seasons'' and implies it serves seasonal *kaiseki* delicacies. Lunch course from ¥2,500. Special free green tea and sweets service on Mondays and Wednesdays when you order lunch. English menu. 11 A.M.–9 P.M.; closed Dec. 29–Jan. 2.

[11] **Junsei** 順正 左京区南禅寺草川町60 ☎(075)761-2311
One of a number of restaurants serving *yudofu* (simmered tofu), bean, and vegetarian dishes near Nanzenji Temple, but this is one of the oldest, dating from 1834. ¥2,150 up; 11 A.M.–8 P.M.

[12] **Koan** 壺庵 左京区南禅寺福地町86-16 (075)771-2781
Vegetarian delicacies in a temple atmosphere with a garden, including noodles made from soybean flour. ¥2,500; lunch only; 11 A.M.–4:30 P.M.; closed Wed.

[13] **Izeki** いぜき 中京区先斗町通四条上ル中程鴨川ぞい ☎(075)221-2080
Pretty *kaiseki* dishes in an informal setting overlooking the equally pretty Kamogawa River. Lunch set menus in the ¥2,500 range. Select from what's in the window outside, or from a picture-menu. Popular with Kyoto housewives, who seem to gather here in flocks for lunch. Right on narrow Pontocho. Noon–8:45 P.M.; closed Wed.

[14] **Minokichi** 美濃吉 左京区栗田口鳥居町65 ☎(075)771-4185
Famous old (1716) restaurant serving Kyoto specialties amid folk art in an old farmhouse. Near Miyako Hotel. ¥5,500 up; 11:30 A.M.–9 P.M.

[15] **Natsuka** ナツカ 先斗町四条上ル 栞ビル2F ☎(075)255-2105
When you're tired of Japanese food, this little French bistro offers tasty morsels, plus a view of the Kamogawa River from the second floor. On Pontocho. Special lunch ¥1,500; dinner ¥3,500–¥6,000; 11:30 A.M.–2:30 P.M., 5–9 P.M.; closed Wed.

[16] **Hagi** 波ぎ 東山区高台寺通下河原町463 ☎(075)531-4551
Coffee, tea, or juice from either tables or *tatami* mat overlooking a pretty garden. Great place to take a break while strolling from Kiyomizudera Temple to Maruyama Park. Japanese set lunches from ¥800 to ¥1,500 during the noon lunch hour. 10 A.M.–5 P.M.; closed Thurs.

KYOTO SHOPPING

The main shopping drag is **Kawaramachi Dori** between Shijo and Oike Dori, along with two covered shopping arcades that parallel Kawaramachi to the west. Shops selling Kyoto specialties such as dolls, pottery, lacquerware, silks, brocades, damascene, cloisonné, and incense are concentrated here. Antique lovers should not miss two areas: **Shinmonzen Dori**, just east of the Kamogawa River between Sanjo and Shijo streets, and Teramachi Dori, between Oike Dori and the Old Imperial Palace. These are probably the greatest concentrations of old things for sale in all Japan. A flea market is held at **Toji Temple**, southwest of Kyoto Station, on the twenty-first of each month. Textile fans can see how the city's *nishijin ori* and *yuzen* silks are made at centers where the processes are explained. The **Nishijin Ori Kaikan** explains *nishijin* silk weaving and sells items made from the fabric. **Kodai Yuzen-en** demonstrates how designs are hand-painted on this type of silk. At **Nihon Shishukan** you can view and buy Japanese embroidery. If you enjoy the bustling activity of a morning food market, take an early-morning stroll through **Nishiki-no-Ichiba**, an alley which parallels Shijo Dori just to the north from Teramachi Dori to Horikawa Dori.

17 **Tanakaya** 田中彌 下京区四条通柳場馬東入ル
Right on Shijo Dori, this shop specializes in Kyoto dolls in their full splendor. Also has a demonstration corner. 10 A.M.–6:30 P.M.; closed Wed.

18 **Oi Hyotan** 大井ひょうたん 東山区清水3
A six-foot-high gourd at the entrance tells what's inside—dried gourds in a wide array. Gourds were once used by the samurai to carry their saké on their belts—the sure sign of a playboy. 10 A.M.–6 P.M.

19 **Erizen** ゑり善 下京区四条通河原町西入ル
Kimono maker to Kyoto's old families since 1584, and a gorgeous display, indeed. For about US$2,000 you can order a nifty number in which you can slink around in your own bedroom. 10 A.M.–6 P.M.; closed Mon.

20 **Ishikawa Take-no-mise** 石川竹の店 右京区嵯峨天竜寺造路町35
Out in Arashiyama, the Sagano district is thick with bamboo, and this shop has about 1,000 different things crafted with the wood—flower baskets, dolls, even holders for your teacup. 9 A.M.–6 P.M.; closed Wed.

21 **Tomatsuya** 十松屋 上京区京都御所堺町御内の西
One of the oldest fan dealers, turning out silver and gold works of art for the Imperial Household, classical Japanese dancers—or you. 9 A.M.–8 P.M.; closed Sun.

22 **Tachikichi** たち吉 下京区四条富小路角
On Shijo Dori, a famous pottery shop using old methods to make modern ceramics. The third floor has a nice selection of Kyoto's own

Kiyomizu-yaki (Kyo-yaki). 10 A.M.–7 P.M.; closed Wed.

23 Higashiyama Kogei 東山工芸 東山区高台寺北門入ル

Near Yasaka Shrine, all of Kyoto's folk-art specialties—masks, dolls, clay bells—are stocked here. 10 A.M.–6 P.M.

24 Shogo-in Yatsuhashi 聖護院八ッ橋 左京区聖護院山王町6

Kyoto's most famous pastry is a cinnamon and sugar-flavored rice cake known as *yatsuhashi*, and this old shop created it back in 1689. 8 A.M.– 6 P.M.

25 Inaba Shippo 稲葉七宝 東山区三条通白川橋西入ル 今小路町86

One of the most famous cloisonné shops in all Japan. Hand-painted enamelware on jewelry, cigarette cases, vases, etc. 9 A.M.–5 P.M.

26 Kyoto Craft Center 京都クラフトセンター 祇園四条通花見小路東

Not to be confused with Kyoto Handicraft Center below, this shop offers up-to-date, modern crafts by Kyoto's best designers, and there's always an alluring array to choose from. Coffee shop on first floor. 11 A.M.–6 P.M.; closed Wed.

27 Kyoto Handicraft Center 京都ハンディクラフトセンター 左京区熊野神社 東入ル

Built especially for foreign visitors, the tour buses never fail to bring you to this spot behind Heian Shrine. All the famous Kyoto products, but not necessarily for discriminating tastes. Let your eye be your guide. 9:30 A.M.–6 P.M.; Dec.–Feb., 9:30 A.M.–5 P.M.

NARA, UJI, OHARA, AND MT. HIEI

A thirty-three-minute ride from Kyoto on the Kinki Nippon Railways limited express train (¥900) brings you to **Nara**, Japan's first permanent capital and the door through which much Chinese influence came during its brief heyday from A.D. 710 to 784. The city's chief attractions are widely scattered, perhaps the most important being **Horyuji**, reached from Nara on the JR Kansai Main Line (¥230, Horyuji Station). The worldly-wise Prince Shotoku, who founded the temple in A.D. 607, made this place the fountainhead of Japanese art and culture. Its main hall

102

may be the oldest surviving wooden structure in the world, and the treasure hall is filled with priceless objects from the period. The octagonal Yumedono (Hall of Dreams) is where the prince meditated on Buddhist principles. By taking the JR Sakurai Line south from Nara to Sakurai (¥310), then the Kinki Nippon Railways about ten minutes east to Hasedera (¥150), you'll find **Hasedera Temple**, which is reached by climbing a steep hill through a forest of peony trees and is one of the most breathtakingly situated in all Japan. Nara lords used to flock out here for a rest, and you'll have no trouble understanding why. In Nara proper your first stop should be **Todaiji**, headquarters of the Kegon sect and all its temples in the provinces, and site of the country's biggest Buddha, almost fifty feet high. On the grounds is the **Shoso-in** (Treasure Depository), which is kept tightly sealed, except for a week in the fall when the rare works from the Nara period are put on view. The **Nara National Museum** near the entrance to **Nara Park** is open all year. Nearby, **Kofukuji Temple**'s five-story pagoda, especially its reflection in Sakusawa Pond, is practically a symbol of Nara. **Kasuga Shrine** is remarkable for some 3,000 stone lanterns which line its paths and are lit twice a year (Feb. 3 or 4 and Aug. 15).

The Keihan Electric Railway will take you from Kyoto's Keihan-Sanjo Station to **Uji** in forty minutes (¥250). **Byodo-in**, once the villa of Fujiwara Michinaga in the tenth century, became a monastery in 1052 and is today the finest example of architecture from the Fujiwara period (A.D. 794–1192). Some architects have called its main hall the most beautiful building in the world. It houses a sculpture of the Amitabha Buddha in sublime repose. On your way back to Kyoto you might stop off at **Daigoji Temple** to see Kyoto's oldest structure, a five-story pagoda, and the celebrated **Sambo-in**, as the buildings and garden are a great example of the warlord Hideyoshi's extravagant taste.

Two easy trips north of Kyoto are to **Ohara**, a small village still retaining its country charm, and **Mt. Hiei**, site of the great Enryakuji Temple and a Kyoto landmark. From Kyoto Station or Keihan-Sanjo Station it's a one-hour bus ride to Ohara (¥450). You'll want to see **Sanzen-in**, noted for its lush garden full of pastels in the spring and rich reds and yellows in the fall. Some of the buildings were reconstructed from the ceremonial hall of the Old Imperial Palace. Across the valley is **Jakko-in**, a secluded nunnery founded by an empress dowager who became a nun after her son's demise.

Mt. Hiei can be reached by bus from either Kyoto Station or Keihan-Sanjo Station in about one hour (¥720). The **Enryakuji Temple** there was founded in A.D. 788 at the top of this mountain by Saicho, founder of the Tendai sect, to protect Kyoto from the evil spirits which were suppose to come from the northeast. It later became a center of militant Buddhism, and its monks often swept down the mountain to stage raids, sometimes even threatening the Imperial Palace.

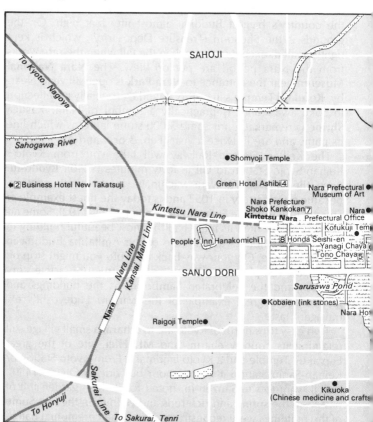

NARA SLEEPING

[1] **People's Inn Hanakomichi** ピープルズイン 花小路 23 Konishicho, ☎(0742)23-8753. Western-style. Near the Kintetsu Nara Station. Singles ¥5,600; twins ¥11,600.

[2] **Business Hotel New Takatsuji** ビジネスホテル ニュー たかつじ 5 Shiba-tsujicho 4-chome 12, ☎(0742)34-5371. A short walk from the Kintetsu Shin-Omiya Station. ¥5,500 per person. ¥700 breakfast.

[3] **Wakasa Ryokan** わかさ旅館 14 Oshiagecho, ☎(0742)22-3143. ¥8,000–¥10,000, ¥12,000, ¥15,000 with two meals.

[4] **Green Hotel Ashibi** グリーンホテル 馬酔木 16-1 Kitamachi 1-chome, Higashimuki, ☎(0742)26-7815. Western rooms. Singles from ¥5,150, twins from ¥9,270.

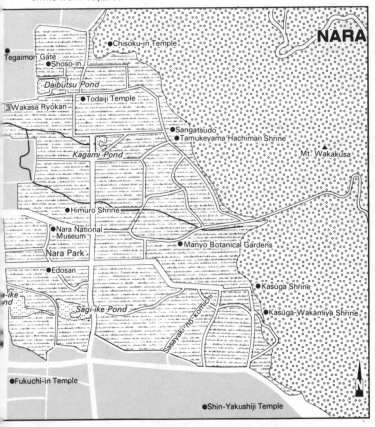

NARA EATS AND DRINKS

5 **Tono Chaya** 塔の茶屋 登大路町47 ☎(0742)22-4348
A special *kayu bento* lunch for ¥2,500 is served on antique plates in this teahouse. 11:30 A.M.–9 P.M.; closed Tues.

6 **Yanagi Chaya** 柳茶屋 登大路町4-49 ☎(0742)22-7460
Save up for this one. ¥6,000 will get you a special lunch course of fried tofu in *miso* sauce, green tea, and rice soup, along with several other dishes—all overlooking a beautiful garden behind Kofukuji Temple. 11:30 A.M.–6 P.M.; closed Wed.

NARA SHOPPING

7 **Nara Prefecture Shoko Kankokan** 奈良商工観光館 登大路町38-1
A display hall of Nara handicrafts, including dolls, lacquerware, and masks. On Sanjo Dori. 10 A.M.–6 P.M.; closed Mon.

8 **Honda Seishi-en** 本田青紫園 東向通中町
A local folk-art shop offering Nara's own carved wooden dolls and gorgeous fans used for dancing—or as a decoration on your TV set. 9 A.M.–6 P.M.

OHARA SLEEPING

Minshuku Ohara-Sanso, 民宿 大原山荘 17 Kusaocho, Sakyo-ku, Ohara, ☎(075)744-2227. Fifteen minutes from Ohara bus stop, beside Jakko-in. ¥5,500 with two meals.

Minshuku Ohara-no-sato, 民宿 大原の里 41 Kusaocho, Sakyo-ku, Ohara, ☎(075)744-2917. A quiet retreat just outside Kyoto at the entrance to Jakko-in. ¥6,000 (¥6,500 Sat., Sun.) with two meals.

Pension Yase Ohara, ペンション 八瀬大原 116-1 Yase Nose-machi, Sakyo-ku, Ohara, ☎(075)722-6041. New pension convenient to Jakko-in and Sanzen-in. Just beside Yase Yuenchi bus stop. ¥4,900 per person without meals, ¥7,400 with dinner, breakfast; ¥8,400 July 20–Aug. 31 and at New Year's. Extra ¥1,500 single service charge.

OSAKA

大 阪

NEW IMAGE IN SIGHT

Osaka, with an area population of 13.5 million, is the leading city of the history-rich Kansai area that includes Kyoto and Kobe. It has for so long taken the brunt of nasty jokes by Tokyo dilettantes, it has developed an inferiority complex. However, the city planners aren't down yet. A "Twenty-first Century Plan" is under way to put Japan's "second city" (the city proper now ranks third behind Tokyo and Yokohama in population) into the international big leagues.

For the foreign visitor expecting a factory town, surprise! The evidence is everywhere that beautification is being taken seriously. The greenery sprouting up around the new buildings in front of mammoth Osaka Station and down imposing Midosuji Boulevard, lined on both sides with ginkgo trees, and around Nakanoshima Island at the city's very heart, rivals anything Tokyo's business centers have to offer. True, there is virtually no sightseeing attraction worthy of the name, but then, neither is there a true "must-see" sight in Tokyo. Accept Osaka for what it is—a maze of commercial excess—and the true big-city hedonist can have just as good a time here as in Tokyo.

Getting your bearings is certainly far easier in Osaka. There are really only two main sections you need bother yourself with: North (**Kita**), also known as **Umeda**; and South (**Minami**), also known as **Nanba**. The two beehives of buying/selling are split by the aforementioned Nakanoshima, a long and skinny island that runs east and west between the Dojimagawa and Tosaborigawa rivers. They are connected by that stately boulevard

OSAKA

To Shin-Osaka Tenjinbashisuji 6
Tokaido Main Line
Nakazakicho
Osaka Loop Line Tenma
Sakuranomiya
Ogimach

Osaka ● Hankyu Dept.
Umeda Higashi-Umeda
Nishi- Sonezaki 8 Daimi
Umeda ● Dai-Ichi Hotel
Fukushima Sonezaki Shinchi Nishi-Tenma Minami-Morimachi
London 11 Umeshin East 1 Toko Hotel 3
Tea Room Hotel 16 Nihon Kogeikan Mingei Fukyubu
Musica 10 12 Samboa Bar ● Tenmangu Shrine
Dojima Hotel 2 9 Wakaba
Dojimagawa ● City Hall Keihan Main Line Kyobashi
River Nakanoshima ● Museum of Katamachi
Higobashi Yodoyabashi Oriental Ceramics ● Fujita Art
● Osaka Univ. 4 Nakanoshima Inn ● Nakanoshima Park Museum
Kitahama
Tenmabashi
Edobori Osaka
Castle
Kitahama

Chuo Line
Awaza Chuo Odori
Honmachi Sakaisuji Honmachi Tanimachi 4
Moriomiya

13 Bistro Eventhia
6 Hotel Do Sports Plaza Tanimachi 6
14 Tokuoka's Wine
Hotel Nikko Osaka Shinsaibashi Nagahoribashi
Hotel California 5 7 Ark Hotel Tamatsukuri
Yotsubashi ● 15 Bar Be-in
AMERIKA ● Daimaru Dept.
MURA YOROPPA MURA
Dotonborigawa River 17 Japan Life
Shiomibashi ● Kani DOTONBORI
Doraku ● National Bunraku Theater
Namba ● Nippombashi Tanimachi 9
Shin-Kabukiza Theater ● Tsuruhashi
● Takashimaya Dept. Uehonmachi

● Osaka Stadium

Yoshiharabashi

Daikokucho Shitennoji-mae Momodani
Imamiya-Ebisu ● Imamiya-Ebisu Shrine
Imamiya Ebisucho ● Shitennoji Temple
● Tsutenkaku
Tower
Shin-Imamiya ● Osaka ● Tennoji Park
Municipal
Art Museum
Dobutsuen-mae
Tennoji Teradacho
To Nara

N

108

called Midosuji, under which runs an air-conditioned subway line by the same name that will take you almost everywhere worth seeking out.

Should you base yourself in Umeda or Minami? Both have a myriad of shopping opportunities, large office complexes, and a wealth of restaurants and clubs to choose from. Although Umeda is fast sprucing up and now has even a Hilton International Hotel as evidence of its current status, Minami still gets the nod for the fashion-conscious—a sort of Harajuku and Roppongi rolled into one.

If you're coming from Tokyo or Kyoto, you'll probably arrive via the Shinkansen (Bullet Train) which stops at Shin-Osaka Station, not the big Osaka Station in Umeda. Smack in the middle of a Japanese "new town," Shin-Osaka provides no reason to tarry. Hop aboard a Midosuji Line subway which runs north and south below Shin-Osaka, to either Umeda or Shinsaibashi Station, the latter in the center of the Minami area.

You'll need a map of Osaka. If you haven't picked up one from TIC in either Tokyo or Kyoto, you should make your first stop the **Osaka Municipal Tourist Information Office** in Osaka Station (8 A.M.–7 P.M., every day). It's located at the very east end of the long concourse that runs the full length of the station behind the new ACTY Building and Daimaru department store. Someone is usually on hand who can handle a foreigner. JAL also publishes a *Kyoto/Osaka & Kobe Shopping and Dining Guide*, available at English-language bookstores throughout Japan, which is especially valuable for its close-up maps of both the Umeda and Minami areas.

Whether above ground—or below—the sheer volume of things to buy, places to eat, and people to see can keep you running through Umeda for at least half a day. Start at the neighborhood's flashiest evidence of new prosperity—**Daimaru Department Store** (closed Tuesday), with fourteen floors, including a host of restaurants on the fourteenth story. If you still can't find something to eat, go up two more floors to the sixteenth floor, the "ACTY Osaka" restaurant floor (10 A.M.–9 P.M.; closed Tuesday).

Across the street from Daimaru to the left is the older, old-world **Hankyu** department store (closed Thursday), which has an English video recording to help you find your way. Hankyu is a private railway company which can take you by express train at cheaper prices and in faster times than JR to Kyoto, Kobe, Takarazuka, and Senri from the big terminal behind the department store. Adjacent to the Hankyu main store are two boutique-filled subsidiaries: **Navio Hankyu** (closed third Thurs. each month), and **Hankyu Five** (closed third Tues. each month), where you'll find the wares of Japan's trendiest fashion designers in its basement "Designer's Collection." Hankyu also goes well underground behind its railway station in a complex called **Hankyu Sanbangai**, which has a "river" flowing amid the eating spots on the very bottom level.

Sanbangai is a good introduction to the three kilometers of **underground arcades** that fan out in several directions from the Osaka and Hankyu terminals. This is Japan's biggest underground shopping complex and, in spots at least, its most attractive, with open plazas gurgling water and flashing lights. It's a good place to escape on one of Osaka's steamy summer days. The Dojima Chika Center tunnel will take you almost to Nakanoshima Island. There are signs in English at the main intersections of the underground complex, but expect to remain hopelessly lost.

When the sun sets, Kita's office workers do what Japanese office workers all over the country do—pour into the thousands of bars in the area to unwind. Only Tokyo's Ginza outdazzles Kita's **Sonezaki-Shinchi** quarter for expense-account glitz. If one of Japan's big companies isn't paying the bill, you'd be wise to keep out of this area's watering holes, but a walk through the streets—especially **Shinchi Hondori**—just south of National Route 1 and west of Midosuji is as exhilarating for its show of managers in blue or gray suits and bar hostesses in both Western and Japanese finery as any nightspot in the country.

The junior execs and just plain folks concentrate in **Sonezaki** proper, just south and a little east of the Hankyu conglomeration, and especially along the narrow covered alley that runs north and south roughly down the middle of the neighborhood. There's a good sprinkling of the sleazy, and the touts here hawking flesh don't even take a break during broad daylight. Again, it's an interesting place to observe Japanese life, but you're better off observing, not trying to participate.

Just a short ten-minute walk south, but a world away from the tawdriness, is **Nakanoshima**. A Parisian will quibble, but this long, narrow island, if it does not resemble the Ile de la Cité in appearance, at least holds the same associations. There are the imposing civic buildings with their neo-Greek and Roman façades; Nakanoshima Park, Osaka's oldest (from 1891), which lacks the trees of the little park below Pont Neuf, but makes up for it with its rosebeds in bloom from May to November; and at the west end, the Osaka Royal Hotel, gathering place for the city's rich and powerful.

Not to be missed if you're even remotely interested in oriental ceramic art is the new **Museum of Oriental Ceramics** at the west end of the Park. Its Korean celadon collection is considered the best outside Seoul, and, although not as numerous, the Chinese pieces are among the very best in Japan. This is the world-famous Ataka Collection, given to the city by the Sumitomo Group, and housed in a building created especially for it. The first-floor coffee shop has its own entrance from the street and affords a fine view of the park and Dojimagawa River below.

From the nearby Yodoyabashi Station, just south of Nakanoshima on the Midosuji Line of the subway (this station is also the Osaka terminus for the Keihan Railway line from Kyoto), you can board a southbound train and be in Shinsaibashi Sta-

Osaka Castle

Nakanoshima

tion, gateway to the **Minami** area, in just a few minutes. With three major department stores and a covered shopping arcade boasting some of Osaka's best shops, Shinsaibashi has been the city's classiest shopping area since World War II. **Daimaru** (closed Wednesday), in an elegant Art Deco building whose first-floor chandeliers alone are worth the effort of entering, and neighboring **Sogo** (closed Thursday) sit right on top of the station. The Osaka store of Japan's famous **Takashimaya** (closed Wednesday) is at the next station south down the Midosuji Line, known as Nanba.

The big treat for trendy young shoppers and sippers are the very up-to-date boutiques and eating/drinking places popping up on both sides of tree-lined Midosuji. On the east side behind the shopping arcade is **Yoroppa Mura** (European Village), boasting shops obviously influenced by the Continent; on the west side a little south of JAL's Nikko Osaka Hotel is **Amerika Mura** (American Village), with a more laid-back ambience. You don't have to be very old to be too old for these two relatively new commercial developments. But if you're homesick, you'll like the feel. There are some really well-designed café bars that will prompt you to give more attention to Japan's current international design sense.

For more traditional Japanese nightlife, follow the shopping arcade south to **Dotonbori**, the neon-festooned canal holding high-spraying fountains colored at night by underwater lights. They don't cram together this much neon anyplace else in the world. After a thorough blinding, cross the bridge and take a left into the pedestrian thoroughfare that parallels the canal to the south. On the corner you can't miss the flapping claws of the sizable crab that adorns the entrance to **Kani Doraku**, a famous crab-specialty restaurant.

Walking east, there is every Japanese taste treat imaginable, and a few that are not. At the next bridge on the left, pick up a small tray of *takoyaki* from the outdoor stall. *Tako* is octopus, and *takoyaki* are balls of egg batter that contain bits of octopus and spices. It was allegedly invented in Osaka, inspired a hit song back in the early seventies—and has since gone nationwide.

Dotonbori and the adjacent alleys are packed with bars, some of them reputable, some of them not. There are also a number of movie theaters. If you are looking for the kind of theater the Japanese used to like, there is Osaka's own Kabuki theater, the **Shin-Kabukiza**, down by Takashimaya. Farther east from Namba near Nipponbashi Station is the **National Bunraku Theater**, home to Japan's famous *bunraku* puppets, notable for their beauty and the fact that you can see their operators dressed in black deftly moving the puppets across the stage. *Bunraku* was born in Osaka, and both *bunraku* and Kabuki flourished as entertainment for the merchant class from the seventeenth to the early nineteenth centuries. Your chances of catching a performance are slim, however, as the two theaters seem most often to be closed.

To round out your mental picture of Japanese society, a trip to what is probably the most famous day-laborers' quarter in the country is an eye-opener. True, the vast majority of Japanese think of themselves as middle-class. But a few, of course, don't follow the strict rules imposed on them. Escaping from society—and in many cases their families—they go to Osaka's **Shin Sekai** (New World), the center of which runs north from Dobutsuen-mae Station on the Midosuji Line approximately to Tsutenkaku Tower, one of Japan's first observation towers (now there's one in practically every Japanese city), just west of the Tennoji Park Zoo.

Osakans insist foreigners have no business in the area. True, clip joints flourish, many of them run by *yakuza*, Japan's families of gangsters. But a brisk walk past the rows of cheap theaters, counter-only restaurants, mah-jongg parlors, discount clothing stores, and old-time theaters where males take female parts in the early evening before the place is awash with drunks, will assure you that Japan, too, has its dropouts. If you tend to your own business, it's not likely anyone will bother you here.

History? Emperors once lived on the site where the ferroconcrete **Osaka Castle** now stands, but it was Hideyoshi Toyotomi, the sixteenth-century warlord, who saw the location's strategic value, consolidated many of the feudal clans to the west, and built a castle of proportions so grand that the Japanese had never seen anything like it. The great stone revetments are even now reminders that in the war-torn Japan of the late sixteenth century, mammoth meant might. Hideyoshi also coerced the prosperous merchants from nearby Fushimi (near Kyoto) and

113

Sakai to move in, assuring them that during the next 250 years the city would become Japan's most important distribution center. Rice went first to Osaka, and then to the rest of the country. There are museums on the second and seventh floors of the castle donjon with personal artifacts of Toyotomi, armor, and folding screens (¥400; 9 A.M.–4:30 P.M.)

Like Tokyo, Osaka has a myriad Buddhist temples and Shinto shrines popular with the people who live in their immediate surroundings. None of them rival the famous landmarks in nearby Kyoto and Nara, but if you happen upon one when a neighborhood festival is in progress, you'll quickly capture the ebullience of the participants as they lug around the portable shrine in a gesture of bringing the locally venerated gods out to the people.

The city's most famous festivals take place in July. The **Tenjin Matsuri**, held July 24–25, is one of the country's three biggest. On the evening of the twenty-fifth the shrine and costumed historical characters are carried by a fleet of boats up and down the Okawa River, northeast of Nakanoshima, followed by fireworks. Then on July 30–August 1 the **Sumiyoshi Shrine** (Sumiyoshi-koen Station, Nankai Main Line) stages the city's last big summer festival, with the local kids hauling small shrines across the nearby Yamatogawa River and an evening fish market. As is true all over Japan, this Sumiyoshi Shrine, headquarters for all shrines of the same name, is especially popular with the country's seafarers—its stone lanterns were donated by sailors and shipowners. Before land was reclaimed, it stood near the water's edge: Sumiyoshi Park to the west was once a beach.

Osaka's most famous Buddhist sanctuary is **Shitennoji**—

Tenjin Matsuri

called Tennoji for short—because it claims to be Japan's oldest. Prince Shotoku, who encouraged the introduction of Buddhism from China, founded it in A.D. 593, fourteen years before the more famous Horyuji Temple in Nara. But earthquakes, fires, and the last war have left Tennoji's present artificial atmosphere of concrete replicas totally bereft of charm.

Inveterate museum-goers will find a variety of small exhibition halls in Osaka, most of them, however, tucked away in hard-to-find corners that make the final viewing almost not worth the effort. Notable for fine art is the tiny storehouse of the late Baron Fujita, the **Fujita Art Museum** (across the street from Taikoen Restaurant—also on the baron's land—near Tenmabashi Station, Keihan Railway Main Line Tanimachi subway line).

Unquestionably Osaka's best "sight" is the Osakan, a breed of Japanese unto himself, known for his acute business acumen and gutsy, brawling lust for life—a sort of lovable tramp with a heart of gold. He/she likes to have a good time, dress with flair, and above all, eat well, spending his/her last yen for a bowl of noodles. These very qualities that, frankly, put off the non-Osakan are the same qualities with which the Osakans endear themselves to a foreigner. Just when you begin to think there is not a Japanese in the land who will look you straight in the eye and tell you what he/she thinks, you meet a man/woman from Osaka, shattering your notions of the Japanese race. Very refreshing.

Once laced with canals, the city's lifeline used to be these waterways. The low-slung, see-through-top **Aqua Liner** pleasure boats will take you on a 60-minute spin through the canals past Osaka Castle (April–September; 10 A.M.–5 P.M. weekdays, to 7 P.M. Fri., Sat., Sun., holidays; ¥1,540; from Yodoyabashi, Tenmabashi, or Osakajo). The city's railroads, however, will take you farther. In addition to the six subway lines, there are five private railways, plus the JR loop line, to assure that you're never very far from your destination. Again, you buy your tickets from machines, the fare calculated by the distance traveled, with fare maps in English posted near the machines at most stations.

A new international airport is destined for a manmade island out in Osaka Bay. The current international airport is JAL's second international hub in Japan, with flights to most corners of the world. The best thing about it is that it's only thirty minutes by bus from either Umeda's Osaka Dai-Ichi Hotel in front of the JAL office or the Hotel Ichiei, Nanba. Buses stop in front of the domestic check-in counter, from which its a short walk back to the international terminal. Buses are also available to the airport from Shin-Osaka Station, Kyoto, and Kobe (remember, this airport serves the whole Kansai area).

MUSEUMS FOR THE SPECIALIST

Osaka Municipal Art Museum 大阪市立美術館 (Tennoji Station, Tanimachi subway line, JR Kansai Main Line). Interesting for the Jomon-type pottery and ancient artifacts dug up from around the city, and also has modern Japanese artwork. (¥200; 9:30 A.M.–5 P.M.; closed Monday).

Fujita Art Museum 藤田美術館 (Tenmabashi Station, Keihan Main Line, Tanimachi subway line). Top-quality Japanese decorative art treasures from the collection of the late Baron Fujita displayed in a tiny storehouse. Have a look at the baron's garden behind the Taikoen Restaurant across the street. ¥500; 10 A.M.–4 P.M., closed Mon.

Craft Museum 日本工芸館 (Namba Station, Midosuji, Yotsubashi, and Sennichimae subway lines). Small but good collection of Japanese folk art in an interesting building.

Farmhouse Museum 日本民家集落博物館 (Ryokuchi-koen Station, Kita Osaka Kyuko Railway, a northern extension of the Midosuji Line). A collection of some fifteen Japanese rural houses reconstructed in Hattori Park. ¥400; 9:30 A.M.–4:30 P.M.; closed Mon.

National Museum of Ethnology 国立民俗学博物館 (Senri Chuo Station, Midosuji, Kita Osaka Kyuko lines, then Hankyu bus to Expo '70 Memorial Park). An entertaining way to learn about the world's cultures with a library of video films available to individuals in a stunning building designed by Kisho Kurokawa. Two other museums face the garden outside, a legacy from Expo '70 held at the site.

OSAKA SLEEPING

There are a wealth of business hotels in this business-minded metropolis—some of them imaginatively designed as well as convenient. The following were chosen with an eye to ambience as well as accessibility to public transportation.

[1] **Umeshin East Hotel**, 梅新イーストホテル 4-11-5 Nishi Tenma, Kita-ku, ☎(06)364-1151. A good ten-minute walk to the nearest subway station, Umeda on the Midosuji Line, but the slight inconvenience is worth it if you're sensitive to surroundings. This striking new building has a dramatic lobby with high ceilings, rough ceramic tile walls, and a view of a garden through the plate glass. Restaurant, tiny bar on the premises. On a street lined with antique shops and galleries, and a short walk to Nakanoshima Park. Singles from ¥6,800, twins from ¥10,000.

117

[2] **Dojima Hotel**, 堂島ホテル 2-1-31 Dojimahama, Kita-ku, (06)348-0111. A bit of the Continent in, of all places, Osaka! This hotel dates from 1984, but it has a definite old-world feel inside, and the rooms are bigger than the usual business hotel cubbyhole. Continental and Japanese restaurants. Dojima Club offers entertainment. Halfway between Higobashi and Nishi-Umeda stations, Yotsubashi Subway Line, handy to Nakanoshima business offices. Singles from ¥11,000, twins from ¥20,000.

[3] **Toko Hotel**, 東興ホテル 1-3-19 Minami-Morimachi Kita-ku, ☎(06)363-1201. A basic no-frills operation with sparsely furnished, small rooms. There's a restaurant and bar. Right above Minami-Morimachi Station, Sakaisuji and Tanimachi subway lines. One of a chain. Singles from ¥6,300, twins from ¥11,400.

[4] **Nakanoshima Inn**, 中之島イン 1-13-10 Edobori, Nishi-ku, ☎(06)447-1122. Run by the Osaka Royal Hotel, so good service is assured, but don't expect the luxury touches of the mother hotel at these prices: singles from ¥7,000, twins from ¥11,000. Right above Higobashi Station, Yotsubashi Subway Line, and handy to Nakanoshima business establishments, as the name implies.

[5] **Hotel California**, ホテル カリフォルニア Daihojicho, Nishinocho 24, Minami-ku, ☎(06)243-0333. Too cute for words, but if you can stand all the affected casualness—and the kids who fill the first-floor café bar—you're steps from fashionable Shinsaibashi shopping and smack in the heart of Amerika Mura. Three minutes to Shinsaibashi Station, Midosuji Subway Line. Singles from ¥6,790, twins from ¥13,590.

[6] **Hotel Do Sports Plaza**, ホテル ドゥ スポーツプラザ 3-3-17 Minami-Senba, Minami-ku, ☎(06)245-3311. You guessed it. This is where those

so inclined "do sports" in the ninth-floor athletic club. You don't have to "do sports," however, to enjoy the handy location on the northern fringes of the Shinsaibashi shopping area and in what's left of Osaka's wholesale garment district, and the low rates: singles from ¥8,500, twins from ¥11,000. Five minutes to Shinsaibashi Station, Midosuji Subway Line.

7 **Ark Hotel**, アークホテル 1-19-18 Shimanouchi, Minami-ku, ☎(06)252-5111. In place of Noah's animals, this "Ark" offers herds of the human species in what's always a busy lobby. Big for a business hotel (381 rooms), but right above Nagahoribashi Station, Sakaisuji Line, close to the Bunraku Theater and a short walk to Minami's Yoroppa Mura. Singles from ¥6,000, twins from ¥10,300.

OSAKA EATS AND DRINKS

Ah, food. Osakans live to eat—or so they say. But if you're used to the Tokyo variety of Japanese cuisine, the Kansai variety served in Osaka may take some getting used to. The dishes themselves are basically the same—sushi, eel, tempura, sukiyaki. The difference is in the flavor, which is lighter and sweeter. You may long for a salt shaker. Some Japanese dishes are supposed to have been invented here, such as *okonomiyaki*, a sort of cabbage and tidbit pancake. There are many foreign restaurants as well—a good place to indulge in something familiar before you head again into the hinterlands.

8 **Daimi** 大巳 北区曽根崎2-5-23 ☎(06)315-0160

Eel, Osaka-style, and freshness is practically guaranteed, since you have to pass through the first-floor eel market before reaching the stairs to this second-floor workingman's favorite. Prices start at ¥950 for the *nami* over rice in a box, up to ¥1,500 for the *tokujo*. 11 A.M.–9:30 P.M., till 7:30 P.M. on holidays; closed Sun.

9 **Wakaba** 和佳葉 北区堂島浜1-4-27 ☎(06)345-5743

Office workers from the Dojima and Nakanoshima areas flock into this basement room for low-priced, quality Japanese noodles starting at ¥380 for *udon* with vegetables. Tempura over noodles is just ¥1,000. 11:30 A.M.–9 P.M.; closed Sun., holidays.

10 **Musica** ミュージカ 北区堂島1-5-17 ☎(06)345-5414

The decor suggests Eastern Europe, but this place is actually connected with a shop by the same name in Sri Lanka, and that means fine teas—not only from Sri Lanka. Also desserts. 10 A.M.–10 P.M.; closed Sun., holidays.

11 **London Tea Room** ロンドン・ティー・ルーム 北区堂島2-2-38 ☎(06)347-0107

This place could have been plucked off London's Regent Street. Authentic English tea served English-style amid old-world charm. Also a good

English breakfast served in the morning, a nice alternative to your hotel, if you can wait until opening time. 9 A.M.–10 P.M.; 11:30 A.M.–6 P.M. Sun., holidays.

[12] **Samboa Bar** サンボア・バー 北区堂島1-5-40 ☎(06)341-5368
Osaka's oldest Western-style bar from 1918, the present version an authentic English-style pub where most customers stand amid well-varnished wood and polished brass. 5–11 P.M.; Sat., 4–10 P.M.; closed Sun., holidays.

[13] **Bistro Eventhia** ビストロ・エヴァンチア 南区南船場3-2-6 ☎(06)243-9141
The unusual name belongs to the French wife of the owner, and a more laid-back spot for French food is hard to find in Japan. No pretense, just good food in the ¥3,000–¥5,500 range for dinner, less than ¥2,000 for lunch. 11:30 A.M.–2:30 P.M., 5:30 P.M.–9:30 P.M.; closed Sun., holidays.

[14] **Tokuoka's Wine** 徳岡ワイン 南区南船場3-5-26 ☎(06)251-4560
A café-style wine bar behind a liquor store near Shinsaibashi's glitter. Come with a friend, buy a bottle of wine from ¥1,400, bread, and cheese, and you can have a light dinner here. 5–10 P.M.; closed Sun., holidays.

[15] **Bar Be-in** バー ビー・イン 南区東清水29 ☎(06)252-4475
This bar is a beauty: two long counters of cherry wood amid gray concrete and granite under an arched ceiling with a large plate- glass window behind one counter overlooking a Japanese garden. Designed by Takashi Sugimoto, who made a name for himself in Tokyo. All those familiar cocktails known to Westerners, plus a light snack menu. Popular with Osaka fashion-plates under thirty. 6 P.M.–1 A.M.; Sun., 5–11 P.M.

OSAKA SHOPPING

Like Tokyo, there is nothing in this world you can't find in commercial Osaka. Many of Japan's major department stores were born here. There's no neighborhood quite as chic as Tokyo's Harajuku-Omotesando district. But Yoroppa Mura is fast on the rise for sophisticated city slickers. The following offer something special.

[16] **Nihon Kogeikan Mingei Fukyubu** 日本工芸館民芸普及部 北区西天満4-7-15 ☎(06)362-9501
If you haven't purchased Japan's charming folk art in Tokyo or Kyoto yet, this small shop offers more of the same: rustic pottery, textiles, craft paper, small wooden chests. On a street with the city's best galleries near the Umeshin East Hotel. There's a branch near Takashimaya in Minami. 10 A.M.–6 P.M.

[17] **Japan Life** ジャパンライフ
Not a shop, but a sleek complex of the best in Japanese modern design, mostly for the home. There's an inside atrium where you can sit down

and take a breather from the crowds outside in the Shinsaibashi arcade. Located behind Holiday Inn. 11 A.M.–8 P.M.; closed third Wed. each month

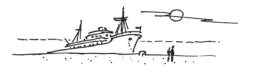

KOBE: LAST FOOD STOP

Kobe provides an added dimension to the diverse Kansai megalopolis, Western Honshu's powerhouse: There is something Western here for the Japanese to ogle. The foreign visitor intent on discovering what the Japanese find exotic is also welcome.

This is Western Japan's chief port, just as Yokohama is eastern Japan's gateway to the water. Both cities were opened to foreign trade in 1859. The foreigners in Kobe were at first allowed to live only in a waterbound district near the harbor, eventually moving farther up the steep slopes of Mt. Rokko. It's this hillside district known as Kitanocho in which at least a few foreigners still live, and to which young fashion-conscious Japanese now flock to look at such romantic objects as homes with castlelike turrets topped by weathercocks and bay windows with mullion panes. The single best reason for the foreigner to hop off the Bullet Train (*Shinkansen*) here is to feast on Western delicacies, as well as authentic Indian and Chinese cuisine, that are practically impossible to find anyplace farther west.

The following suggested walking tour will provide a peek at the importance of the city's shipping industry to Japan, and its Western impact on the Japanese mind. The **Kobe City Museum** (¥1,000; 10 A.M.–5 P.M.; closed Mon., day after holidays), just south of the Oriental Hotel and the best of its type, offers an analysis of both Western and Eastern influences on Japan with very comprehensible English descriptions of exhibits. The museum is especially famous for its paintings by Japanese artists of the foreign explorers and missionaries who began coming to

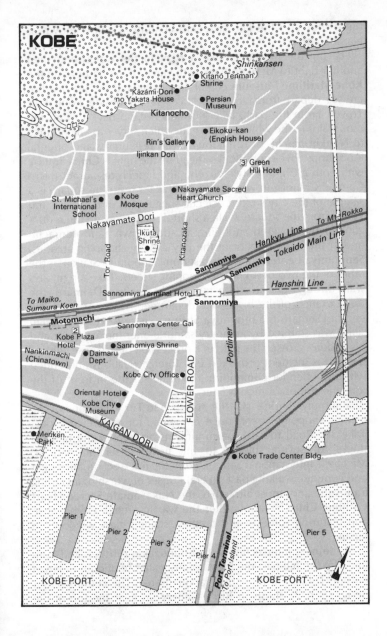

KOBE

Shinkansen

● Kitano Tenman Shrine

Kazami Dori no Yakata House

● Persian Museum

Kitanocho

● Eikoku-kan (English House)

Rin's Gallery ●

Ijinkan Dori

3 Green Hill Hotel

● Nakayamate Sacred Heart Church

St. Michael's ● International School

● Kobe Mosque

Nakayamate Dori

Tor Road

Ikuta Shrine ●

Kitanozaka

Hankyu Line To Mt. Rokko

Sannomiya Sannomiya Tokaido Main Line

Hanshin Line

To Maiko, Sumaura Koen

Sannomiya Terminal Hotel 1

Sannomiya

Motomachi

Sannomiya Center Gai

2 Kobe Plaza Hotel

Nankinmachi (Chinatown)

● Sannomiya Shrine

● Daimaru Dept.

● Kobe City Office

Portliner

FLOWER ROAD

Oriental Hotel ●

Kobe City ● Museum

KAIGAN DORI

● Meriken Park

● Kobe Trade Center Bldg.

Pier 1

Pier 2

Pier 3

Pier 4

Pier 5

Port Terminal To Port Island

KOBE PORT

KOBE PORT

N

these shores in the late sixteenth century, a genre known as Namban art.

Leaving the museum, take a right to the waterfront, then another right to **Meriken Park** with views of the harbor and the **Kobe Maritime Museum** celebrating Kobe and the sea. Harbor cruises depart from adjacent Naka Wharf beside Kobe Port Tower. From the park, take Nishimachi Dori back toward the mountains to the white marble gate which serves as an entrance to **Nankin-machi**, or Chinatown, with restaurants and oriental food shops. Five short blocks ahead on the right is **China Square** with both a Chinese-style gazebo and French restaurant Bistro Comme Chinois, in which you can take a rest. The square is a sample of the city's often eclectic suggestions of both East and West. From the square, walk a short distance toward the mountains to the covered shopping arcade known as **Motomachi**, one of the most elegant of the city's many shopping arcades. **Sannomiya Center**, running west from Sannomiya Station, is the other of the two best-known shopping streets. Take a right and walk through the arcade a few blocks back to **Daimaru**, the Kobe branch of the big Osaka department store. At the other end of Daimaru is **Sannomiya Shrine**, where in 1868 a foreign sailor was stabbed by an angry samurai after the foreigner and his buddies crossed the path of a procession of Japanese fighting men. This incident provoked bad foreign relations and ended with the offender committing ritualistic suicide in front of the foreigners about a month later.

Sannomiya Shrine is at the entrance to **Tor Road**, one of the leading shopping streets once renowned for its foreign goods. Take Tor Road toward the mountains and under the railroad tracks for several blocks to the first intersection past St. Michael's International School. From the intersection, turn right and continue walking past several houses of worship, including a **mosque** and, most attractive, the **Nakayamate Sacred Heart Catholic Church**, rebuilt after the war in French Gothic style and featuring some of the prettiest stained glass windows in Japan.

At the next intersection with **Kitanozaka**, turn left and continue up the hill past the most sophisticated boutiques in Japan outside Tokyo's fashionable Harajuku area. The country's best designers have shops in **Rin's Gallery** up near the top of the

Kitanocho

street on the right. Along **Ijinkan Dori**, which crosses Kitanozaka below Rin's, there are more smart boutiques and foreign restaurants.

From the top of Kitanozaka, take a left and walk to the second
narrow lane, which climbs the hill on the right. This is the beginning of a well-trodden trail for wide-eyed young Japanese to see
how the non-Japanese used to live. Now in a historic preserva-
tion district, the **foreigners' houses**, or *ijinkan*, are in various
stages of repose. Some have been turned into museums and
been given names like "American," "English," "Persian," and
"Oriental." Each charges a small admission fee for seeing things
like Western paintings, Persian ceramics, and old Victorian furniture foreigners threw away. Commercialization is gradually
ruining the charm of the quarter, but there are still pockets of
unspoiled beauty, including the **Kazami** ("Weathercock") **Dori
no Yakata House**, the setting of a TV drama about a German
baker married to a Japanese that popularized the neighborhood
throughout the country.

Find your way back down the steep slopes to Kitanozaka.
This street leads all the way downhill to **Sannomiya Station**, the
city's main transportation center from which JR, the Hankyu
and Hanshin private railways, and the Portliner computer-
operated overhead railway run. A ride on the Portliner offers a
quick overview of the bustling port before making a circle
around the man-made Port Island, which serves both freighters

around its waterfront rim, and people at the glamorous Portopia Hotel, International Exhibition Hall. Minami Koen, a small park at the south edge provides spots to peek through the underbrush at the Inland Sea.

The visitor with more time, when favored by good weather, might well seek out two famous views: one from the top of **Mt. Rokko**, which forms the city's dramatic mountain backdrop to the north, and the other from the waterfront at **Maiko** from which big Awaji Island in the Inland Sea can easily be seen. Mt. Rokko's upper reaches are most easily visited by taking the Rokko Cable Car from Rokko-Keiburushita Station, a ten- or fifteen-minute bus ride from Hankyu's Rokko Station, or the JR Rokkomichi Station, east of Sannomiya. Maiko is a twenty-minute ride on the JR Sanyo Main Line local train west of Sannomiya. McDonald's lovers can feast on the familiar while they view the Inland Sea and Awaji Island, and there is a waterfront walk squeezed between the seawall and a pine-tree-filled park. If you're in Kobe during cherry blossom season, join the throngs at **Sumaura Koen**, a park that climbs the last of the Rokko Mountain chain's slopes, called Hachibuse, above Sumaura-koen Station. It is an easy stopover to or from Maiko.

There are, of course, Buddhist temples and shrines common to all Japanese cities. All will be an anticlimax after nearby Kyoto. Do what the Japanese do. Gape at exotica in the foreign quarter and partake of some of the best Western food available in this country.

The **Kobe Tourist Information Office** beside the west exit of the JR Sannomiya Station (east exit of the Hankyu Line) usually has English-speaking staff on hand who can give you English pamphlets and maps of the city. If you're more serious about seeing things properly, invest in copies of *An Exploration of Historic Kobe* by Makoto Tanabe and Kris K. Shibuya, and the very detailed "Map of Kobe" published by Kobe International Association, both available at the Tourist Information Office.

KOBE SLEEPING

[1] **Sannomiya Terminal Hotel**, 三宮ターミナルホテル 8-chome, Kumoi Dori, Chuo-ku, ☎(078)291-0001. One of the JR chain, and right on top of handy Sannomiya Station, convenient to all of Kobe. Singles from ¥8,157, twins from ¥15,862.

2 **Kobe Plaza Hotel**, 神戸プラザホテル 1-chome, 13-12 Motomachi Dori, Chuo-ku, ☎(078)332-1141. Older business hotel, but handy location in front of Motomachi Station near the center. Singles from ¥6,600, twins from ¥13,000.

3 **Green Hill Hotel**, グリーンヒルホテル 2-chome, 5-16, Kanoucho, Chuo-ku, ☎(078)222-1221. You won't see the "green hill," but you're close to Shin-Kobe Station where the Bullet Train stops, and the foreigners' quarter in Kitanocho. There is also a nearby annex. Singles ¥5,800, twins from ¥11,000.

KOBE EATS AND DRINKS

Head straight for Kitanocho for a Western food fix. In this small quarter you'll find nearly authentic French, German, Italian, Moroccan, and Indian food, not to mention Japanese sukiyaki and *shabu shabu* made with famous Kobe beef. **Gaylord**'s, the famous Indian restaurant of London, San Francisco, and Los Angeles, has two branches in Kobe, one just across the street from the City Hall near Sannomiya.

HIMEJI: IDYLLIC CASTLE

There's just one reason to get off the Bullet Train (Shinkansen) at Himeji about a half hour west of Kyoto: The city has the finest extant Japanese castle in all the land.

During the bloody sixteenth century, castles were built all over Japan. Practically every *daimyo*, or regional lord, had one. Commonly there was a keep of several stories perched on either a natural or man-made hill supported by great stone revetments laid in a graceful curve from bottom to top. The donjon was surrounded by outbuildings; tile-topped plaster walls and a series of moats slowed down an attacker's approach.

When things settled down in the seventeenth century under the Tokugawa shogun, the castles became less important as defense structures than as administrative headquarters for the region. Many a Japanese city grew up around a castle, with Tokyo the supreme example.

Himeji Castle (¥500; 9 A.M.–4 P.M.) is not only still standing, but gorgeous, thanks to an eight-year repair job completed in 1964. Because of its stark white walls topped by dark-gray tiles and the gentle curves of the roofs, the Japanese call it *Shirasagi-jo* or *Hakurojo* ("Egret Castle"). At a distance the structure does indeed look like a bird swooping over the rice fields.

If you can take your eyes off the donjon long enough, you'll discover a series of long structures and walkways spiraling up the hill. These separate buildings were the living quarters and dungeons, and this is the only castle where such buildings have survived. The buildings to the west of the donjon were built for Senhime, the daughter of the second Tokugawa shogun and the wife of the son of the castle's *daimyo* in the early seventeenth century.

Himeji as we see it today was constructed between 1601 and 1610 by Ikeda Terumasa, son-in-law of Tokugawa Ieyasu, the first of the Tokugawa shoguns. But the castle's origins can be traced to 1333 when a fortress was built there. That complex, with the addition of a three-story donjon, was used by Toyotomi Hideyoshi to conquer western Japan. It was from this castle that the great general launched an attack against the assassins of Oda Nobunaga, who was murdered at Honnoji Temple in Kyoto in 1582.

NAGOYA

名古屋

SHRINES AND CORMORANTS

Nagoya, Japan's fourth largest city, was the stomping ground of the Tokugawa shoguns until the beginning of the Meiji period, which saw the classic castle town become the classic factory town. Reduced to rubble in World War II, Nagoya is now perhaps the best-planned of Japan's big cities. None of this makes the city very interesting for the foreign visitor, however. **Nagoya Castle** (¥400; 9:30 A.M.–4:30 P.M.), the home of Tokugawa Ieyasu's son and his descendants until the Meiji Restoration, is now a concrete replica serving as a museum for Tokugawa-period art objects, especially paintings on sliding doors.

Nagoya, however, is right in the center of a number of interesting sights within a day's journey. **Ise-Shima National Park** includes **Ise Shrine**, closely associated with the emperor and the most venerated in all Japan; Toba, home of the Mikimoto pearl domain; and a group of breathtakingly beautiful, pine-clad islands. Uji-Yamada, the station closest to the shrine, can be reached in an hour and twenty-eight minutes by Kinki Nippon Railways limited express over a scenic route from Nagoya (¥2,120). There are actually two shrines here, inner and outer sanctuaries connected by bus. Most visitors spend their time at the inner shrine, located in a magnificent grove of old Japanese cypress through which the clear Isuzugawa River flows. The chief building, called the Nai-ku, is an extraordinarily simple structure made of cypress wood. It is dedicated to the sun goddess, Amaterasu, divine ancestor of the emperor, and holds the

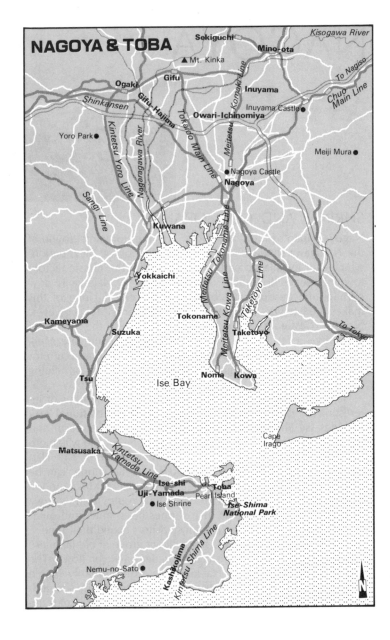

NAGOYA & TOBA

Kisogawa River

Sekiguchi

Mino-ota

To Nagiso

▲ Mt. Kinka

Ogaki

Gifu

Inuyama

Chuo Main Line

Shinkansen

Gifu-Hajima

Owari-Ichinomiya

Inuyama Castle ●

Yoro Park ●

Kintetsu Yoro Line

Nagaragawa River

Tokaido Main Line

Meitetsu Komaki Line

Meiji Mura ●

● Nagoya Castle

Nagoya

Sangi Line

Kuwana

Yokkaichi

Meitetsu Tokoname Line

Kameyama

Tokoname

Meitetsu Kowa Line

Taketoyo Line

To Tokyo

Suzuka

Taketoyo □

Tsu

Noma Kowa

Ise Bay

Cape Irago

Matsusaka

Kintetsu Yamada Line

Ise-shi

Toba

Uji-Yamada

Pearl Island

● Ise Shrine

Ise-Shima National Park

Nemu-no-Sato

Kashikojima

Kintetsu Shima Line

N

sacred mirror which, along with the sword and jewel, constitutes the regalia of the Japanese Imperial Throne. The Atsuta Shrine in Nagoya holds the sword; Tokyo's Imperial Palace, the jewel. The small shrine is typical of Japanese architecture before Chinese influence prevailed. It's rebuilt every twenty years in accordance with ancient custom.

Just twenty minutes from Ise Kintetsu Station by train (¥230) is **Toba**, a picturesque town situated on the hills above the sea. **Pearl Island**, just offshore, demonstrates how Kokichi Mikimoto developed the process of making oysters produce pearls. The oysters are traditionally brought up from the seabed by women divers called *ama-san*. From Toba you can return to Nagoya via a hydrofoil to Gamagori (¥2,700), then by JR train to Nagoya Station (¥950).

At Gifu, twenty-six minutes by train from Nagoya, the major nightly event between May 11 and October 15 is watching **cormorants** fishing for *ayu* (sweetfish) in the Nagaragawa River. You can hire a longboat at the landing beside Nagara Bridge (¥2,400 per person; June–Aug., ¥2,800, ☎[0582]02-0104) and let the boatmen steer you toward the action. There's a long wait during which you are served food and drink. Then the birds, with cords around the base of their necks to keep them from swallowing the fish, are brought down the river in a flotilla of boats, each manned by four men, one of whom is at the bow,

Toba

Atsuta Shrine

while two watch the birds and the fourth takes care of the fire used to lure the fish. However, the fish are not attracted to the fires under moonlight, so don't go during a full moon. One cormorant can catch from two to four fish each time it's put in the water. Cormorant fishing is an old Japanese custom which can also be seen at Arashiyama and Uji near Kyoto, and Hakata in Kyushu.

The sport can also be seen on the Kisogawa River at nearby **Inuyama**, a city famous for its small white castle dating from 1440, the oldest in the country, from which there is a fine view of the river's rapids. The part of Kisogawa River between Inuyama and the villages of Rhine-Yuen and Imawatari upstream is known as Japan's Rhine. **Imawatari** is a fifty-five-minute train ride on the Meitetsu Line from Shin-Nagoya Station (¥630). There are public and private boats for hire (¥2,700), and you can shoot the rapids to Inuyama in about two hours.

Southeast of Inuyama is **Meiji Mura** (Meiji Village) (¥1,240; 10 A.M.–5 P.M.; Nov.–Feb., 10 A.M.–4 P.M.), an outdoor museum of buildings from the Meiji period, Japan's Victorian age. There are fifty-four structures in all, and especially interesting is a small-town Kabuki theater and the original façade from Tokyo's famous Imperial Hotel, designed by American architect Frank Lloyd Wright—not a Meiji-period building, but here nevertheless. Meiji Mura can also be reached by Meitetsu Express Bus direct from its Nagoya bus terminal to the gate (¥1,180). The trip takes sixty minutes.

An hour and a half from Nagoya on the JR Chuo Main Line will bring you to Nagiso, from where it's short bus or taxi ride to **Tsumago**, one of Japan's best-preserved old towns, nestled in a mountain valley on the old stone-paved Nakasendo Road, which was used as an alternate route between Edo (Tokyo) and Kyoto during the Tokugawa period. The town shares the limelight with **Magome**, another old village (a twenty-minute bus ride or a two- or three-hour hike away), for being unspoiled, but Tsumago gives a better sense of the past in a mountain road stage stop: a single street of old wooden shops and homes. There are many *minshuku*. For example, at Kameyama, ☎(02645)7-3187, a twenty-minute walk from Tsumago, the owner serves fresh trout, mountain greens, and pickles (¥5,000 with two meals).

Meiji Mura

131

Shooting the rapids on
Kisogawa River

NAGOYA SLEEPING

Nagoya Crown Hotel 名古屋クラウンホテル 1-8-33 Sakae, Naka-ku ☎(052)211-6633. Five minutes from the Fushimi Subway Station. Singles from ¥4,940, twins from ¥8,430.

Dai-ichi Washington Hotel 第一ワシントンホテル 3-18-28 Nishiki, Naka-ku, ☎(052)951-2111. A few minutes from the Sakae Subway Station. Singles from ¥6,458, twins from ¥11,330.

Dai-ni Washington Hotel 第二ワシントンホテル Nishiki 3-chome, Naka-ku, ☎(052)962-7111. A few minutes from the Sakae Subway Station. Singles from ¥6,458, twins from ¥11,330.

Nagoya Chisan Hotel 名古屋チサンホテル 1-12-8 Noritake, Nakamura-ku, ☎(052)452-3211. A few minutes, walk from Nagoya Station. Singles from ¥5,047, twins from ¥9,270.

Parkside Hotel パークサイドホテル 3-6-15 Nishiki, Nakaku, ☎(052)971-1131. Handy location near Sakae Subway Station. Situated right in front of the TV tower. Singles from ¥6,000, twins from ¥10,000.

Eki-mae Monblanc Hotel 駅前モンブランホテル 3-14-1 Meiki, Nakamura-ku, ☎(052)541-1121. Three minutes from the JR Nagoya Station by taxi. Singles from ¥6,300, twins from ¥10,800.

Nagoya Plaza Hotel 名古屋プラザホテル 3-8-21 Nishiki, Naka-ku, ☎(052)951-6311. Brand-new, just beside the Sakae Subway Station. Singles from ¥4,800, twins from ¥8,800.

TAKAYAMA

LIFE IN THE MOUNTAINS

Four-fifths of the Japanese archipelago is covered by mountains—some gentle like those around Kyoto, some wild and rugged like the Japan Alps. Probably no single topographical feature of the land has had a greater impact on the Japanese mind.

For practically all Japanese, home was or is a valley. Many villages are built beside a swiftly running stream. Every patch of level land beside the water is planted with something, principally rice, and in some areas the paddies are built on terraces right up the mountainside.

And where the valleys were especially broad grew the major cities. Tokyo, Osaka, Nagoya—each was built on a marshy plain through which sweep several rivers.

Takayama is special because, perhaps more than any other town in the mountains, it's been able to preserve its old houses, shops, and godowns—not a single isolated wooden house overpowered by a concrete monstrosity next door, but whole blocks full of wooden slat façades and deep, overhanging roofs. Many of the houses are open to the public, providing a great opportunity for the visitor to learn how people lived in the mountains, where life was never exactly easy and winters are long and hard.

Right in front of the exit from Takayama Station is the **Tourist Information Office**, which can give you an English map of the town and make a *minshuku* reservation. Also in front of the station you can rent a bicycle for ¥250 per hour or ¥1,250 for the

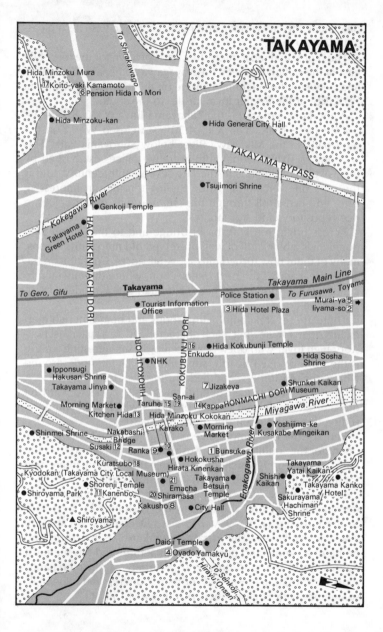

TAKAYAMA

- Hida Minzoku Mura
- 17 Koito-yaki Kamamoto
- 6 Pension Hida no Mori
- Hida Minzoku-kan
- Hida General City Hall
- Tsujimori Shrine
- Genkoji Temple
- Takayama Green Hotel
- Kokegawa River
- HACHIKENMACHI DORI
- TAKAYAMA BYPASS

To Shirakawago

Takayama Main Line

To Gero, Gifu

Takayama

To Furusawa, Toyama

- Police Station
- Tourist Information Office
- 3 Hida Hotel Plaza
- Murai-ya 5
- Iiyama-so 2
- 16 Enkudo
- Hida Kokubunji Temple
- Hida Sosha Shrine
- Ipponsugi Hakusan Shrine
- NHK
- 7 Jizakeya
- Shunkei Kaikan Museum
- Takayama Jinya
- HIROKOJI DORI
- KOKUBUNJI DORI
- San-ai
- Taruhei 15 19
- 14 Kappa HONMACHI DORI
- Miyagawa River
- Morning Market
- Kitchen Hida 13
- Hida Minzoku Kokokan
- Shinmei Shrine
- Nakabashi Bridge
- Susaki 12
- Ranka 9
- 10
- Karako
- Morning Market
- Yoshijima-ke
- Kusakabe Mingeikan
- Enakogawa River
- Kuratsubo 18
- Kyodokan (Takayama City Local Museum)
- 1 Bunsuke
- Hokokusha
- Hirata Kinenkan
- Shorenji Temple
- 11 Kanenbo
- 21
- Emacha
- Takayama Betsuin Temple
- Shishi Kaikan
- Takayama Yatai Kaikan
- Shiroyama Park
- 20 Shiramasa
- Kakusho 8
- City Hall
- Takayama Kanko Hotel
- Sakurayama Hachiman Shrine
- ▲ Shiroyama
- Daioji Temple
- 4 Oyado Yamakyu

To Senkoji

Hirayu Onsen

To Hirayu Onsen

day. Since the city is small and relatively traffic-free, it's a pleasant place to cycle.

The oldest and most interesting parts of town for the tourist lie east of the station between the Miyagawa and Enakogawa rivers and between the Hachiman Shrine on the north and Shiroyama Park, site of the former local castle, to the south.

A good place to start is the **Takayama Jinya** (¥300; 8:45 A.M.–5 P.M.; Nov.–Mar., 8:45 A.M.–4:30 P.M.; closed Wed.) on the west bank of the Miyagawa River below Shiroyama Park. This was one of sixty regional administrative offices established by the Tokugawa shoguns in the late seventeenth century, and is the only one remaining. After passing through an impressive gate, you can stroll through the *tatami* rooms of the offices, a rice repository, and storehouses.

Across bright red Nakabashi Bridge and to the left on Sannomachi is a block full of well-preserved **old merchants' shops**, many of them now turned into souvenir stores. Continue on the same street across the next intersection, where the nineteenth-century-Japan mood continues, although a few modern intrusions have crept in.

There are several combination shops and homes of rich merchants open for viewing, each characterized by a spacious, two-story-high foyer with open-beam ceilings. An interesting feature is the *irori*, or open hearth, sunk into the *tatami* floor, around which the customers huddled during the frosty winters. A screen was often placed behind the guests' backs to ward off drafts. The family lived in smaller rooms which are behind the sliding doors and open out onto small gardens.

Perhaps the most impressive of the three merchants' homes open to the public is the **Kusakabe Mingeikan** (Kusakabe Folklore Museum), which, despite the name, is more interesting for the building than the folk art it contains (¥309; 9 A.M.–5 P.M.; Dec.–Mar., 9 A.M.–4:30 P.M.). If you want to see more of this interesting architecture, also drop by the **Yoshijima-ke**, next door to the museum (¥250; 9 A.M.–5 P.M.; Dec.–Feb., 9 A.M.–4:30 P.M.; closed Tues.). The **Hirata Kinenkan** was the shop and home of a candle and pomade manufacturer and has the most interesting of the museums, with a variety of old merchants' tools, fabrics, Japanese and Korean pottery, and paintings, sometimes with English labels (¥200; 9 A.M.–5 P.M.).

The fine wood with which these homes were built comes from the surrounding timber-rich mountains. Commoners were forbidden to cut the trees during the Tokugawa period. The restriction was lifted, however, during the Meiji period, and rich merchants like the Kusakabes and Yoshijimas took the opportunity to build their dream-house/shops.

A short walk from the Kusakabe and Yoshijima homes is **Hachiman Shrine**, one of the many shrines with the same name in Japan devoted to the god of war. Next door is **Takayama Yatai Kaikan** (¥460; 8:30 A.M.–5 P.M.; Dec.–Feb., 9 A.M.–4:30 P.M.), with several ornately decorated floats on display when they are not being paraded during the spring festival, April 14 and 15, or the fall festival, October 9 and 10, two of Japan's most colorful pageants. At the **Shishi Kaikan** below Hachiman Shrine is a new museum devoted to those grotesquely humorous *shishi* (lion) masks worn by merrymakers at festivals throughout Japan (¥430; 8:30 A.M.–5 P.M.).

There are more small museums for the inveterate museum-goer. At the **Kyodokan** (Takayama City Local Museum; ¥200; 8:30 A.M.–5 P.M.; Dec.–Feb., 9 A.M.–4:30 P.M.; closed Thurs.), more regional folk art and archaeological material are on display, with a small room devoted to the seventeenth-century priest-sculptor Enku, whose primitive carvings are mysteriously powerful. Nearby, the **Hida Minzoku Kokokan** (¥300; 7 A.M.–

Morning market, Takayama

Takayama street scene

7 P.M.; Dec.–Feb., 8 P.M.–5 P.M.) has a small collection of fine art. This is the only surviving samurai's house in Takayama and, after seeing the merchants' houses, you need no reminder as to which class was better off during the late Tokugawa and early Meiji periods.

The **Hida Kokubunji** (¥200; 9 A.M.–4 P.M.), with a fine three-story pagoda, is the oldest temple in the city. Founded in 1588, it was one of the provincial temples put under the direction of Todaiji Temple in Nara. An enormous ginkgo tree, pure gold in autumn, dominates the small grounds.

A bicycle will be handy to reach the **Hida Minzoku Mura** (¥500; 8:30 A.M.–5 P.M.; Nov.–Mar., 8:30 A.M.–4:30 P.M.), a village of country houses about one mile from the station. This is the most accessible place in all of Japan to grasp the conditions in which the vast majority of the mountain common people—chiefly the farmers and craftsmen in the Tokugawa period—eked out their frugal lives.

The high-pitched thatched roofs, called *gassho-zukuri* (in the shape of hands in prayer), kept the snow from piling high. In the multistoried versions of these homes the upper floors, dark and dry from the smoke of the *irori* on the main floor, were used to rear silkworms, an occupation that kept the families busy during the summer months. As many as fifty or sixty people sometimes lived in the structures. Another house features strong beams supporting a shingle roof over which stones were laid to keep the wind from ripping it off. A rice storehouse and the homes of a village headman and a Buddhist priest are also open to the public. From the site there is a fine view of the usually snow-capped Alps.

On a mountaintop just east of the city (a fifteen-minute bus ride to Shukokan-mae, then about a one-hour hike uphill) is **Senkoji**, an old temple neglected over the years, but once a stopping-off place for the much-traveled priest-sculptor Enku, whose works are on view at the Kyodokan. More of his sculpture can be seen at the adjacent **Enku Exhibition Hall** (¥400; 8:30 A.M.–5 P.M.).

If you want to see thatched-roof houses still occupied, you'll have to venture to **Shirakawago Gassho Mura** (¥500), where eight of these homes were transported from a dam site and are open from 8:30 A.M.–6 P.M. (Aug., 8 A.M.–6 P.M.; Dec.–Mar., 9

A.M.–4 P.M.). It's an hour-and-thirty-five-minute bus ride from Takayama to Makido (¥1,700), then another hour by JR bus (¥1,200) to Ogimachi, site of the village and several *minshuku*.

A scenic one-hour bus ride (¥1,300) to **Hirayu Onsen** will bring you to one of the country's less-spoiled mountain spas. About twenty *ryokan* (Japanese inns) and *minshuku* are clustered here at the foot of Mt. Norikura, and some of them feature outdoor baths from which you can gaze at the midnight stars.

When a Japanese takes a holiday, it's often at an *onsen*. The volcanic island chain has thousands of natural hot springs emitting waters believed to be good for one ailment or another. Feeling better is part of the lure. But the hot spring conjures up romantic images—relaxing in the hot water with a view of nature's wonders, strolling around the area in your cotton kimono, and, for the men, perhaps a flirtation or two with a hot-spring geisha à la Yasunari Kawabata's *Snow Country*.

Today, however, any hot spring that can be reached by bus—and that includes most of them—will probably disappoint you. The old wooden inns have mostly been replaced with high-rise hotels, and are filled with armies of drunk and over-happy octogenarians and business-minded bar hostesses. The scenery, thank God, is still there. Before you eagerly head for a hot spring, try to find out what the place is like.

TAKAYAMA SLEEPING

From the City Tourist Office at the station exit you can get help for accommodations either in Takayama or up in the moutains at Hirayu Onsen. The following are only a few suggestions.

[1] **Bunsuke** 文助 77 Shimoichinocho, ☎(0577)33-0315. ¥5,500 per person with two meals.

[2] **Iiyama-so** いいやま荘 262-2 Honobucho, ☎(0577)33-4863. ¥8,000– ¥10,000 with two meals.

[3] **Hida Hotel Plaza** ひだホテルプラザ 2-60 Hanaokacho, ☎(0577)33- 4600. New, well-designed 152-room hotel with rooms in two separate

low-rise towers. Rustic charm of Takayama captured in restaurant, shopping arcade. Hot-spring bath, swimming pool. Three minutes from Takayama Station. Singles from ¥7,000, twins from ¥15,000.

4 **Oyado Yamakyu** お宿山久 58 Tenshoji, ☎(0577)32-3756. Fifteen minutes by foot from the JR station at the foot of the mountains. Nice garden. ¥5,300–¥6,000 with two meals.

5 **Murai-ya** 村井屋 148 Honobucho, ☎(0577)33-4823. ¥5,000 with two meals.

6 **Pension Hida no Mori** ペンション ひだの杜 3349 Shingucho, ☎(0577) 34-6575. Western-style rooms. From ¥7,500.

TAKAYAMA EATS AND DRINKS

In this mountain area the specialties are mountain greens (*sansai*), lake trout (*masu*), and various types of mushrooms and nuts. Be sure and try the *mitarashi dango*, small rice cakes roasted on a stick over a charcoal fire.

7 **Jizakeya** 地酒屋 末広町2番街 ☎(0577)34-5001
Japanese snacks such as grilled meat (*yakiniku*, ¥1,200) and tofu—and thirteen kinds of local saké. ¥3,000–¥4,000; 4 P.M.–2 A.M.

8 **Kakusho** 角正 馬場2-98 ☎(0577)32-0174
Their ¥9,000 vegetarian lunch of mountain vegetables, noodles, mushroom soup, and sugared nuts is not exactly in the bargain category, but save up for this special treat. The food is served in a teahouse overlooking a garden. Lunch only; 11:30 A.M.–1:30 P.M.; closed Thurs; reservations required.

9 **Ranka** 藍花 上三之町93 ☎(0577)32-3887
Coffee (¥400) and good ice cream (¥500) in an old mud-walled warehouse. 9 A.M.–9 P.M.

10 **Karako** 唐子 上三之町90 ☎(0577)32-0244
Japanese green powder tea (*matcha*) and sweet-bean cakes sold in sets from ¥450; also *amazake*, a sweet, thick saké served warm (¥400); in a rustic Hida setting. 9 A.M.–5 P.M.; closed Wed.

11 **Kanenbo** 嘉念坊 堀端町8 ☎(0577)33-0776
More vegetarian food served in Shorenji Temple. ¥5,000, ¥6,000, and ¥7,000 courses. 11 A.M.–6 P.M.; reservations required.

12 **Susaki** 洲さき 神明町4-14 ☎(0577)32-0023
Sansai—greens fresh from the nearby mountains—is the specialty of this quality establishment. ¥8,500 course. 11:30 A.M.–6:30 P.M.; closed Tues; reservations required.

13 **Kitchen Hida** キッチン飛騨 本町1-66 ☎(0577)32-5406
Beef from the area's mountain grazing lands served in courses in the ¥5,000–¥7,000 price range. 11:30 A.M.–9 P.M.; closed Wed.

14 **Kappa** かっぱ 朝日町23 ☎(0577)33-8909

Izakaya drinking place with *kushiyaki* (meat and vegetables grilled on bamboo sticks) and *sansai* as the specialties. 5–11 P.M.; closed Sun.

15 **Taruhei** 樽平 有楽町46 ☎(0577)32-5490

A *nomiya* drinking place which draws the locals for saké fresh from the keg. ¥2,500 range; 5–11:30 P.M.; closed Fri.

TAKAYAMA SHOPPING

Several types of pottery are produced in Takayama, the most striking of which is *shibukusa-jiki*, a fine white porcelain with hand-painted deep-blue designs. The **Hokokusha** shop selling this ceramic is across the intersection and a few doors to the right on the same street where the Hirata Kinenkan is located. The town is also famous for its *shunkei-nuri*, a clear lacquerware which allows the wood's natural grain to show through. You can see the full array of the latter at the **Shunkei Kaikan Museum**. In a region full of fine timber, wood carvings are naturally common. Antique shops loaded with odds and ends from the last century are scattered throughout the old neighborhoods. Don't miss the **morning markets** either in front of Takayama Jinya or along the Miyagawa River. Country people from the surrounding mountains are here from 7 A.M. until noon with fresh vegetables, fruit, and crafts.

139

16 **Enkudo** 円空洞 天満町6 飛騨国分寺境内

Just inside the main gate of Kokubunji Temple, this tiny old farmhouse is the working place of master wood-carver Toshiro Miwa, who creates surprising likenesses of the Buddhas carved by Enku that you saw at the Kyodokan. Also miniatures of Takayama's festival floats, folk toys, and dolls made of Japanese paper. 8:30 A.M.–9 P.M.

17 **Koito-yaki Kamamoto** 小糸焼窯元 上岡本町1037

Located at Hida Minzoku Mura, potter Mitsuro Hasekura's rustic works are for sale here—all with a country flavor. 9 A.M.–5 P.M.

18 **Kuratsubo** 倉坪 上一之町8

A thirty-year-old antique shop offering pottery, chests, and old housewares from the region, not necessarily at a poor man's prices. Browse anyway. 8:30 A.M.–5:30 P.M.

19 **San-ai** 山愛 相生町23

Easy to spot with a waterwheel outside, this shop has all the local goodies—folk art, including pottery, straw hats, Hida pickles, and bean paste. 8 A.M.–9:30 P.M.

20 **Shiramasa** 志良政 馬場町1

Rustic antiques from the not-too-distant past.

21 **Emacha** 江間茶 上一之町66

A curio shop offering possibilities for your living-room shelf. 9 A.M.–8 P.M.

KANAZAWA

CLASSY CASTLE TOWN

Of the many Japanese cities built around a castle, Kanazawa is outstanding. It was dominated during the Tokugawa period by the Maeda *daimyo*, the richest in all the land by virtue of the amount of rice grown in their territory. Such stature brought culture. It also created what is common to potentates everywhere: paranoia. To the Tokugawa shogun, the Maedas were outside lords not to be wholly trusted. So the Maedas quite naturally did everything possible to prevent the shogun from giving vent to his wrath.

The Maeda castle was not only protected by the usual high walls and moats; it was also surrounded by winding, twisting streets. The two rivers on either side acted as further barriers. And for good measure, Buddhist temples were placed at the approach from Edo on the other side of the Saigawa River. One of these was not really a temple at all, but an escape route connected by tunnel to the castle. Tokugawa spies were everywhere in the land, passing on to Edo any information hinting of insurrection.

With a population as eager as any in Japan to be "modern," Kanazawa is not totally a city of the past. But thanks to having been spared the bombings of World War II, there is enough left to give quite a clear picture of life in a Japanese castle town. All you need is a little imagination to replace what are now modern buildings.

Start at Kanazawa's reason for being, the castle, now the site of Kanazawa University. Unfortunately, all that's left of the castle is **Ishikawa Gate**, merely the back door during its heyday. The cautious Maedas were always ready for the worst. Those lovely white tiles on the roof could be melted down for ammunition if necessary.

Kanazawa's great sightseeing attraction is **Kenrokuen** (¥300), across the street from Ishikawa Gate. This garden is considered, along with Okayama's Korakuen and Mito's Kairakuen, to be one of Japan's three greatest stroll gardens. Landscaping began as early as 1670 under the fifth Maeda *daimyo*, but it wasn't completed in its present form until the early nineteenth century under the thirteenth Maeda lord.

The Japanese have given a name to practically every tree, rock, and blade of grass here. The tourists rush through in groups, their leaders giving the details through a megaphone as they go by. The gates open at 6:30 A.M. (close at 6 P.M.) April through September, and if you're an early bird, you can avoid the pandemonium (Oct.–Mar., 8 A.M.–4:30 P.M.).

Seisonkaku Villa (¥500; 8:30 A.M.–4:30 P.M.; closed Wed.), a sumptuous Japanese-style home built by the thirteenth lord for his elderly mother, stands inside the garden and is well worth a few minutes' peek to see how comfortable a home for an elderly woman can be.

Just outside the garden and behind Seisonkaku is the **Ishikawa Prefectural Art Museum** (¥350; 9:30 A.M.–5 P.M.; closed Dec. 29–January 3), which houses a permanent collection of Kutani ceramics, one of the city's most famous products. Kutani ware has had its ups and downs: Its makers were patronized by the Maeda family from around the mid-1600s, but for reasons unknown, production stopped entirely, then was revived about one hundred years later. The old Kutani (Ko-Kutani) is highly prized and extraordinary for its rich color combinations of corn yellow, deep green, and lavender. Today Kutani ware is produced in amazing variety and every tourist shop has it. Ko-Kutani, however, can these days be found only in the most expensive antique shops. Some of the modern potters produce ware with colors and patterns that approximate the old ware.

Before wandering away from Kenrokuen, stop at **Gyokusenen Garden** (¥400; 9 A.M.–4 P.M.; closed Dec.–Mar.), another stroll garden, but on a far more manageable scale. You'll feel a lot more comfortable ambling over the stepping-stones

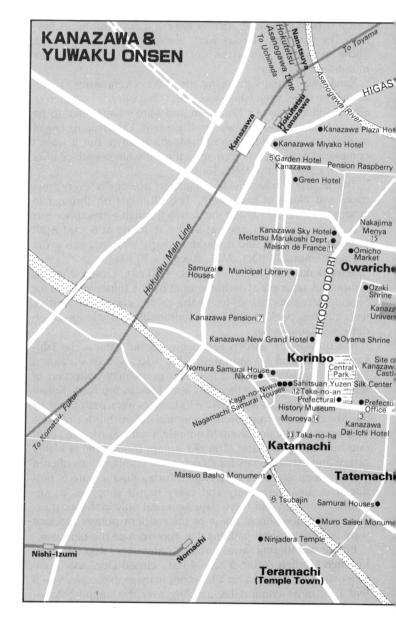

KANAZAWA & YUWAKU ONSEN

Nanatsuya

Hokutetsu Asanogawa Line
To Uchinada

To Toyama

Asanogawa River

HIGAS

Kanazawa

Hokutetsu Kanazawa

●Kanazawa Plaza Hot

●Kanazawa Miyako Hotel

5 Garden Hotel Kanazawa

Pension Raspberry

●Green Hotel

Hokuriku Main Line

Kanazawa Sky Hotel●
Meitetsu Marukoshi Dept. ●
Maison de France 11

Nakajima Menya 15

●Omicho Market

Samurai Houses ●   Municipal Library ●

HIKOSO ODORI

Owaricho

●Ozaki Shrine

Kanaza Univers

Kanazawa Pension 7

Kanazawa New Grand Hotel ●

●Oyama Shrine

To Komatsu, Fukui

Korinbo

Central Park

Site o Kanazaw Castl

Nomura Samurai House ●
Nikore ●

Kaga-no-Niwa

Nagamachi Samurai Houses

●●●Sahitsuan Yuzen Silk Center
12 Take-no-an
Prefectural ●   ●Prefectu
History Museum   Office

Moroeya 14

Kanazawa
Dai-Ichi Hotel

3

13 Taka-no-ha

Katamachi

Matsuo Basho Monument ●

Tatemachi

8 Tsubajin   Samurai Houses ●

●Muro Saisei Monume

● Ninjadera Temple

Nishi-Izumi

Nomachi

Teramachi
(Temple Town)

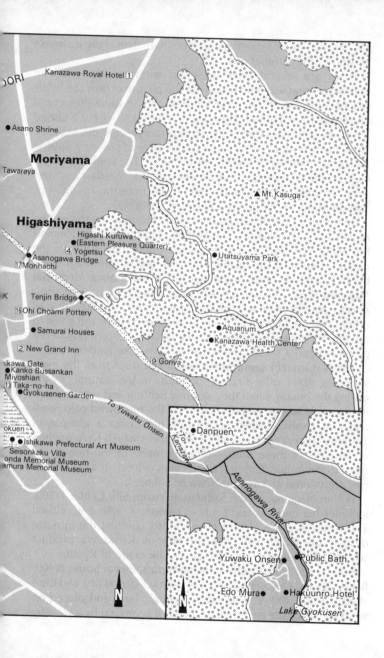

DORI
Kanazawa Royal Hotel 1

● Asano Shrine

Moriyama

Tawaraya

Higashiyama

Higashi Kuruwa
(Eastern Pleasure Quarter)
4 Yogetsu
● Asanogawa Bridge
17 Morihachi

▲ Mt. Kasuga

● Utatsuyama Park

K   Tenjin Bridge ●

16 Ohi Choami Pottery

● Samurai Houses

2 New Grand Inn

● Aquarium
● Kanazawa Health Center

ikawa Gate
● Kanko Bussankan
Miyoshian
13 Taka-no-ha
● Gyokusenen Garden

9 Goriya

To Yuwaku Onsen

okuen

● Ishikawa Prefectural Art Museum
● Seisonkaku Villa
onda Memorial Museum
amura Memorial Museum

● Danpuen

To Kanazawa

Asanogawa River

Yuwaku Onsen ● ● Public Bath

Edo Mura ● ● Hakuunro Hotel

Lake Gyokusen

N

N

and through the moss and maple trees here than at the *daimyo*'s version of the same above.

There are several small museums within a short walk of Kenrokuen that will help round out the picture of how the lord's retainers lived. Just down the hill from the Ishikawa Prefectural Museum is the **Honda Museum** (¥500; 9 A.M.–5 P.M.; closed Thurs. except Mar.–Oct.). The Honda family were the Maedas' chief advisers and were given a sizable slice of property outside the castle in the early seventeenth century. The family treasures include the trousseaux and dowries of the Maeda daughters who married into the Honda family, gifts from the Tokugawas, and uniforms of the family's personal firefighters.

Below a steep wall behind the Honda Museum are the wilting remains of a villa garden that belonged to the Hondas (behind the MRO Building) and a few homes and mud walls of the family's retainers. Up against the wall and off the main street behind two big office buildings is the **Nakamura Memorial Museum** (¥300; 9 A.M.–4 P.M.; closed Tues.), home of a prosperous saké brewer who collected tea ceremony utensils and other Japanese fine art. The house was moved here and given to the city in 1974. The admission fee covers a cup of powdered green tea and a small cake while you view the garden.

The **Nagamachi samurai houses**, a few steps from the main shopping street, offer a rare opportunity to see samurai city life during the period when they stopped fighting and settled down in the castle towns next to their lord. The mellowed gold mud-and-straw walls, topped with black tiles, offer a glimpse of austerity. Except for a couple of tea parlors which have opened up in parts of these houses recently, none of the homes are open to the public. Green tea and cakes in a set, or a cup of coffee, are offered at **Kaga-no-Niwa** or **Nikore**.

Within Nagamachi, the **Saihitsuan Yuzen Silk Center** (¥500, includes tea and sweets; 9 A.M.–12 noon, 1–4:30 P.M.; closed Thurs.) gives you a chance to see artists painting the intricate designs on *yuzen* silk, another famous Kanazawa product which differs slightly from the *yuzen* silk made in Kyoto.

Adjacent to Nagamachi is the **Nomura samurai house** (¥400; 8 A.M.–5 P.M.; Dec.–Feb., 9 A.M.–4:30 P.M.; closed first and third Wed.), a fine 200-year-old house brought here and placed on what was once the exclusive property of a samurai by a wealthy industrialist from Daishoji town. The house is built around a lovely small garden with a winding stream, which can also be viewed from the coffee shop next door.

On the other side of the Saigawa River and a ten-minute walk from the main shopping street lies **Teramachi** (Temple Town), the spot where the Maeda *daimyo* placed temples favored by the Tokugawas as an additional defense measure. Most of these temples are run-down and of little interest except for the silence they offer, but one is the biggest tourist attraction next to Kenrokuen. Called **Myoritsuji** (¥400; 9 A.M.–4:30 P.M.; Nov.–Mar. till 4 P.M.), it's more popularly known as **Ninjadera** (Ninja Temple) after the Tokugawa spies who rampantly sniffed out any malcontent. The innocent-looking temple is loaded with secret chambers, trapdoors, hidden staircases—all built around a well which was a tunnel to the Saigawa River and the castle. Reservations are necessary to see it (☎[0762]41-2877).

145

Save time for strolling along **the quays** on either of the two rivers, the stretch between the Asanogawa River Bridge and Tenjin Bashi beside the Asanogawa River being especially nice. Another breathing space is **Central Park** just beside the shopping area. Park yourself on a bench, and within minutes you'll be attracting students from nearby Kanazawa University who want to see if they can understand your English.

Outside Kanazawa, it's well worth the ¥510, forty-five-minute bus ride to **Yuwaku Onsen**, a tiny hot-spring resort distinguished for the fanciful, luxurious Hakuunro Hotel, a Spanish-Chinese architectural marvel hanging off a verdant cliff, and **Edo Mura**, a group of buildings from the Edo period. The bus stops in front of the hotel. A short walk up the road will bring you to the Edo Mura entrance (¥1,000; 8 A.M.–6 P.M.; Oct.–Mar., 8 A.M.–5 P.M.). Among the structures brought here are a country inn where the emperor Meiji once stayed and several homes of farmers, merchants, and samurai. The Hakuunro is too expensive for the bargain traveler, but have a snack in the coffee shop before you head back to town. In Yuwaku village below you can try the public bath (¥200; 7 A.M.–10 P.M.).

JAL and the Kanazawa Language School have teamed up to offer two weeks of Japanese language and culture study in this old castle town, with lots of free time to explore on your own and at a reasonable price of from ¥125,000 to ¥138,000, depending on single or double occupancy. The program is subsidized by the Society to Introduce Kanazawa to the World, a non-profit organization of volunteers. Contact JAL offices anywhere, or in Tokyo, Domestic Creative Tours (DCT) (03)284-2920.

KANAZAWA SLEEPING

[1] **Kanazawa Royal Hotel** 金沢ロイヤルホテル 3-28 Koganemachi, ☎(0762)52-7151. Five minutes from Kanazawa Station. Singles from ¥5,000, twins from ¥9,000.

[2] **New Grand Inn** ニューグランドイン 3-7 Kenroku Motomachi, ☎(0762) 22-1211. Convenient and quiet location, very near Kenrokuen, with a good coffee shop serving a ¥1,200 Western breakfast. Singles ¥5,800, twins ¥11,500.

[3] **Kanazawa Dai-ichi Hotel** 金沢第一ホテル 1-2-25 Hirosaka Dori, ☎(0762)22-2011. Also right beside Kenrokuen. Singles ¥4,800, twins ¥9,000.

[4] **Yogetsu** 陽月 1-13-22 Higashiyama, ☎(0762)52-0497. A *minshuku* in an old geisha house in the city's classiest geisha quarter. ¥5,500 with two meals.

[5] **Garden Hotel Kanazawa** ガーデンホテル金沢 2-16-16 Honmachi, ☎(0762)63-3333. Right in front of Kanazawa Station. Singles from ¥6,600, twins from ¥11,000.

[6] **Pension Raspberry** ペンションラズベリー 22-24 Takaokamachi, ☎(0762)23-0757. Convenient to the Musashi section, run by a charming couple who have traveled all over Europe. ¥5,500 including breakfast. ¥8,000 with two meals. Beds, not *futon*.

[7] **Kanazawa Pension** 金沢ペンション 8-4 Nagamachi 3-chome, ☎(0762) 61-3489. A cozy *minshuku* in the Nagamachi samurai house quarter and a ten-minute walk to Kenrokuen. ¥3,900 per person with bath, twins ¥7,900.

KANAZAWA EATS AND DRINKS

[8] **Tsubajin** つば甚 寺町5-1-8 ☎(0762)41-2181
Jibuni, a stew made with chicken stock, is the specialty. A great winter warmer-upper in this snowy region. Courses from ¥15,000; 11 A.M.–10 P.M.; last order at 7 P.M.

[9] **Goriya** ごり屋 常盤60 ☎(0762)52-2288
As the name implies, the river fish known as *gori* is dished out here. ¥6,000; 11:30 A.M.–7:30 P.M.; last order at 7 P.M.

[10] **Miyoshian** 三芳庵 兼六町1-11 ☎(0762)21-0127
Right in Kenrokuen, this famous place offers *kaburazushi*, fermented turnips and yellowtail fish layered with rice. Tastes better than it sounds. Lunch from ¥1,500; 10 A.M.–3 P.M. *Kaiseki* from ¥6,000 with reservation, 6–8 P.M.

[11] **Maison de France** メゾン・ド・フランス 金沢名鉄丸越デパート ☎(0762)60-2454

On the second floor of the Meitetsu Marukoshi Department Store, the famous Japanese *chanson* singer Yoshiko Ishii offers French-style omelettes. 10 A.M.–6 P.M.; closed Thurs.

[12] **Take-no-an** 竹の庵 香林坊2-12-10 ☎(0762)61-3393
Kanazawa's best noodles, the locals insist. All homemade. Try their tempura *zaru soba* (cold buckwheat noodles with tempura on top) for ¥1,350; 11:30 A.M.–3 P.M.; 5–7 P.M.; closed Sun.

[13] **Taka-no-ha** 鷹の羽 兼六園店 兼六町2-20 ☎(0762)22-5188.
Inexpensive *jibuni* at two locations—one near Kenrokuen, the other in the Katamachi shopping area. Lunch from ¥1,600; 10 A.M.–6 P.M., closed Thurs. Nov.–Mar.

KANAZAWA SHOPPING

[14] **Moroeya** 諸江屋 片町1-3-22
Probably the best selection of Kutani ware in town, with a museum-like third floor. They'll pack and ship. ¥1,000 up, up, and up. 9 A.M.–8 P.M.; closed Wed.

[15] **Nakajima Menya** 中島めんや 尾張町2-2-18
The oldest toy store in the area, with dolls of the region. 9 A.M.–6 P.M.; closed Thurs.

[16] **Ohi Choami Pottery** 大樋長阿弥 大手町9-19
Specializing in the strange orange-and-green tone Ohi ceramics, of course. Nice selection, reasonable prices. 8 A.M.–6 P.M.

[17] **Morihachi** 森八 尾張町2-12-1
A famous Japanese cake shop with a 300-year history. Beautifully wrapped, fascinatingly crafted cakes, mostly made with sweet beans to eat with green tea. Nice gift for a Japanese friend. ¥800 up; 9 A.M.–7:30 P.M.; closed first and third Sun.

KURASHIKI

GODOWN GALLERIES

If you like your art stylishly displayed, you'll like Kurashiki, where the town's old rice granaries, distinctively covered halfway up their walls with black clay tiles deeply set in white mortar, have been turned into art and archaeological museums and attractive shops.

All of the city that matters for the visitor is a compact area on either side of a willow-lined canal about a ten-minute walk from Kurashiki Station. Away from the restored old buildings this is a growing industrial center making synthetic fiber, cotton yarn, petroleum, steel, machinery, chemicals, and cement.

The chief attraction is the **Ohara Art Museum** (¥600; 9 A.M.– 5 P.M.; closed Mon.), whose original building in neo-Greek style is impossible to miss amid the white walls and black-tile roofs. The collection was put together by the late Magosaburo Ohara, president of what is now Kurabo Industries Ltd., and includes works by the best-known French impressionists as well as El Greco's *Annunciation*.

Within the grounds are also the **Ohara New Art Museum**, with a small but interesting group of paintings by Japanese artists influenced by the impressionists (works by Shigeru Aoki, Ryuzaburo Umehara, Sotaro Yasui, and Tsuguji Fujita are especially worthy of note); the **Ohara Pottery Hall**; **Munakata Gallery**; **Serizawa Gallery**; and **Far Eastern Gallery**.

The latter are in a group of old granaries whose interior designs are as stunning as what's exhibited. The Ohara Pottery Hall holds ceramics by the three great folk potters Shoji

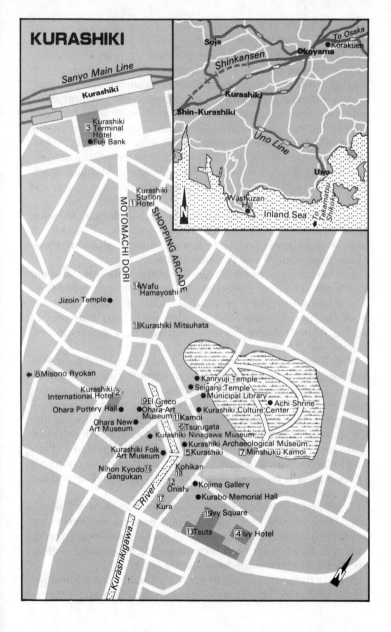

KURASHIKI

Sanyo Main Line

Kurashiki

3 Kurashiki Terminal Hotel
● Fuji Bank

MOTOMACHI DORI

Kurashiki Station Hotel 1

SHOPPING ARCADE

14 Wafu Hamayoshi

Jizoin Temple ●

18 Kurashiki Mitsuhata

8 Misono Ryokan ←

Kurashiki International Hotel 2
9 El Greco
Ohara Pottery Hall ●
Ohara Art Museum
Ohara New Art Museum ●
11 Kamoi
6 Tsurugata
● Kurashiki Ninagawa Museum
Kurashiki Folk Art Museum ●
5 Kurashiki
Nihon Kyodo 16 Gangukan
Kohikan
10
12 Onishi
17 Kura
13 Tsuta

● Kanryuji Temple
● Seiganji Temple
● Municipal Library
● Achi Shrine
● Kurashiki Culture Center
Kurashiki Archaeological Museum
7 Minshuku Kamoi

● Kojima Gallery
● Kurabo Memorial Hall
15 Ivy Square
4 Ivy Hotel

River

Kurashikigawa

Inset map

To Osaka
Soja
Okayama ● Korakuen
Shinkansen
Kurashiki
Shin-Kurashiki
Uno Line
Uno
Washuzan Hill
Inland Sea
To Takamatsu, Shikoku

Hamada, Kanjiro Kawai, and Kenkichi Tomimoto, plus some by the famous English potter Bernard Leach. The Munakata and Serizawa galleries are perhaps the best spots in all Japan to discover these famous artists, Munakata creating Buddhist-influenced woodblock prints and Serizawa stencil-dyed designs.

A few steps away from the Ohara compound are three other fine museums, each specializing in a different field. Although lodged in the usual Kurashiki godown, the interior of the **Kurashiki Ninagawa Museum** (¥600; 8:30 A.M.–5 P.M.; June–Aug., 8:30 A.M.–6 P.M.) would be quite at home in Paris or Vienna. The Ninagawa family collection of Western, Middle Eastern, and ancient Mediterranean art includes ceramics, mosaics, and sculptures.

150

Across the canal is the **Kurashiki Archaeological Museum** (¥300; 9 A.M.–5 P.M.; Dec.–Feb., 9 A.M.–4:30 P.M.; closed Mon.), with a small collection of Japanese artifacts, plus some pre-Columbian pottery and Peruvian textiles.

Farther along the canal the **Kurashiki Folk Art Museum** (¥500; 9 A.M.–5 P.M.; Dec.–Feb., 9 A.M.–4:15 P.M.; closed Mon.) has a wide assortment of Japanese folk art—rustic ceramics, glass, textiles, bamboo and wooden ware, plus examples of rooms from Japanese homes—displayed in a group of connected warehouses.

You'll also want to wander a short distance from the canal to **Ivy Square**, a group of revitalized nineteenth-century red-brick cotton mills, the first factory of Kurabo Industries. The complex now includes a hotel, restaurants, shops, and more small museums. The **Kurabo Memorial Hall** tells the history of the company. The **Kojima Gallery** displays Western-style works by Okayama Prefecture native Torajiro Kojima, who lived in Paris and helped Ohara purchase his French paintings. The courtyard of Ivy Square is paved with old bricks from the factory and is a good spot to rest.

The standard shopping mall which is a feature in practically every Japanese city gets an extra plus here for the interesting craft shops at the Ohara Museum end. Look for woven reed products and Bizen ware, a rustic, deep-chestnut-colored pottery spotted with ash residue from wood-fired kilns.

Thanks to the patronage of the town's native sons, Kurashiki has several good examples of modern Japanese architecture.

The **Kurashiki International Hotel**, designed by Kurashiki-born Shizutaro Urabe, who now works in Osaka, features a three-story lobby filled with large murals by Munakata. The exterior, using the familiar black tiles set in white mortar, was designed to blend in with the nearby godowns. Urabe also designed Ivy Square.

The peaceful canal with the swans was once busy with barges hauling rice from the warehouses to the Inland Sea, then to Osaka, the distribution center for all of Japan during the Tokugawa period. The surrounding fertile plain did and still does produce great quantities of rice.

For an overall look at the black-tile roofs of Kurashiki, climb the steps to **Kanryuji Temple**. Just an hour and twenty minutes by bus from Kurashiki Station is **Washuzan Hill**, one of the best lookouts for a panorama of the island-dotted Inland Sea, now dominated by the Seto Ohashi Bridge to Shikoku island. The view may inspire you to linger, and a number of cruise-ship and ferry services operate from the ports nearby. The Setouchi Kisen Line (☎[0822]55-3344) operates a daily service, April–November, from Onomichi (about one hour west of Kurashiki by JR) to **Setoda Island** (¥1,440; departs 10 A.M., arrives at Setoda 10:35 A.M.). From Setoda you can return to Onomichi, or you can continue through the pine-clad islands on another SKK ship to Omijima Island, Hiroshima, and Miyajima Island.

Onomichi

Itsukushima Shrine gateway

Kurashiki canal

152

Folk Art Museum

Omijima is the site of **Oyamazumi Shrine**, in feudal times a popular stopping point for soldiers off to battle, and containing some 80 percent of Japan's most valuable armor. The boat called *Akinada* departs from Setoda Island at 1:30 P.M., stopping at Omijima at 2:00 P.M. There's an hour-and-a-half stopover on Omijima to see the shrine and admire the fine scenery. The boat departs again at a 3:30, arriving in Hiroshima at 5 P.M. and Miyajima at 5:36 (Setoda to Miyajima, ¥6,380). Taped explanations in English of the sights along the route are available. You can also start in Miyajima or Hiroshima and make the trip to Onomichi.

Except for the **Peace Memorial Museum** (no charge; 9 A.M.–4:30 P.M.), which chronicles the events of that fateful day, August 6, 1945, when the city was virtually flattened by the atomic bomb blast, and makes a plea for world peace, there is no reason to tarry in Hiroshima proper. Lying in a river delta, it's never been a naturally scenic spot, and little was done to rebuild the city in an attractive way after World War II.

The chief attraction in the Hiroshima area is **Miyajima** (Itsukushima), noted both for its beautiful scenery and **Itsukushima Shrine**, whose great red *torii* gates lie anchored in the water a short distance away from the attractive buildings with the their connecting open corridors. Miyajima-guchi can be reached from Hiroshima by JR in twenty-five minutes, and from there it's a ten-minute ferry ride across to the island. There is also a direct boat service from Hiroshima.

KURASHIKI SLEEPING

[1] **Kurashiki Station Hotel** 倉敷ステーションホテル 2-8-1 Achi, ☎(0864) 25-2525. Three minutes from the station, a short walk to the Ohara Museum. Singles ¥5,000, twins from ¥10,000.

[2] **Kurashiki International Hotel** 倉敷国際ホテル 1-1-44 Chuo, ☎(0864) 22-5141. Delightful, small Western-style hotel, decorated with folk art. Just behind the Ohara Museum. Singles from ¥7,500, twins from ¥12,500.

[3] **Kurashiki Terminal Hotel** 倉敷ターミナルホテル 1-2-901 Achi, ☎(0864) 26-1111. New. On top of an office building beside the station. Singles ¥5,800–¥6,700, twins ¥11,300–¥12,300.

[4] **Ivy Hotel** アイビーホテル 7-2 Honmachi, ☎(0864)22-0011. Attractive rooms done up with local folk art, all tucked behind the red brick walls of the former Kurabo textile mill. Part of the Ivy Square complex. Singles) ¥8,000, twins ¥12,000 with bath, cheaper without bath.

[5] **Kurashiki** 倉敷 4-1 Honmachi, ☎(0864)22-0730. A fancy *ryokan* in the old town near the museums. ¥15,000–¥30,000 with two meals.

[6] **Tsurugata** つるがた 1-3-15 Chuo, ☎(0864)24-1635. Another nice *ryokan* right in the old town and handy for all the sights. ¥15,700–¥25,000 per person with two meals.

[7] **Minshuku Kamoi** 民宿 カモイ 1-24 Honmachi, ☎(0864)22-4898. Cozy *minshuku* with Japanese flavor at foot of Achi Shrine and just a short walk to the canal. ¥5,000 per person with two meals.

[8] **Misono Ryokan** 御園旅館 3-4-1 Ojmatsucho, ☎(0864)22-3618. For the big splurge, try this famous *ryokan* with fine food and its own garden. 10 minutes from the station and the old town. ¥15,000 per person with two meals.

KURASHIKI EATS AND DRINKS

[9] **El Greco** エル・グレコ 中央1-1-11 ☎(0864)22-0297
This landmark coffee shop has ivy-covered walls outside, high ceilings, and warm woods with fresh flowers arranged in handsome Japanese ceramics inside. Right beside the Ohara Museum entrance. 10 A.M.–5 P.M.; closed Mon.

[10] **Kohikan** 珈琲館 本町4-1 ☎(0864)24-5516
Coffee with a view of the old town and served by an attractive mama-san. 10 A.M.–5:30 P.M.; closed Mon.

[11] **Kamoi** かも井 中央1-3-17 ☎(0864)22-0606
This *sushiya* (raw fish shop) specializes in fish slightly steamed in a bam-

boo container. There is an adjacent coffee shop. Right across from the Ohara Museum. 9 A.M.–7:30 P.M.; closed Mon.

12 **Onishi** おおにし 本町5-29 ☎(0864)22-8134

Homemade Japanese noodles from ¥380. Try their *zaru udon*, cold noodles which you dip in a spicy sauce, during the summer months. 10 A.M.–6 P.M.

13 **Tsuta** 蔦 本町7-2 倉敷アイビースクエア内 ☎(0864)22-0011

Japanese-style lunches from ¥900. But the specialty is a course of several fish and vegetable dishes served up in fine style for ¥6,000; 7:30–9:30 A.M., 11:30 A.M.–2 P.M., 5–9 P.M.

14 **Wafu Hamayoshi** 和風 浜吉 阿知2-19-30 ☎(0864)21-3430

Lunch ranges from ¥800–¥3,000; dinner ¥5,000–¥15,000; 12–2 P.M., 5–10 P.M., closed Mon.

154

KURASHIKI SHOPPING

15 **Ivy Square** アイビースクエア 本町7-2

The complex includes several shops. One sells a nice selection of Japanese folk art, including reed crafts and *washi* paper. 8 A.M.–7 P.M.

16 **Nihon Kyodo Gangukan** 日本郷土玩具館 中央1-4-16

Toys from everywhere for ¥300 up. 8 A.M.–5 P.M.

17 **Kura** 倉 本町5-25

A godown full of crafts just beside the canal. 9 A.M.–5:30 P.M.; closed Mon.

18 **Kurashiki Mitsuhata** くらしき 光畑 本町4-21 ☎(0864)25-6522

Nice local souvenirs in the ¥300–¥1,000 range near Ohara Art Museum. 9 A.M.–7 P.M.

MATSUYAMA

松 山

A BATH BENEATH THE CASTLE KEEP

Few feudal castles in Japan dominate the cities below them more than **Matsuyama Castle**. Others are more sprawling, their keeps more lofty. None, however, seem to be set so high on their aeries as Matsuyama's. At 132 meters above the flat plain below, the castle hill is thickly forested. From nearly everywhere in town you can look up at the greenery and, if at the proper distance, see the three-story tower fortress, especially impressive after dark when its illuminated upturned tile roofs seem suspended in the night sky.

Matsuyama—indeed, all of Shikoku Island—has never been caught up in the country's tumultuous history. The castle was put into the hands of two feudal lords favored by the military dictators of their time. Kato Yoshiakira, who happened to side with Tokugawa Ieyasu in the decisive battle of Sekigahara, which would put Japan in Ieyasu's clutches, began constructing the castle in 1602, but its original five stories weren't completed for twenty-six years. In 1635 it was given to Matsudaira Sadayuki, to be reconstructed to its present three stories. Like so many of the country's castles, it's seen numerous fires. Lightning destroyed it in 1784, and the donjon was not rebuilt until 1820. Most of the present structure dates from 1854. Castles had long since given up their function as means of defense against attacks, but Matsuyama Castle's circuitous access and series of gates along the approach suggest that nineteenth-century builders were still taking war seriously. A 1933 fire destroyed a second keep adjacent to the main three-story one, and it wasn't reconstructed until 1968. The two donjons, several gates, and turrets are designated Important Cultural Properties by the Japanese government.

You can climb the steep hill, but the town fathers have thoughtfully installed a gondola and a chair lift up the east slope to a landing just below the gently curving stone ramparts. There's still a climb ahead, however, its strain on one's calves

MATSUYAMA

Sun Garden Matsuyama [2]

HEIWA DORI

Matsuyama Castle

[6] Toei Inn

JR Matsuyama

Ehime Prefectural Offic

ANA Hotel Matsuyama

Prefectural Art Museum

Manhattan Cl
City Hall

Matsuyama New [4]
Grand Hotel

Matsuyam
P.(

[11]
Grays

To Uchiko and Uwajima [14] and [7]

Matsuyama City Station

Gintengai Arcad

lessened to some extent by the fine views of the city and distant mountains and sea (castle, ¥260, 9 A.M.–5 P.M.; ropeway/chair lift, ¥570/¥310, including entrance fee to castle, 8:30 A.M.–5:30 P.M.).

The flat-topped castle ramparts are a good place to sort out where the city's action centers lie. Directly west toward the Inland Sea is JR's Matsuyama Station with a City Information Of-

Kawakichi Besso
Yunomachi   Kosen
           Takada Towel
Dogo Onsen

Shiki Memorial Museum

To Ishiteji

Ichibancho

Hotel Top Inn
Mitsukoshi Dept.
Kento's
Flying Scotsman
Kushihide
tsuretsutei

Okaido Arcade

N

fice (8:30 A.M.–9:30 P.M.), a good neighborhood to locate a business hotel for the night, but little else. Directly below to the south is the main shopping and entertainment district, which centers on Okaido, an up-to-date shopping arcade which finally makes a sharp right turn to become Gintengai, another arcade leading all the way past less fancy shops to Matsuyama City Station (Matsuyama *Shi Eki*), dominated by the Iyotetsu Sogo Department Store built over Iyotetsudo's rail and bus terminal. In front of Sogo lies Matsuyamachika Town, an underground arcade packed with inexpensive eating places. Directly east lies Dogo Onsen, Matsuyama's other must-see attraction—a spa which claims to be the oldest in Japan with a history of 3,000 years. And just north are Ehime University and Matsuyama University of Commerce, their campuses spread out on a broad plain beneath the mountains.

The landmarks are connected by a streetcar system with several different lines that circle the castle and roll east to Dogo Onsen and west to Matsuyama Station (¥150, regardless of distance traveled; board from the rear). You can reach **Dogo Onsen** in just ten minutes from Okaido. Legend attests the first bather at the spa was a white heron which discovered the water's healing powers when he dipped his injured leg into a crevice gushing hot water. The creature has become a symbol of the place, its graceful physique resting from atop the old public bath-house Shinrokaku and on the shopping bags from the souvenir shops.

Dogo has seen Japan's greats, from emperors to military dictators, and you can join the list of luminaries who have taken to its waters by checking into one of a raft of Japanese-style hotels or, more simply, by going to **Shinrokaku**, a landmark 1894 Momoyama-style building with three floors and two baths open to the public. A ¥1,240 ticket entitles you to go "first class" with a tatami room of your own where you can change clothes on the third floor; a stiffly starched cotton kimono; access to either the first-floor Kami-no-yu or the second-floor Tama-no-yu baths, made of granite stone; and Japanese sweets and green tea back in your room after your bath. It's the "first class" rooms which were the choice of Meiji-era novelist Natsume Soseki during his time in Matsuyama as a schoolteacher. In his novel *Botchan*, relating his Matsuyama experiences, Soseki wrote, "If you went first class, you could get a bathrobe and wash by the servant as well. Moreover, a pretty maid would serve you tea in a cup called tenmoku." All but the back scrubbers and pretty maids remain—even the third-floor room where Soseki unwound nearly every evening after work. It can be viewed for the price of the ticket.

Anyone can afford a bath at Shinrokaku. For ¥220 you're entitled access into the changing room and a big granite bath "as large as a fifteen-mat room," said Soseki. For ¥620 you're pointed to the second-floor changing room, can dip in either of the two baths, and are given a cotton kimono, tea, and cakes.

Although Shinrokaku reeks with atmosphere of bygone days and should not be missed, the late-model 1984 **Tsubaki-no-yu** public bath-house (just a minute away down the Yunomachi arcade) has even larger granite baths and seems to draw more locals than tourists. You buy your entrance ticket for ¥220 from a machine at the entrance. The lady to whom you hand your ticket will give you a towel and soap, the towel to be returned after use, for ¥50.

The **Yunomachi** arcades are jammed with look-alike souvenir shops selling local products which no Japanese dares return home without. And beyond the bath-houses and arcades, you're surrounded by ugly postwar high-rise concrete hotels whose exteriors belie the fact that within they're purely Japanese. The tour buses roll up at the doors in the evenings and disgorge their loads to take a quick bath, eat, and sing together in their cotton kimonos, hit the hay, swallow their breakfasts whole, then jump back on the bus again for the next leg of their journey. Although Shinrokaku is the ultimate in Japanese public bath-houses, Dogo town itself is a carbon copy of the most famous hot-spring resorts. You don't check in at one of these hotels to get away from it all. For a price, you can find an oasis of tranquillity or two. Check the Matsuyama hotel listings at the end of this section.

The whole of Matsuyama must have been terribly tranquil once. Soseki, a Tokyo city slicker, had a ball poking fun at the town's rustics in *Botchan*. Matsuyama's own great Meiji-era literary figure, Masaoka Shiki, born of a lowly samurai family and brought up in the town, seemed to share Soseki's sentiments in his writings. He could hardly wait to leave for Tokyo.

Matsuyama is rightfully proud of Shiki, a local boy who lead a group of poets that together revolutionized haiku and tanka poem-writing by shaking it free of its stodginess at the time and dragging it into the modern era. In the short thirty-five years of his life from 1867, the year before the emperor Meiji was restored to power replacing nearly 250 years of rule by the Tokugawa shoguns, he'd watched his country transform itself, and in the area of literature he'd helped revive.

The **Shiki Memorial Museum** in Dogo Park, just a few minutes' walk from Shinrokaku, traces his life in remarkably clear English, although you won't be able to appreciate any of his writing on display unless you can read Japanese. For years until his death of spinal tuberculosis in 1902 he lay bedridden, writing a lively diary that belied his agony—and longing to see the newfangled wonders of Tokyo, including motion pictures, bicycle races and stunts, lions and ostriches in the zoo, automatic telephones and red postboxes, a beer hall, and an athletic meet for girl students.

Shiki was no doubt well acquainted with the pilgrims dressed in white from the Shingon sect of Japanese Buddhism. In honor of the sect's founder, Kukai, posthumously known as Kobo Daishi, who was born at Zentsuji on Shikoku, now the sect's headquarters, the pilgrims have for centuries traveled round the island, visiting eighty-eight temples. Eight of the eighty-eight are located in Matsuyama, the most famous of which is **Ishiteji**, just a ten-minute walk up the road from the Shiki Memorial Museum.

Although perhaps Matsuyama's most venerable, with a history dating from A.D. 728 and a two-story gate decked out with giant straw sandals, the type of which are worn by the pilgrims, and a fine specimen of a pagoda dating from the fourteenth century, Ishiteji has no buildings, nor has it the dramatic setting of any temples in Kyoto or Nara. Still, it offers solace between the busloads of tourists who come, and it's a likely spot to see the pilgrims themselves arriving on buses.

Before you head into the Shikoku hinterlands, you'll want a taste of Tokyo life, if not the kind Shiki longed for, and the place to go is **Okaido**, the streetcar stop at the entrance of the big shopping arcade. the neighborhood is Matsuyama's Ginza and Roppongi rolled into one, and has a lot of the shop names you'll have already seen in Tokyo or one of the other provincial cities. La Foret Harajuku, like the Tokyo original, is jammed with teenyboppers à la Shikoku. Mitsukoshi lies just across the arcade. Issey Miyake and Rei Kawakubo's Commes des Garçons are next door. Matsuyama's a backwater? You could stock up on English-language books at Tokyo's Kinokuniya, but you'll find another one in Chifunemachi 5-chome down by Matsuyama Shi Eki.

Just forty-two minutes away by express train on the JR Yosan Main Line lies **Uchiko**, a village of 13,000 the world had nearly passed by until it was linked directly with Matsuyama with the opening of a rail tunnel through the steep mountains only a few years ago. Although the town fathers are valiantly trying to attract visitors, it's not yet a large mark on the tourist map, and well worth a half day of the foreigner's time to capture the flavor of country Shikoku.

Uchiko's two architectural jewels, while a little dusty, are its street of merchants' houses dating from the last 150 years or so and known as Yokaichi, and a Kabuki theater called Uchikoza dating from 1916 when Kabuki troupes still played the boards in country towns.

Uchiko Station is just a piddle stop. There are no coin lockers, but you can check your bag with the JR man on duty for ¥260. Although there are no English signs in town, the village is small, and by merely pronouncing the names Yokaichi or Uchikoza, the natives will no doubt take you by the hand and lead the way. Take the street downhill from the station past the supermarket and head left on the first street, then across a stream. You're now in downtown Uchiko. The old Kabuki theater **Uchikoza** is down the street and up the hill on the left, the alley leading to it marked with big banners sticking out of the ground.

The old hall is in pristine condition, still used for concerts at times, although Kabuki doesn't stop here anymore, and you can almost picture the fifty geisha and their patrons who used to flock in for performances during the town's busier days. The stage turntable still works. Local patrons have donated a colorful theater curtain. Board floors lie where tatami mats used to be, but otherwise you're in a Japanese time capsule.

Back down to the main street, with a growing number of new restaurants and shops geared for visitors, you continue down the avenue to the recently spruced-up Iyo Bank, then take a left, climbing uphill to **Yokaichi**. There are a few eyesores here from recent times, but the mood of a street of old merchants' houses remains. Most outstanding for its interesting architecture of whitewashed clay and stone walls is the **Kamihaga-tei** house (9 A.M.–4:30 P.M., closed Wednesday). This is the building you've seen plastered on every piece of Uchiko tour propaganda, and it's worth the ¥210 admission charge to see how a well-off country merchant lived in this part of Japan. Some of the old houses have been converted into shops and restaurants. At the **Shokokan** (¥310, 9 A.M.–4:30 P.M., closed Wednesday) you can wander through folk art. Up at the top of the street, just to the right beyond the fork in the road, you can watch a fifth-generation candle maker named Omori plying his trade at the **Omori Rosokuten**. Uchiko's tradesmen were mostly candle makers, the candles are curious to Westerners because they taper from the bottom up rather than from the top down, the logic being that the drippings don't fall on the candle.

162

Back to the fork and immediately uphill to the right is **Kosho-ji**, a Buddhist temple of the Tendai sect with a lushly planted courtyard behind the entrance gate.

At **Iyo-Ozu**, the next stop south on the JR Yosan Line and just twelve minutes by express from Uchiko, you have yet another chance to see cormorants catching *ayu* fish, an old tradition in Japan known as *ukai*, from June through September 20. You'll need to make a reservation to board a longboat for a fee of ¥2,500 from the landing at Kameyama Koen Shita (phone [0893] 24-3133).

Uwajima, another one hour and a half down the west coast of Shikoku by express train, beckons with bullfights, a small castle and stroll garden, and a Shinto shrine with a museum of erotica for wishful baby-makers, all in a laid-back sub-tropical torpor. Hop off the train and you'll think you've mistakenly arrived in Beverly Hills or Palm Springs—the main street is lined with tall Washingtonian palm trees. You needn't look far beyond the palm fronds, however, to realize you're deep in the Japanese countryside.

This little castle town, once ruled by a branch of the Date lords of Sendai is, like Matsuyama, dominated by a castle hill, its approach equally steep—and without gondolas or chairlifts. The climb affords a walk through dense foliage and, once you've reached the top, a fine view of Uwajima Bay and the very near mountains, plus a **miniature castle keep** that's been around since 1665 (free). A short stroll south brings you to **Tenshaen**, another stroll garden built for the feudal lord and his guests, now nearly submerged behind a baseball diamond (¥210, 8:30 A.M.–4:30 P.M., till 5 P.M. April–June).

At the foot of the mountain to the north, facing the stream, are two Shinto shrines. **Ware Shrine** is imposing for the stone bridge which leads to a flight of steps and into a simple court-yard where bantam fowl strut as though they owned the place. Just west along the stream past the bridge, a narrow lane on the right leads to **Taga Shrine** with a courtyard full of phalluses offer-ing immediate indication of what's venerated. Such shrines are not unique to Uwajima—nor are they unique to Japan. The ad-joining Taga Aimaru Museum of erotica (¥600, 8 A.M.–5 P.M.) is one of the country's more bizarre collections, an assortment of phalluses from around the world, along with scenes of bliss on china, in photographs, and in woodblock prints that climb walls and cover ceilings. It's more of a laugh than a turn-on. Don't miss it if you're in town.

163

Uwajima's main claim to fame are its sumo matches for bulls, known as *togyu* hereabouts. The bulls size each other up, then charge, trying to push the other out of the circular ring, egged on by cheering fans surrounding them. There's rarely blood—and no matador's life is at stake. Worth the time, if you happen to be in town, which is unlikely unless you plan well ahead. Togyu is staged only six times each year. Check with the Japan National Tourist Office at home or at their TIC offices at Narita, Tokyo, or Kyoto before you head south.

Shikoku is now more accessible from Honshu Island with the completion of the Seto Ohashi Bridge, the first road and rail link spanning the Inland Sea between the two islands. Changing to the Seto Ohashi Line at Okayama, you can be on Shikoku in forty-five minutes, and in Matsuyama in three hours and twen-ty minutes via an express train. Matsuyama also has hydrofoil and ferry service from Hiroshima, and ferry service from Osaka, Kobe, and Beppu on Kyushu Island.

Most visitors spend their time on Shikoku along the Inland Sea. **Takamatsu**, the island's second city, was also a castle town, the remains of its castle surviving as reminders in Tamamo Park near the shore. **Ritsurin Park**, once the summer villa of the Matsudaira lords, takes advantage of its surrounding natural scenery from the slopes of Mt. Shuin, adding small lakes, hills, and gnarled trees to create one of Japan's best stroll gardens.

West of Takamatsu at the south end of Seto Ohashi are two religious centers: the aforementioned **Zentsuji**, birthplace of the great priest Kobo Daishi and headquarters for the Shingon sect of Buddhism with many seventeenth-century buildings holding Buddhist sculpture, art, and manuscripts in the priest's hand; and **Kotohiragu Shrine** at Kotohira, a religious center popular with the island's long line of seafarers and voyagers, its buildings connected by a very long flight of 1,300 steps over a hillside.

The JR Dosan Main Line rolls south from Kotohira through scenic Iyadani Gorge with sheer rock walls along the Iya River to **Kochi**, Shikoku's southernmost major city, in two hours and twenty minutes. The Yamanouchi lords ruled here for sixteen generations, and their five-story **castle keep** offers a view of the town and surrounding scenery. Built on a steep slope, **Godaisan Park** is dotted with temples, a pagoda, and botanical garden. Following narrow Urado Bay to the Pacific, you're in **Katsurahama**, the area's most popular beach, situated in a wide cove of rock formations and pines.

For lovers of seascapes, the two wide peninsulas jutting out into the sea east or west of Kochi are lush with subtropical vegetation, with **Cape Ashi Zuri** being perhaps the more spectacular.

There's no direct rail service between Kochi and Matsuyama, but JR express buses connect the cities in a little over three hours. By changing buses at Mimido, you can continue up **Mt. Ishizuchi** by road to Ishizuchi Tsuchigoya, then via a gondola to within a two-hour hike to the summit of Shikoku's highest peak at 1,892 meters. On a clear day the whole of the island is visible, from the Inland Sea to the Pacific. There are six buses per day between Ishizuchi Tsuchigoya and Matsuyama's JR Station.

MATSUYAMA SLEEPING

1 **ANA Hotel Matsuyama** 全日空松山ホテル 3-2-1 Ichibancho, ☎(0899) 33-5511. The best Western-style hotel in town, and the handiest loca-

tion at Okaido. Singles in the rear annex begin at ¥6,500; twins from ¥15,500.

2 **Sun Garden Matsuyama** サンガーデン松山 3-2-10 Heiwadori, ☎(0899) 26-4411. On the nothing (north) side of Matsuyama Castle hill, but new and clean, and within walking distance of the gondola and chair lift. Singles ¥5,500; twins ¥15,000. Western or Japanese breakfast for an extra ¥700.

3 **Hotel Top Inn** ホテルトップイン 1-5 Ichibancho, ☎(0899)33-3333. New business hotel with flash, and steps from Okaido. Singles ¥5,000; twins ¥8,800.

4 **Matsuyama New Grand Hotel** 松山ニューグランドホテル 3-4-1 Niban-cho, ☎(0899)33-3661. Older business hotel, but in a handy location near Okaido, and there's a sauna on the first floor. Singles ¥5,000; twins ¥8,500.

5 **Kawakichi Besso** かわきち別荘 1-13 Dogosagidanicho, ☎(0899)31-1171. On oasis of Japanese tranquillity in the midst of Dogo Onsen's concrete squalor. Ask for a room in the original *kyukan* dating from the 1930s, and you'll swear you're in Kyoto. For the big splurge at from ¥18,000 per person with two meals—figure close to ¥20,000 per person with taxes. Worth every single yen, if you've been grubbing in business hotels or *minshuku* for a stretch.

6 **Toei Inn Matsuyama** 東映イン松山 1-34-1 Miyatacho, ☎(0899)24-2121. One of a chain of business hotels, and your best bet among the cluster of these hotels near the JR Matsuyama Station—just a few minutes' walk north. Singles ¥5,200.

7 **Hotel Ishibashi** ホテルイシバシ 2-4-14 Sakaimachi Minato, ☎(0895) 22-5540. Not the newest, but the most spectacularly located business hotel in Uwajima, overlooking the harbor with its ferries to outlying islands moving to and fro. Singles ¥4,500; twins ¥8,000.

MATSUYAMA EATS AND DRINKS

8 **Kushihide** くし秀 二番町3-2-8 ☎(0899)21-1587. There are two Kushihides just west of the Okaido arcade, the one nearest the arcade specializing in *yakitori* chicken pieces or small bits of vegetables grilled on a stick. ¥1,500 will buy a selection of five chicken pieces, rice, pickles, and a beer. Down the street on the corner behind chic white walls is Kushihide's elegant fresh-fish parlor. You sit at a wraparound counter and select from the tank behind. ¥5,000 or so per person. 4:30–11 P.M.

9 **Katsuretsutei** かつれつ亭 ☎(0899)41-6318. Located between the two Kushihides, this attractive spot done up in folk art is for meat lovers, serving grilled steak or deep-fried pork cutlet (*tonkatsu*) with prices from around ¥1,500.

10 **Flying Scotsman** フライング・スコッツマン 大街道2-5-9 ☎(0899)47-6527.

Coffee and snacks in a fake San Francisco cable car on the Okaido arcade, and open at nearly the crack of dawn for a caffeine fix. 7:30 A.M.–11:30 P.M.

11 **Grays** グレイズ 千舟町4-6-2 ☎(0899)43-5700. Good coffee and great homemade cakes in a shop of antiques from the early part of this century. Just beside JAL Plaza on Chifunemachi Dori. 10:30 A.M.–8 P.M., closed Wed.

12 **Manhattan Club/Suntory Jigger Bar** マンハッタンクラブ・サントリー・ジガー・バー 二番町3-10 ☎(0899)21-4058. A casual bar for a quick snort of the sort of things you drink at home. 6 P.M.–3 A.M. It's a coffee shop from 8 A.M. to 4 P.M.

13 **Kento's** ケントス 二番町3 チャイムシンワビルB1 ☎(0899)21-4067. Live bands hurtling tunes from the '50s and '60s from 7:35 P.M. until the wee hours. This is one of a chain, the original in Tokyo's Roppongi. 6 P.M.–2 A.M.

14 **Bizenya** 備前屋. Yokaichi Not-so-old Japanese antiques and coffee in one of those old merchants' houses in Uchiko. Charming. The owner is fond of Bizen pottery, hence the name. 9 A.M.–8 P.M.

MATSUYAMA SHOPPING

Two forms of folk art originating in the Matsuyama area still thrive: blue *ikat* cotton cloth known as **Iyo-gasuri** (Iyo was the old name of much of what is now Ehime Prefecture) and mostly lightly glazed blue and white stoneware called **Tobeyaki**—named after the village of Tobe, where it's still made just south of the city. You can see Iyo-gasuri made and find mounds of it for sale at the **Iyo-gasuri Kaikan**, just up the road north of Kiyuyama Station on the Iyotetsudo private line heading for Mitsuyama, or an Iyotetsudo bus, both from *Matsuyama Shi Eki* (City Station). Tobeyaki is available along the main street of **Tobe town**, but if you can't make it that far, there's plenty in every souvenir shop in Matsuyama, including those to Dogo Onsen. The thing to bring to Japanese friends is the local tart (*taruto*), a citrus-flavored confection with a swirl of sweet bean jam in the center. The best selection of souvenirs in Matsuyama's center is in the Okaido arcade or around Matsuyama Shi Station. In Dogo it's Yunomachi, the arcade stretching from Dogo Station, terminus for the streetcar, all the way to the Shinrokaku bath-house.

15 **Kosen** 古泉 道後湯之町13-14 ☎(0899)31-8205. Not the largest, but the most discriminating selection of local crafts in the Yunomachi arcade at Dogo, including fine *tobeyaki* and a nice assortment of *Iyo-gasuri*. 8:30 A.M.–10 P.M.

16 **Takada Towel** 高田タオル 道後湯之町 ☎(0899)21-0760. Folksy hand towels for camouflage in the public baths up the street at low, low prices from ¥130. They make a fun and easy-to-pack gift. In the Yunomachi arcade at Dogo.

NAGASAKI

長 崎

PEEPHOLE TO THE OUTSIDE

Although a thoroughly Japanese city to the foreigner's eye at this time in its history, Nagasaki stirs visions of exoticism in the Japanese. No city in the country has had more contact with foreigners over a longer period of time. The Portuguese were the first to come in the late sixteenth century—attracted by the mountain-surrounded harbor and a local feudal lord friendly to Christianity. After the foreign religion was banned once and for all by the Tokugawa shogun in the mid-seventeenth century, the Dutch were allowed to trade from a tiny manmade island called Dejima. For the next two centuries the ships sailing into the port once or twice a year brought news of what was happening in the West. British merchants in Nagasaki did much to help the country at last open its doors to the outside world in the mid-nineteenth century. Finally, this city was the target of the world's second atomic bomb on August 9, 1945.

Hints of the rich history remain. You will at first be struck by the city's lovely setting, squeezed between narrow valleys and climbing up mountains facing the narrow channel to the sea. Next, you'll be awed by the familiar. Few non-Japanese actually live here anymore. But the heritage remains in churches, nineteenth-century European-style homes, and romantic restaurants filled with antiques from faraway places. The Madame Butterfly story immortalized in the Puccini opera is probably untrue. But it is close enough to the many sad Nagasaki liaisons between Japanese and foreigners in days gone by to touch the romantic heart.

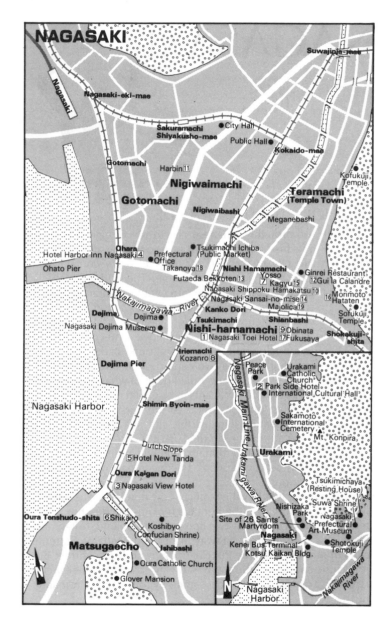

The **Glover Garden** on a slope overlooking the snug harbor is a good place to start. Chiochio-san is there in statue waiting for Lt. Pinkerton. The garden is named after Thomas Glover, whose 1863 house is the oldest among the wooden Western houses that have survived. While the Glover house is the chief purpose for the pilgrimage up the hill, it is not alone. Several merchants' homes from the same period, along with a rest house for the crews of Mitsubishi Heavy Industries, have been moved from other locations. On exiting from the grounds you will pass through an exhibition hall displaying the colorful European and Chinese floats used in the city's biggest festival, held each October 7 to 9. (Garden admission ¥600; 8 A.M.–6 P.M.; Dec.–Feb., 8:30 A.M.–5 P.M.)

Adjacent is **Oura Catholic Church** (¥250; 8 A.M.–6 P.M.; Dec.–Feb., 8:30 A.M.–5 P.M.), Japan's oldest Gothic-style wooden church, built in 1865 to commemorate the deaths of twenty-six Christian martyrs in 1597. The six foreigners and twenty Japanese were crucified in a purge by Hideyoshi on Nishizaka, a hill just above present-day Nagasaki Station, which could once be seen across the valley from Oura Church. Legend says the men hung on their crosses for eighty days, during which many miracles happened. They were canonized in 1862 by Pope Pius IX. Christians from all over Japan gather here on February 5, the date of the executions, and Pope John Paul II paid a visit on his historic trip to Japan in 1981. **Nishizaka Park**, with a monument to the twenty-six martyrs and a small museum (¥200; 9 A.M.–5 P.M.) outlining the tragedy and other missionary endeavors in Japan, is more easily visited when seeing the monuments to world peace in connection with the atomic blast.

Below Glover Garden and Oura Church you can begin exploring Nagasaki's many Chinese-influenced attractions. The old Hong Kong and Shanghai Bank sits on the waterfront. **Shikairo**, rising like a pagoda next door, is one of the oldest Chinese restaurants in the city, and the first-floor lounge with mother-of-pearl inlaid furniture imported from the Chinese mainland is worth a look, even if you don't eat there.

China's great port of Shanghai is just a 900-mile voyage across the East China Sea from Nagasaki. The Chinese immigrants were always allowed more freedom of movement than the resident Europeans, and their presence is still felt. A short walk north and east from Shikairo is Koshibyo, the **Confucian Shrine** and **Chinese Museum of History** (¥515), easy to spot with its yellow-tiled roof and bright red walls. It opened in 1983 on the ninetieth anniversary of the shrine, and the small museum holds artifacts and china on loan from the People's Republic, the exhibition changing each year. Nagasaki's Chinese restaurants, with most of their cooks from Fukien Province, are clustered behind four big gates near the downtown shopping area.

More romantically Chinese are a series of bridges spanning the Nakajimagawa River adjacent to the shopping quarter, the most famous being **Meganebashi**, or "Spectacles Bridge," whose two arches reflected in the water look like a pair of glasses. It was built in 1634 by one of the first Chinese priests at Kofukuji up the hill. A flash flood in 1982 swept some of the original stones away, but most of them were retrieved, and the bridge was well restored with seventeenth-century techniques. Both **Kofukuji** and **Sofukuji** in the *teramachi*, or temple town, above the downtown area should be visited for their bold Chinese architecture in contrast with the more somber Japanese temples nearby. Sofukuji's Ming-style red gate is a local landmark. The two temples belong to Obaku, the youngest of Zen Buddhist sects to come to Japan in the early seventeenth century.

Also adjacent to the business section is **Dejima**. The island is gone, lost to a landfill operation in the nineteenth century. On

Chinese dragon dance

Meganebashi

the site a scale model of the fan-shaped trading compound has been built inside a small park, and across the street the **Nagasaki Dejima Museum** (no charge; 9 A.M.–5 P.M.; closed Mon.) contains reminders of the city's Dutch and Portuguese past. The white walls surrounding the park and school across the street mark the approximate location of the original island. At **Ginrei Restaurant** (☎[0958]21-2073) on the upper fringes of the business section next to the temple town you can pretend you're in an Amsterdam town house while sipping coffee or having a meal (10 A.M.–9 P.M.). A new commercial enterprise with a Dutch theme has opened on the western shores of Omura Bay northwest of the city. Known as **Holland Village**, it has restaurants, shops, and a replica of an old Dutch trading ship, along with a few foreign live models to give the Japanese the impression they've crossed the ocean. (¥2,570 for an open ticket to all attractions. There is double-decker bus service from the Nagasaki Bus Terminal in the center of town—¥600, ¥100 extra for the upper deck. It's about an hour-and-a-half ride each way, so you'll need at least a half day).

171

Reserve at least a few hours to retrace the tragic events of August 9, 1945, when the atomic bomb fell on a narrow strip of land between the mountains and the harbor north of the city center. At the **International Cultural Hall** (¥50; 9 A.M.–6 P.M.), just above Hamaguchi Station on the No. 3 or 5 streetcar line, a museum graphically explains the human misery of the world-altering event. Some 75,000 people died. Many more were injured. The Nagasaki museum lacks the flair for display of its Hiroshima counterpart, but it still stirs thoughts. Just down the street a sleek marble column stands in a park at the hypocenter of the blast, and in the same park the shattered remains of Urakami Church were brought to offer more evidence of the horrors of nuclear war. The church was rebuilt and sits on a hill about a ten-minute walk from the park. Close to the epicenter in a separate location is Peace Park, with a famous statue and fountain symbolizing world peace. It was created by residents in 1955.

The easiest way to get around Nagasaki proper is by streetcar. Four lines rattle along at the bottom of the city's narrow valleys and beside the shoreline. Major stops are well marked in English. The fare is only ¥100 per ride, regardless of distance.

For ¥500 you can buy an all-day pass. From the stop, it's usually a short walk uphill to your destination.

With the sound of the ships honking in the harbor, you'll want to go to sea. There is an **excursion boat** which departs several times a day year-round from Ohato Pier. If you want to be spared the recorded explanations in Japanese and have more than the fifty minutes it takes for the sightseeing boat, take a thirty-five-minute ride to **Ioshima**, a small island at the entrance to Nagasaki Harbor. You can explore the village, with its pretty church and the rice paddies climbing the steep hills in terraces, then go back to Ohato Pier on another ferry. With more time, there is another ferry to the **Goto Islands**. The trip takes four hours one-way.

All of Nagasaki Prefecture is spectacularly scenic, a touch of the French Riviera or California with its mountains tumbling into the sea. Possiblities for further sightseeing include the **Arita** area where the famous Imari ware export china was made. Especially worthwhile is the trip to **Hirado Island**. Buses leave from the Kenei Bus Terminal across the street from Nagasaki Station for Sasebo Station (¥1,350), from where you catch a local bus to the nearby port of Kashimae. Here you board the **Kobaruto Line** ferry for a slow one-and-a-half-hour ride among the ninety-nine islands to Hirado (¥2,890). This large island off the west coast of Kyushu also has links with British, Dutch, and Chinese traders. The small village has several *minshuku*, a rebuilt castle at the harbor entrance, a fine museum of art objects belonging to the local *daimyo*, another Catholic church associated with the island's Christian history, and quiet pedestrian pathways winding over the hills above the town.

East from Nagasaki you can take a two-hour-and-ten-minute Kenei Bus ride to **Unzen-Amakusa National Park** (¥1,750), a high-altitude (717-meter) scenic resting spot with views of the sea on all sides. Established in 1934, this was Japan's first national park, and was once a gathering place for old American and European "China hands" who came here to escape the heat in Shanghai, Hong Kong, and Manila. En route to Shimabara by bus you can spot **Hara Castle** on the plain near the shore, where some 30,000 Christians held out against the Tokugawa forces in 1641—the last time they fought before going underground. Nothing remains of the original castle, but a

Model of Dejima

Nagasaki Harbor

concrete version houses an interesting exhibit about the revolt with explanations in English, as well as Christian icons made by Japanese. From Shimabara there is a Kyushu Shosen ferry (¥810) to Misumi across Shimabara Bay.

You can pick up English information about Nagasaki and the surrounding area from the **Nagasaki Trade and Tourist Association** on the second floor above the Kenei Bus Terminal in front of Nagasaki Station. Most of it is free. Invest in a copy of *Your Guide to Nagasaki,* put together by the city's Interpreters Association. It's your best single source of tourist information, with a map in English showing all the streetcar-stop names.

NAGASAKI SLEEPING

[1] **Nagasaki Toei Hotel** 長崎東映ホテル 7-24 Doza, ☎(0958)22-2121. The best in the business hotel category of hostelries with which Nagasaki abounds. New, and in the center of shopping, sightseeing. Near public transportation. Singles ¥6,200, twins ¥12,000 or ¥15,000.

[2] **Park Side Hotel** パークサイドホテル 14-1 Heiwamachi, ☎(0958)45-3191. Out of the way, but in a pretty and quiet location overlooking the epicenter park beside the International Cultural Hall. Singles ¥6,600, twins ¥13,200.

[3] **Nagasaki View Hotel** 長崎ビューホテル 2-33 Ouramachi, ☎(0958)24-2211. The waterfront rooms have great views of the harbor, as does the grand bath on the tenth floor. Handy to Glover Garden, Orandazaka.

¥10,000 per person with two meals. Slightly higher during peak seasons.

4 **Hotel Harbor Inn Nagasaki** ホテルハーバーイン長崎 8-17 Kabashimamachi, ☎(0958)27-1111. Singles ¥5,150, twins from ¥8,240.

5 **Hotel New Tanda** ホテルニュータンダ 2-24 Tokiwamachi, ☎(0958)27-6121. Cozy hotel popular with foreigners at the foot of Dutch Hill and just a five-minute walk to Oura Church and Glover Mansion. Singles from ¥7,300, twins from ¥14,700.

NAGASAKI EATS AND DRINKS

6 **Shikairo** 四海楼 松ヶ枝町4–5 ☎(0958)24-4744

A local institution since 1899. Chinese students going to school in Nagasaki used to frequent the place. Claims to have invented the hearty soup noodle dish *Nagasaki champon*. Tour groups here can be overwhelming, but at least look at the handsome first-floor lounge. 11:30 A.M.–8 P.M.

7 **Yosso** 吉宗 浜町8–9 ☎(0958)21-0001

You eat on the wide tatami floor in this old (1866) restaurant. Small lunch courses in the ¥1,000 range. *Chawanmushi*, an egg custard flecked with vegetables in a fish stock, is the specialty. 11 A.M.–8:30 P.M.; closed Tues.

8 **Kozanro** 江山楼 新地町12–2 ☎(0958)21-3735

One of a half dozen or so Chinese restaurants clustered together near the shopping area, this one with inexpensive *champon* for ¥600 or ¥800, depending on size. 11 A.M.–9 P.M.

9 **Obinata** オビナタ 船大工町3 ☎(0958)26-1437

Extensive menu of Japanese-style Italian dishes, heavy on pasta, but the draw here is the romantic atmosphere. Dinner by candlelight amid European and Japanese antiques. Average ¥5,000 for dinner, but can be less if you order carefully. 6–10 P.M.

10 **Nagasaki Shippoku Hamakatsu** 長崎卓袱浜勝 鍛冶屋町6–50 ☎(0958)26-8321

Shippoku ryori, a mixture of Chinese, Japanese, and Western dishes that originated in Nagasaki, is what draws customers here. ¥3,800 course; 11:30 A.M.–8:30 P.M.

11 **Harbin** ハルビン 興善町2-27 ☎(0958)22-7443
A Russian and French menu including caviar in crepes among the listings. A beautiful setting for a romantic dinner, like being invited to a rich man's home. The owner once lived in Harbin. ¥1,000–¥3,000 for lunch; dinner à la carte or in a set course from ¥3,000; 11 A.M.–2:30 P.M.

12 **Gui la Calandre** ギィ・ラ・カランドル 鍛冶屋町6-10 ☎(0958)24-9080
Coffee and cakes with a fireplace in the winter and a view of a small garden. Great place for a rest after trooping through nearby *teramachi* or shopping. 10 A.M.–11 P.M.

NAGASAKI SHOPPING

13 **Futaeda Bekkoten** 二枝べっ甲店 浜町3-26
One of many shops selling tortoiseshell jewelry and hair ornaments, but this is among the oldest, and it's easy to find on the lower end of the Hamanomachi Arcade. 10 A.M.–8 P.M.

14 **Nagasaki Sansai-no-mise** 長崎三彩の店 丸山町7-1
A local porcelain in a combination of three colors. Eguchi Shuzan is the potter. 10 A.M.–6 P.M.; closed Sun.

15 **Kagyu** 臥牛 鍛冶屋町1-10
Kagyu ware, a rustic pottery running to calm shades of brown, beige, and a soft blue-green, is made in Sasebo, and this Nagasaki branch shop has a good selection of mostly smaller pieces. 10 A.M.–8 P.M.; closed Thurs.

16 **Morimoto Hataten** 森本ハタ店 鍛冶屋町6-44
Nagasaki's only kite maker, busy during the city's kite festivals every Sunday and on April 29 and May 3. 8:30 A.M.–8 P.M.

17 **Fukusaya** 福砂屋 船大工町3-1
The city's most famous *castella* sponge cake maker. 8:30 A.M.–8 P.M.; closed Mon.

18 **Takanoya** 高野屋 築町1-16
The Japanese line up here for *karasumi*, a cod-roe sausage which is sliced thin before serving. 9 A.M.–7 P.M.

19 **Majolica** マヨリカ 油屋町1-4
A basement full of antique glass, china, and some furniture both from Europe and the Far East. Great for browsing. Just off Hamanomachi Arcade at the upper end. 10:40 A.M.–8 P.M.

KAGOSHIMA

鹿児島

SMOKE AND SPIRIT

Looming over this southernmost big city in Japan (population 510,000) like some angry god is the still very active volcano on Sakurajima, whose smoke and fine ashes drift across the bay to the city when the wind is wrong. Kagoshima folks carry umbrellas, and contact lens wearers complain. But the constant threat lends special character to this old castle town which was ruled by twenty-nine generations of the Shimazu clan—a total of 695 years—before the Meiji Restoration in 1868.

No one defies this volcano, and during their long reign over the area, no one defied the Shimazus either, not even the powerful Tokugawas in Edo. To be sure, the ruling lords of Satsuma, the old name for this area of Japan, kept up the pretense of good relations with the shogunate, as did the Dates in Sendai and the Maedas in Kanazawa.

But the Satsuma rulers were only biding their time. As problem piled upon problem for the Tokugawas in the mid-nineteenth century, the Shimazus saw their chance and, along with the Choshu lords of Western Honshu, were instrumental in overthrowing the shogunate and restoring the emperor to power.

One of the most famous Meiji leaders was Saigo Takamori, a Satsuma native, who gave Japan one more sample of Satsuma spirit in 1877 when he organized a large army of local people and attempted to take over the country. What was happening in Edo, renamed Tokyo, displeased him to the extent that he abandoned his post with the Meiji government and went back to Kagoshima in a huff. The rebellion, Japan's last civil insurrection, failed, but Saigo is admired by the Japanese to this day for his guts.

Kagoshima has another quirk that separates it from other Japanese cities. Since St. Frances Xavier, the famous Jesuit missionary, landed here in 1549, the area has had steady, if infrequent, contact with foreigners. The saint stayed only ten months, eager to move on to Kyoto, but he gave the Shimazus a peek at the outside world—and especially an admiration for Western military technology.

By the time St. Francis Xavier arrived, Portuguese had already reached Tanegashima Island, south of Kagoshima, and with them brought the first muskets Japan had ever seen. The local lord of the island was quick to learn how to make them himself, and soon this new weapon had spread across the country.

As the Tokugawa government faltered in the early nineteenth century, the Shimazus were busily readying themselves to enter the modern world. With translated technical books on modern science, by the mid-nineteenth century they had established factories producing glass, alcohol, and gunpowder. They were also refining oil and building ships.

One of the factories remaining from the industrial complex where once 1,200 men worked still remains and is known as the **Shoko Shuseikan**, now a small museum included in the price of admission to adjacent Iso Teien, a lovely garden that is Kagoshima's foremost beauty spot (¥600).

Just across the road from the museum is the **Ijinkan** (no charge), where English textile manufacturing technicians lived during their stay in 1867 to help the Shimazus set up the Kagoshima Spinning Mills.

Iso Teien, once a seaside villa of the Shimazus, should be your first destination in the city proper. This is another stroll garden built for the enjoyment of lords and ladies. With dramatic Sakurajima so close across the bay you can practically reach out and touch it, the garden proper seems almost incidental. For an additional ¥280 you can take a cable car to the top of Mt. Iso behind, for an even more dramatic view of the volcano and bay.

Kagoshima's shopping and business district lies between Kagoshima and Nishi (West) Kagoshima stations, Shiroyama, the old hilltop castle site, and Kagoshima Bay. From one of the many small hotels, some of which have hot-spring mineral baths piped in, you can easily walk to all the historical sites and shops.

Your starting point in the business area should be the new **Kagoshima Prefectural Museum**, or Reimeikan (¥260); 9 A.M.– 5 P.M.; closed Mon.), which traces the area's history over the past 40,000 years through a series of impressive exhibits. The influence of volcanoes on the local character, and the Satsuma people's foresight in adopting Western technology before it became a national policy, are well outlined. The museum sits on the site of Tsurumaru Castle.

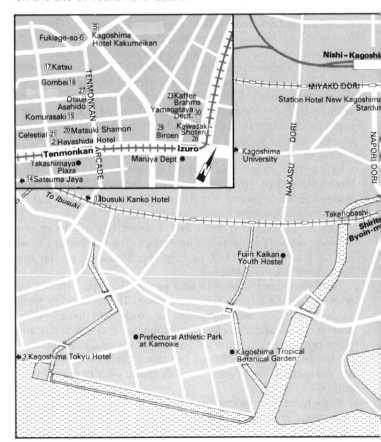

The city is rich with memorials to local leaders in the form of Shinto shrines or statues. At the base of Shiroyama near Reimeikan is **Terukuni Shrine**, dedicated to Shimazu Nariakira, the enlightened lord who gets the credit for introducing Western technology. Down the street is a statue of Saigo Takamori displaying his famed ferocity. A bust commemorating St. Francis Xavier's landing and a church built on the 400th anniversary of the event stand at **Xavier Park** near Takamibara streetcar stop. Yet another statue in front of Nishi-Kagoshima Station commemorates the seventeen young Satsuma men who

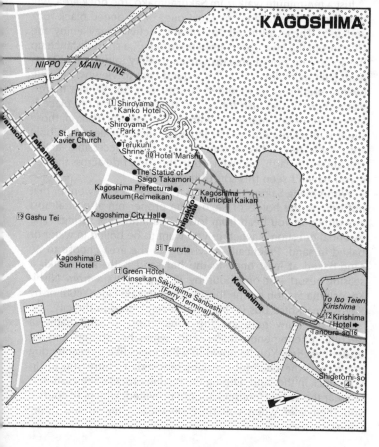

traveled to England in 1865 to learn foreign languages and Western technology under the bequest of the Shimazus, who ignored the shogun and smuggled the men out of the country.

Sakurajima, the city's soul, can be reached in just thirteen minutes by frequent ferry services (¥100) from Sakurajima Sanbashi (pier), near Kagoshima Station. Once an island, the volcano is now connected to the peninsula across from Kagoshima, thanks to a 1914 eruption which shot hot lava down the eastern flank of the mountainside, filling in the narrow isthmus.

Just a ten-minute walk from Sakurajimako, the dock area, will bring you to the lava fields, great piles of hardened black rock and ash. Those addicted to volcanic activity may enjoy the views from the lava observatory (*tempodai*), a short distance up the south side from **Furusato Onsen** (twenty minutes by JR bus from Sakurajimako, ¥270). It's a good spot to view what some twenty eruptions in recorded history can do. Where there's water there is also lush foliage on this island, and the place is famous for its tiny mandarin oranges and gigantic *daikon*, those super-size white radishes the Japanese slice, pickle, and nibble with their rice. This is one of the more accessible active volcanoes on earth, and well worth the short ride across the bay if you haven't seen this sort of thing before.

With boiling Sakurajima setting the pace, it's no wonder that not only in the hotels of Kagoshima proper but also in almost any direction you head from town, you'll find hot springs. The essential question is whether you want to be boiled in water or baked in sand. Practically all visitors to the area choose to be sand-baked at least once in the hot sand baths at Ibusuki, a seaside resort just one hour by JR express train from Nishi-Kagoshima Station on the Ibusuki-Makurazaki Line (¥800) or by Kagoshima Kotsu Bus (¥780) from several stops in the city.

The big draw here are the *sunamushi*, or sand baths, a peculiar phenomenon that occurs when hot springs emerge under beaches. You lie down in what looks like a recently dug grave, and the cheerful assistant proceeds to bury you up to your neck in the sand. During the baking process, the custom is to wear the *yukata* (cotton kimono) provided, which, of course, you shed later when you rinse off those clinging and pesky grains.

There are *sunamushi* along the beach at all major hotels. Try the Kairakuen Hotel, or the indoor sand bath immediately adjacent to the **Ibusuki Kanko Hotel**'s famous jungle bath. The latter hotel is a self-contained resort, often bustling with honeymoon couples dressed in matching clothes and even featuring a Hawaiian hula show. If you can stand all the razzle-dazzle, this is a good place to watch the Japanese enjoying themselves.

The jungle bath and *sunamushi* can be visited separately, in case you're not a guest at the hotel (¥620). The bath spreads out under the tropical plants with some fifteen different pools in various sizes and fruit shapes—all of it glassed in against the winter chill. A sybarite's paradise, and men and women bathe together here.

If just plain old being boiled suffices, the place to head for from Kagoshima is **Kirishima-Yaku National Park**. It can be reached in just fifty minutes by taking the limited express on the JR Nippo Main Line from either Kagoshima or Nishi-Kagoshima station to Kirishima Jingu Station (¥1,420, unreserved seat), the southern gateway to the park. Or take one of the Hayashida Sangyo buses from Nishi-Kagoshima Station and other major points in the city directly to the major hotels in the park (about an hour and thirty minutes), or to Ebino Kogen, a mountain plateau (1,200 meters above sea level) situated handsomely below Karakuni-dake, the highest of the twenty-three peaks that make up the Kirishima Range, in about two hours (¥1,500).

There are few old inns in this park. Instead, each big hotel, usually a high-rise, hangs by itself along the highway up the mountainside. At all these places there are baths the size of football fields, and lest you forget, for the Japanese, the bath is the main reason for checking in. **Kirishima Hotel's bath** at Iodani, for example, is deep enough for swimming—a fountain shoots right up to the vaulted glass ceiling, and smaller pools are set amid the bougainvillea and boulders for the more intimately inclined.

More rugged types may prefer **Ebino Kogen**, Japan's highest hot spring. The facilities are simpler here and spread out in virgin forests with an air reminiscent of the American West. It's the sort of place a horse would enjoy being hitched. It's also a convenient base for hiking up **Karakuni-dake** for fine views of Kagoshima Bay and Sakurajima on a clear day, or of several lakes which have formed in the craters surrounding the peak. Ebino Kogen offers some of the most breathable air in the country, especially during the summer months when the lowlands swelter.

Kirishima Jingu, a Shinto shrine connected with the imperial family, sits imposingly in a grove of old cedar trees about fifteen minutes by bus uphill from the JR Kirishima Jingu Station. The object of worship here is Ninigi-no-Mikoto, a descendant of Amaterasu who, according to legend, formed the Japanese islands. The sun goddess, Amaterasu, is believed to have descended on **Mt. Takachiho**, at the base of which the shrine sits. The present simple structure with elaborate carvings in brilliant colors dates from 1715 and was built by one of the Shimazu feudal lords. But the shrine's origins date back some 1,400 years. Mt. Takachiho, a still-active volcano, can be climbed in about ninety minutes from Takachihogawara, a ten-minute bus ride from the shrine. It is the easternmost peak in the Kirishima Range.

With more time on your hands—and more time is recommended—it's wise to venture farther beyond Kagoshima and its nearby hot-spring resorts to observe life in one of Japan's most isolated regions. The whole peninsula south of the city is breathtakingly scenic. A mountain range covered with bamboo and camphor trees winds from north to south down the peninsula. **Mt. Kaimon**, known as the Mt. Fuji of Satsuma because of its perfect conical shape, dominates the view south from Ibusuki. Beyond Makurazaki to the west is a coastline rivaling California's Big Sur.

The two most worthwhile stops on the peninsula are Chiran, a small village famous for its row of samurai houses, some of which are open to the public, and Bonotsu, once Japan's chief gateway to China, now a sleepy fishing village.

Chiran is obviously a long way from the old capital of Kyoto. But the samurai who resided here were cultivated men of taste. Their Kyoto sojourns are reflected in the rock gardens of some of the homes. This is a perfect spot to contemplate what happens when sophisticated sensibilities reach deep into the provinces. The village is reached by Yamagataya Bus in about an hour and eighteen minutes (¥820) from Kagoshima. The Yamagataya company, which operates buses throughout the Satsuma Peninsula, has its main city terminal adjacent to the Yamagataya department store, a Kagoshima landmark. The bus makes several stops at convenient points in Kagoshima before going to Chiran.

Chiran can be made a stopover en route to Makurazaki, the chief town in the southwest corner of the peninsula and a transfer point for the short twenty-minute bus ride (also Yamagataya) to Bonotsu. These buses make easy connections with trains from Kagoshima or Ibusuki, or direct Yamagataya buses from Kagoshima.

Bonotsu's charm lies in its lovely setting on steep hills rising like the sides of a bowl above a circular bay. This is every foreigner's dream of an idyllic Japanese fishing village, and it was no accident that James Bond film producers chose the spot as a location for *You Only Live Twice*.

Although today Bonotsu sleeps, a lot happened here, and the small **Bonotsu Historic Folklore Museum** (¥210), which sits on the edge of the hamlet, suggests a few of the past events. This was Japan's chief port for Tang dynasty China in the eighth century when the Chinese influence was strong. It was through this area that the famous Chinese Buddhist priest Ganjin (Chien Chen) first set foot in Japan in 753 en route to Nara, which was then capital of Japan, where he founded the Japanese Ritsu sect of the religion with its headquarters at Toshodaiji.

For the next thousand years Bonotsu prospered as the coun-

Cape Sata

Sakurajima *daikon*

try's main port, actively trading with Southeast Asia. This was the harbor through which the luxurious foreign goods destined for Kyoto passed. When Nagasaki was made the official foreign port by the Tokugawa government in 1635, Bonotsu lost its legal license to trade. But it didn't lose its status entirely, as the Shimazus used it as a gateway for illegal smuggling throughout the Edo period.

At **Kurahama-so**, now a *minshuku*, you can still see the second-floor room in which the occupants could hide and observe when one of the shogun's spies happened on the place. This 150-year-old house is the town's oldest, and its septuagenarian grandma owner delights in telling her guests about it (¥5,500, including dinner and breakfast, located right on the waterfront, although there is no view of the harbor from the rooms; ☎[09936]7-0073).

Kagoshima and environs are linked to Southeast Asian cities by direct JAL flights, making it an easy stopover point if you're continuing your journey south from Japan, or entry point, if that's where you're coming from.

The city operates tourist offices in front of both Kagoshima and Nishi-Kagoshima stations that will provide literature and maps in English, as well as advise you about hotels, inns, and local transportation.

KAGOSHIMA SLEEPING

[1] **Shiroyama Kanko Hotel** 城山観光ホテル 41-1 Shinshoin, ☎(0992)24-2211. The city's best, perched atop the hill behind the downtown area where a castle once sat, for fine views of the sea and Sakurajima. Swimming pool. ¥7,000–¥20,000.

[2] **Hayashida Hotel** 林田ホテル 12-22 Higashi Sengokucho, ☎(0992)24-4111. Sleek and modern, right in the heart of the business and shopping district. Built around a tall, plant-filled atrium with piped-in bird calls

that also serves as a restaurant and cabaret. Singles ¥6,300, twins ¥11,500.

3 **Kagoshima Tokyu Hotel** 鹿児島東急ホテル 22-1 Kamoike Shinmachi, ☎(0992)57-2411. One of a chain of business hotels, this one in a quiet location overlooking the bay. Swimming pool. Away from the center. Singles ¥6,800, twins from ¥12,500.

4 **Shigetomi-so** 重富荘 31-7 Shimizucho, ☎(0992)47-3155. Once a villa for the Shimazu lords out by Iso Teien, and the classiest Japanese inn in town. Features a Japanese-style barbecue in the evenings known as *okaribayaki*. From ¥15,000 with two meals.

5 **Kagoshima Hotel Kakumeikan** 鹿児島ホテル鶴鳴館 5-30 Shiroyamacho, ☎(0992)23-2241. One of several small hotels clustered in a green area below Shiroyama, the city's castle hill, and adjacent to the business area. Single ¥10,000, twins from ¥20,000 with two meals.

6 **Fukiage-so** 吹上荘 18-15 Terukunicho, ☎(0992)24-3500. A simple Japanese-style inn in the trees below Shiroyama near Terukuni Shrine. Hot-spring bath. ¥5,000 per person, ¥6,000 with breakfast, ¥9,000 with two meals.

7 **Kagoshima Municipal Kaikan** 鹿児島県市町村自治会館 15-7 Yamashitacho, ☎(0992)26-1010. Bare-bones, no-frills accommodations for folks on the cheap. From ¥2,990 per person.

8 **Kagoshima Sun Hotel** 鹿児島サンホテル 19-14 Horiecho, ☎(0992)25-5511. Another chain operation with no attempt at luxuries. Handy location between downtown and harbor. Singles from ¥4,675, twins from ¥8,240.

9 **Station Hotel New Kagoshima** ステーションホテルニュー鹿児島 6-5 Chuocho, ☎(0992)53-5353. Handy location just in front of Nishi-Kagoshima Station. Singles from ¥5,500, twins from ¥8,000.

10 **Hotel Manshu** ホテル満秀 4-24 Shiroyamacho, ☎(0992)24-1451. Small business hotel with either Japanese or Western rooms in quiet location between business district and Shiroyama. Hot-spring bath in the basement. Singles from ¥4,400, twins from ¥8,000.

11 **Green Hotel Kinseikan** グリーンホテル錦生館 11-4 Izumocho, ☎(0992)25-2525. On the waterfront near Sakurajima Sanbashi for ferries to Sakurajima, with views of the volcano. Hot-spring bath. ¥4,700–¥8,800.

12 **Kirishima Hotel** 霧島ホテル 3948 Takachiho, Makizonocho, Aira, Kagoshima-ken, ☎(09957)8-2121. Your best bet in this mountain resort, if for no other reason than its exotic tropical bath. The name of the bus stop at the bottom of the hill is Iodani for buses from Kagoshima. From ¥12,000, including dinner and breakfast.

13 **Ibusuki Kanko Hotel** 指宿観光ホテル Junicho, Ibusuki-shi, Kagoshima-ken, ☎(09932)2-2131. Lots of hokum in this famous resort hotel with fruit-shaped hot-spring baths in a jungle under glass, steaming sand to

climb in, and hula girls imported from Hawaii. But it's fun to watch the natives going tropical. ¥11,000–¥20,000, including dinner and breakfast, not to mention all the entertainment.

KAGOSHIMA EATS AND DRINKS

14 **Satsuma Jaya** さつま茶屋 山之口町1 ☎(0992)22-0500
An inexpensive place to try local specialities, including *kibinago sashimi* (raw slivers of silverfish you dip in a *miso* sauce), *tonkotsu* (boiled pork rib flavored with ginger), *satsuma-age* (deep-fried fish sausage), and *sakezushi* (slivers of a variety of fish over rice flavored with saké). Drinking is the emphasis, with the usual beer, saké, or the area's own *shochu* made from sweet potatoes. A large room decorated with local folk art on the second floor of a commercial building. Average about ¥2,500 per person. 5:30 P.M.–2 A.M., Sat. to 3 A.M., Sun. to midnight.

15 **Komurasaki** こむらさき 東千石町11 ☎(0992)22-5707
Convenient business center location for Kagoshima's own Satsuma *ramen*, the local version of that ever-popular Chinese noodle dish. ¥700.

16 **Tanoura-so** 田之浦荘 清水町30 ☎(0992)47-1567
Mizutaki, a kind of chicken stew, is the specialty of this old-style restaurant. From ¥2,800.

17 **Katsu** 活 東千石町6-5 ☎(0992)24-1037
One of Kagoshima's best *kushi-age* shops—deep-fried meat and vegetables on a stick. Lunch from ¥700, dinner about ¥2,500. 11:30 A.M.–2 P.M., 5:30–10 P.M., closed Mon.

18 **Gombei** 権兵衛 東千石町8 ☎(0992)22-3867
An unpretentious little place serving tasty *yudofu* (boiled tofu). Nice for cold winter nights. From ¥1,500.

19 **Gashu Tei** 雅集亭 樋之口町10 ☎(0992)23-3717
The locals flock to this small restaurant for good Chinese food at around ¥3,000 per person.

20 **Matsuki Shamon** まつきしゃもん 東千石町12 ☎(0992)24-4487
Famous for not-so-famous *wappa meshi*, tender chunks of chicken and fish placed over a bamboo container of rice, then steamed. From ¥1,000.

21 **Celestial** セレスティアル 東千石町12–22 林田ホテル内 ☎(0992)24-4111
Just beside the Hayashida Hotel's glassed-in third-floor atrium jungle. For atmosphere hard to find in Japan. Filipino bands sometimes play amid the greenery. You have a better chance of finding the Western cocktail of your choice here than anyplace in town. ¥3,000 average.

22 **Stardust** スターダスト 中央町6-5 ニューカゴシマホテル内 ☎(0992)54-5527
Live bands draw steady crowds to this room atop the New Kagoshima

Hotel across the street from Nishi-Kagoshima Station. ¥2,000–¥4,000.

23 Kaffee Brahms コーヒー ブラームス 中町7-9 シゲノビル2F ☎(0992)24-5272

Kagoshima's best coffee, with classical music and a statue of Venus in the corner. ¥400.

KAGOSHIMA SHOPPING

Satsuma porcelains, glazed white and finely crackled, with designs painted over in a wide variety of styles and colors, are one of the more famous of Japanese ceramics outside Japan, since much of it was shipped abroad. But there is also a black variety which may appeal to simpler tastes. The Kagoshima area's other famous products include *oshima pongee*, a lightweight, durable silk in muted colors; *yaku* cedar carvings and furniture; and bamboo products. The latter two items are naturals in a region rich with cedar and bamboo forests. The shops are concentrated on or near the city's shopping arcade known as Tenmonkan, a stop for all streetcar and bus lines.

27 Otsuji Asahido 大辻朝日堂 東千石町8

The biggest selection of Satsuma pots in town in a handy location right on the Tenmonkan arcade. ¥500 and up, up, up.

28 Kawasaki Shoten 川崎商店 城山町2-11-3

Kagoshima Prefecture is Japan's biggest producer of bamboo products, and this shop has a wide variety of baskets, mats, vases, etc., made from the wood.

29 Biroen 美老園 中町5-2

The green tea grown around Kagoshima is among the best in Japan, and this is the place to buy. Ask for *Satsuma homare*. A nice gift for a Japanese connoisseur.

30 Yamagataya 山形屋デパート 金生町3-1

Kagoshima's Macy's, with a gift shop featuring local products on the main floor facing the arcade in the rear.

31 Tsuruta 鶴田 小野町491

Interesting for the lover of simple Asian ceramics. Mostly old things, including sizable rain jars from Thailand and crude white porcelains from China.

187

SENDAI

仙 台

NORTHERN GATEWAY

There was a time when Sendai seemed like the end of the world to Kanto and Kansai residents, let alone foreign visitors. Now the city can be reached in two hours from Ueno Station, by the Tohoku Shinkansen "Yamabiko" (¥11,090), making this attractive city and its nearby Matsushima seascapes, mountain scenery, and historic spots at last easily accessible.

This is the Tohoku region's capital—the place where people from northern Honshu come to shop, do business, and be entertained. It's also an important educational center, seat of Tohoku University. Around the station it looks like all Japanese cities of similar size (population about 600,000). But unlike many other Japanese cities that were firebombed during the war, Sendai has made some effort to beautify, at least in the city center. Aoba Dori, Hirose Dori, and Jozenji Dori—three main avenues between the station and the Hirosegawa River—are tree-lined parkways spreading a canopy of green leaves over the passersby.

The greenery, if not always on the streets, is never far away. A high, thickly wooded ridge—site of the former Aoba castle—dominates to the west beyond the river. From some spots in the city, higher mountains can be seen to the south, west, and north. On a clear day you can see Matsushima Bay's pine-clad islets to the east from the city's high points.

Sendai is another *jokamachi* (castle town)—this one once dominated by one of Japan's most powerful feudal lords during the early Tokugawa period, Date (pronounced dah-tay)

Masamune. The Date clan traces its origins way back to the twelfth century, but they remained small-time until the ninth lord Masamune had the good sense to side with Toyotomi Hideyoshi and Tokugawa Ieyasu, the shogun for whom the Tokugawa period is named. As a reward for his help in battle, Ieyasu gave Date permission to build a fine castle. Masamune finally chose Aobayama, a steep hill above the Hirosegawa River in Sendai, as the site.

Relations with Ieyasu were strained thereafter. Like Maeda in Kanazawa, Date was an outside lord. Ieyasu was forever suspicious of him, as his fief was far from Edo and impossible to control. The policy of permitting powerful outside *daimyo* to build fine castles was calculated to keep them poor. The lords were also required to keep grand estates in Edo, where their wives and first sons were forced to live. Should the outside lords start an uprising, their families would be held in Edo as hostages.

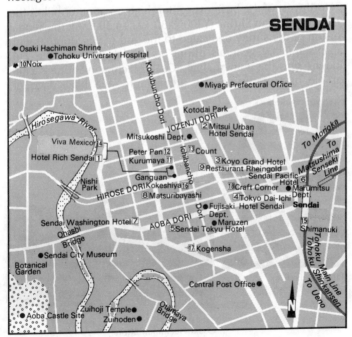

Practically every famous spot in Sendai and nearby Matsushima is connected with the Date clan. **Aoba Castle** is gone, destroyed by Meiji forces in 1875, but visitors still climb Aobayama to see the remaining stone walls and a statue of Masamune on horseback, and to get a fine view of the city and the Pacific Ocean. Masamune looks out over Sendai with his good left eye: He lost the use of his right eye as the result of childhood smallpox.

Below Aobayama, on a small hill called Kyogamine, Masamune, along with Tadamune and Tsudamune, who followed him, is buried. Each has his own small mausoleum, with Masamune's, known as **Zuihoden** (¥515; 9 A.M.–4 P.M.), being the most elaborate. The original was destroyed in the air raids of World War II. An elaborate replica, the brilliant gold metalwork and brightly colored bas-reliefs decorating the roof beams contrasting sharply with the black lacquer walls, now stands on the site.

Northwest of the business center, high on another hill, is the **Osaki Hachiman Shrine** (¥300; 9:30 A.M.–4:30 P.M.), the Sendai version of the shrine dedicated to the god of war popular with Japan's military generals during its feudal era. Like the Zuihoden—only this is an original—Osaki Hachiman Shrine is a fine sample of Momoyama-style architecture—the black lacquer,

Tanabata Festival

Osaki Hachiman Shrine

faded gold, and bright red, green, and blue reminiscent of the Tokugawa mausoleums at Nikko.

Not far from Osaki Hachiman Shrine on Kitayama ("North Mountain") is **Rinnoji**, Sendai's finest Buddhist temple. It was rebuilt to commemorate the 250th anniversary of the death of the wife of an early Date leader after being destroyed by a fire in 1691. Today only the Nio gate dates from the period. The temple boasts one of the finest stroll gardens in northern Japan, which you enter at the right side of the main hall by a turnstile after depositing ¥200. There's something special here in every season—azaleas and peonies in May, irises in June, maple leaves in October, and pines draped in snow in the winter.

Since the city was badly damaged in the war, Sendai is essentially new. If the names of the department stores and specialty shops look familiar, it's because many of them are from Tokyo. What to look for in Sendai are Tohoku's wooden **kokeshi** dolls—mere wooden cylinders with round heads—made in a number of different villages in the region. Experts can tell in which village the *kokeshi* were made by their shape and painted decorations. Some of the shops specializing in *kokeshi* are listed at the end of this section. Marumitsu department store in front of Sendai Station also has a good selection on its first floor.

Kotodai Park, just a few steps from the city's shopping area and in the shadow of the city and prefectural offices, is a popular gathering place for lunchtime brown-baggers and families on weekends. Visitors with more time will want to stroll through **Nishi (West) Park**, just west of the business district and affording fine views out over the Hirosegawa River gorge and up to Aobayama.

Sendai's night town is **Kokubuncho**, and a bustling spot it is after the sun sets. Along Kokubuncho Dori and its side streets are the snack bars, cabarets, coffee shops, and restaurants common to all Japanese cities. Some of the more characteristic places with Tohoku flavor—generally more wild and woolly than in other parts of the country—are listed below. When you've had your last drink, buy an ear of corn brushed with soy sauce and roasted over a charcoal fire off the back of one of the trucks that line the street.

The Sendai environs' prime attraction is **Matsushima Bay**, dotted with tiny islands to which fine specimens of wind-gnarled Japanese red pine cling. Considered by the Japanese to be one of the country's three grand scenic spots, this is relatively unspoiled Japan. **Matsushima Kaigan**, the resort center of the area, has so far been spared the ugly concrete buildings that blight the average resort area. You can spend a delightful day here viewing the little islands from both the surrounding well-maintained shoreline and from the deck of the sightseeing boats that navigate the waters.

Godaido, a tiny temple on an island just offshore and reached by two short bridges, is practically a symbol of Matsushima, and one of the many spots around the seawalk offering views across the water. **Kanrantei** ("Wave-Viewing Pavilion"), a teahouse originally built for Toyotomi Hideyoshi's Fushimi Castle (parts of which you can see in Kyoto), then given to Date Masamune and moved to his Edo home and finally moved to Matsushima by Tadamune, sits on a rocky cliff above the sea. It's another example of Momoyama-period architecture, and may be the largest teahouse surviving from the period (¥200; Apr.–Oct., 8:30 A.M.–5 P.M.; Nov.–Mar., 8:30 A.M.–4:30 P.M.).

Zuiganji has several buildings which are also typical of the flamboyant Momoyama period, four of them "National Treasures." Originally a temple of the Buddhist Tendai sect that played a role in much of Kyoto's history, it has been a monastery of the Zen Rinzai sect for the past seven centuries. Date Masamune had the temple rebuilt at the beginning of the seventeenth century. In addition to the handsome buildings themselves, in the Main Hall (Hondo) there are also some fine paintings on sliding doors by popular Kano-school painters of the Tokugawa period. In front of the Main Hall are two plum trees—one with pink and the other with white blossoms in late February and early March—brought by Hideyoshi, Maeda, and Date from Korea in 1592 after the unsuccessful campaign to capture that country (¥500; Apr.–Sept., 8:30 A.M.–4:30 P.M.; Nov.–Mar., 8 A.M.–4 P.M.).

Two small islands at either end of the town's seawalk—**Oshima** to the south and **Fukurajima** to the east of Godaido—are reached from the mainland by footbridges and offer more viewing possibilities. Years ago the Japanese, with their passion for organizing and naming every natural sight, decreed four

choice vantage points from which to gaze in wonder at Matsushima Bay. They are Tomiyama's **Daigyoji Temple**, **Otakamori** on Miyato Island, **Tamonzan** on Cape Yogasaki, and—
closest to Matsushima Kaigan—**Ogidani**.

Daigyoji is a ten-minute walk from Rikuzen-Tomiyama Station, just ten minutes east of Matsushima Kaigan by JR's Senseki
Line; Otakamori is reached by boat in about one hour from
either Matsushima Kaigan or Shiogama, Sendai's port; you get
to Tamonzan by boat from Shiogama harbor near Hon-
Shiogama Station on JR's Senseki Line; Ogidani is just a ten-
minute bus ride or a twenty-five-minute walk from Matsushima
Kaigan.

A boat ride is recommended for a look at the islands farther
offshore. There are a number of small sightseeing boats seating
from six to fifteen people which offer fifteen-, thirty-, or sixty-
minute pleasure cruises in the immediate vicinity. The larger
Marubun Matsushima Kissen or Matsushima Wan Kanko Kisen
ferries offer one-hour services between Matsushima Kaigan and
Shiogama.

The ferry is recommended at least one-way between the two
towns as an alternative to the train and a chance to see some of
the islands not easily seen from the mainland. The boats operate
regularly between 8 A.M. and 4:00 P.M. from both harbors
(¥1,400 one-way). Tickets are available from a booth outside
Matsushima Kaigan Station or from the individual companies on
the town's seawalk.

If you want to stay in one of the Japanese-style inns in the
area, you can make arrangements at the accommodations desk
outside Matsushima Kaigan Station. Just tell them, or write, the
price you want to pay, and they'll do the searching by
telephone.

Should you find it difficult to leave pretty Matsushima Kaigan,
venture farther east to **Ojika** ("Big Deer") **Peninsula** and
Kinkazan Island at its tip for more of this choice section of
Japan's coastline. There's a toll road over Ojika's mountainous
spine, or a slower prefectural road which hugs the coast above
coves bobbing with small fishing boats all the way down to
Ayukawa village. From Ayukawa it's just a twenty-five-minute
Suzuyoshi Kisen ferry ride (¥780) around the tip of the peninsula
to Kinkazan, an unspoiled mountaintop rising out of the sea. No

193

cars are allowed here, and deer and monkeys roam free. Koganeyama Shrine sits on one side of the mountain and offers sparse but low-priced accommodations.

Ayukawa is best reached by Miyagi Kotsu Bus from Ishinomaki Station, a forty-five-minute ride on JR's Senseki Line from Matsushima Kaigan Station (¥470). There are seven buses per day between 6:55 A.M. and 5:45 P.M., and the trip takes an hour and forty-five minutes and costs ¥1,430.

The tiny village of **Tsukinoura** on Ojika is the site of one of the more peculiar chapters in Japan's history. On September 15, 1613, one Hasekura Rokuemon Tsunenaga, accompanied by several foreign Catholic priests, a Spaniard, 180 Japanese sailors, and some merchants, set sail from the port in a small galleon named the *San Juan Baptista* for Mexico, Spain, and ultimately Rome to visit Pope Paul V under orders from Date Masamune and with the permission of Tokugawa Ieyasu.

Why the voyage was risked remains a mystery. Masamune appeared to have some interest in Christianity, but most historians believe the adventurous journey was made in the interest of establishing trade. Hasekura and some of his men made it to the Pope's throne—and quite a swash they cut in Europe, too—and returned to Sendai in 1620, only to discover that Tokugawa attitudes toward both Christianity and foreign trade had taken a decidedly negative turn.

Tohoku's most glittering man-made wonder is the celebrated **Konjikido** (Golden Hall) (8 A.M.–5 P.M., Nov.–Mar. 8:30 A.M.– 4:30 P.M.) of **Chusonji Temple** in **Hiraizumi**, a small farming community that was the capital of the region in the twelfth century under the Fujiwara family.

Just seventeen feet square in size, the tiny hall was originally coated with black lacquer and plated with gold panned from nearby rivers. The interior contains three gold altars under which are the remains of the Fujiwara leaders Kiyohira, Motohira, and Hidehira. The main pillars are lacquered and inlaid with mother-of-pearl.

Konjikido has been restored in recent years and now dazzles the eye more than ever, though you'll have to content yourself with peeking at it through a plate-glass window. The mausoleum is protected inside a concrete building. The ¥500 admission fee also entitles you to see the treasures, including three

large images of Buddha, inside the Sankozo, just below the Kon-jikido, and the Kyozo (Sutra Hall), a twelfth-century structure just above it. Adjacent to these buildings is one of the few remaining outdoor Noh stages in all Japan, and it's still used for performances.

All these buildings are part of a temple complex known as Chusonji, buried among ancient cedar trees on a steep hill above the surrounding rice paddies. Japan's great seventeenth-century haiku poet Basho paused here during his travels to the north, and you can have a cup of powdered green tea and a sweet-bean cake on the spot where he stopped. Basho's prose-poetry account of his journey, *The Narrow Road to the Deep North*, has been translated into English and makes a fine travel companion while touring Tohoku (see Helpful Reading).

Reflecting on the Fujiwara family's past glory, Basho wrote:

> When a country is defeated, there remain only mountains and rivers, and on a ruined castle in spring only grasses thrive. I sat down on my hat and wept bitterly till I almost forgot time.

> A thicket of summer grass
> Is all that remains
> Of the dreams and ambitions
> Of ancient warriors.

While in Hiraizumi, one more temple is worth your time. It's called **Motsuji** (¥500, 8 A.M.–6 P.M., Sept.–April closes earlier), and although nothing but mounds remain where temple buildings once stood, a fine garden, brilliant with iris in late May and surrounding a sizable pond, offers a chance to see one of the few remaining pleasure spots of the elite from the eleventh century in Japan. The nobles used to ride in small boats on the lake, replicas of which are anchored midpond. The museum holds objects from the Fujiwara family's collection—lacquerware, ironware, and some scrolls. Admission to the temple grounds and museum is ¥500.

It is just two hours from Sendai on the Tohoku Main Line to Hiraizumi Station with a change at Ichinoseki (¥1,590), or you can take the Tohoku Shinkansen "Yamabiko" to Ichinoseki (¥3,840, about thirty minutes), then an Iwate-ken Kotsu Bus direct to Chusonji (¥320, twenty-six minutes).

While in the area, for a greater sampling of the peaceful country scenery, take another Iwate-ken Kotsu Bus from Ichinoseki Station to **Geibikei Gorge** (¥450, twenty-two minutes). From the bus stop, walk downhill along the banks of the Satetsugawa River a few minutes to the Geibikei Kanko Center, which operates a pleasant one-hour-and-thirty-minute cruise in a flat-bottomed boat up the river and back through a magnificent gorge of granite cliffs. Passengers slip off their shoes after entering the craft, then sit on grass mats on the boat's bottom. The boat stops briefly and passengers alight for a quick look at the gorge's farther reaches on foot, then return in the same boat, serenaded by the oarsman. Departures at 10 A.M., 12, and 2 P.M.; ¥1,030. Very special.

Matsushima and Chusonji are the must-see attractions of Tohoku. Those with more time will no doubt want to ex-

Kokeshi dolls

Takinoyu public bath

perience at least one of the many hot springs (*onsen*) in the region. The *onsen* here have not completely escaped the tacky development that's spoiled most mountain resorts since World War II, but there is a better chance of finding the hot spring of your dreams in Tohoku than in any other part of the country. Mixed bathing is also more common here than in any other region; albeit no Japanese woman under sixty would think of crawling into a tub with a bunch of strange men. Voyeurs be warned.

The hot-spring village of **Narugo** might be your perfect choice. The town hasn't escaped modern intrusions, including a few high-rise eyesores, but there are plenty of small inns here proud of their past and determined to maintain the old traditions. Yusaya (☎[02298]3-2565) has just seventeen rooms and prides itself on offering cuisine typical of the region. It costs from ¥12,000 per person with two meals. Owner Masanobu Yusa, who traces his family of innkeepers back some 400 years, speaks English and is pleased to entertain foreign guests with tales of the area.

Just beside Yusaya is the village's public bath, **Takinoyu**, where for ¥100 you can relax in a cypress tub filled with milky sulphurous water which drips from a log connected to a spring outside. The bath's high roof is open to the outdoors under the eaves. People have been bathing on the spot since the year 837.

Like many *onsen* in the Tohoku area, Narugo is also famous for the *kokeshi* dolls there. Some seventy craftsmen are still at work, and a few of them ply their trade in the windows of the shops along the streets. Narugo *kokeshi* are distinguished by their concave bodies, red flower designs, and a head that squeaks when it turns. The sound resembles the cry of a small bird (in Japanese, *narugo*). At the **Nippon Kokeshi Kan** (¥300; Apr.–Dec. 15, 8:30 A.M.–5 P.M.), some 3,000 *kokeshi* from all over Japan are displayed.

The nearby village of **Iwadeyama** was home to Date Masamune for a few years before he built Aoba Castle at Sendai. Predictably, the castle is gone, but the hill on which it sat is still there, and from the park on top there is a fine view of the rice paddies and mountains beyond. Just below the hill is a classic seventeenth-century home built originally as temporary quarters for Masamune's fourth son, Muneyasu, after the castle on the hill burned down in 1663. When a new castle was built, the home became a school used by the children of the lord's retainers to study Chinese classics. It's called **Yubikan**, and you can still visit the home and a handsome stroll garden added at the beginning of the eighteenth century (¥200). The thatched-roof house is the oldest of its type in the country and offers great tranquillity, if you can escape the groups of schoolchildren who descend on it regularly. Iwadeyama is also known for its bamboo basketware, a natural outcome of having a number of lush bamboo groves.

There are direct JR trains from Sendai to Iwadeyama and Narugo (¥1,590, about two hours). You can also take the Tohoku Shinkansen "Yamabiko" to Furukawa (¥1,540, fifteen minutes), then change to a local train to Iwadeyama (¥230) or Narugo (¥640, one hour). The two towns are about thirty minutes apart by train.

If you long for the Tohoku *onsen* experience and have less time on your hands, you might catch the train in Sendai for Sakunami (¥380, forty minutes), from where it's a short bus ride to **Sakunami Onsen**, site of a few hotels along a riverbank in a mountain valley. There's no public bath here. If you are not a guest at one of the inns, you might plead with the man at the front desk of Iwamatsu Ryokan (free minibus service from Sakunami Station) to let you use the inn's outdoor bath at the bottom of the ravine. If the inn is not crowded, they may let you use their *rotenburo* (outdoor bath) for a small fee. There's a bus stop in front of the inns for a Yamagata Kotsu bus back to Sendai Station (¥889; about 1 hour).

You can easily combine Sakunami with **Yamadera**, the next express train stop from Sakunami (¥310, about thirty minutes). As the name in Japanese implies, this is a mountain (*yama*) temple (*tera*), also known as Risshakuji—and what a mountain. The steps from the bottom near the station appear to go right up to Buddhist heaven, with many small temple buildings and alternate paths along the way to divert you from ever climbing all the way to the top. This temple started out in the year 860 as a northern branch of the famed Enryakuji Temple on Mt. Hiei in Kyoto, but was destroyed in the bloody fighting during the fourteenth through sixteenth centuries and was built again early in the Tokugawa period. Yamadera's most famous visitor was that inveterate traveler, the poet Basho, who stopped here in 1689 and wrote a few arresting lines about the Japanese cicada whose incessant screeching in late summer induces insomnia. To the Japanese, it's something akin to music, however. Wrote Basho:

> In the utter silence
> Of a temple,
> A cicada's voice alone
> Penetrates the rocks.

Sendai and its neighboring attractions are well outlined in an excellent English guidebook titled *In and Around Sendai*, written by three American residents (see Helpful Reading). Curiously, this book is easier to find in Tokyo's English-language bookstores than it is in Sendai. Buy it before you head north.

SENDAI SLEEPING

1 **Hotel Rich Sendai** ホテルリッチ仙台 2-2-2 Kokubuncho, ☎(0222)62-8811. Smack in the heart of swinging Kokubuncho for late-night pub crawling. Nothing fancy here, but handy. One of a chain. Singles from ¥5,600, twins from ¥12,500.

2 **Mitsui Urban Hotel Sendai** 三井アーバンホテル仙台 2-18-11 Honmachi, ☎(0222)65-3131. Another marvel of efficiency in tiny spaces, designed for those tiny businessmen. New. Overlooks pretty Kotodai Park. Singles from ¥6,000, twins from ¥12,500.

3 **Koyo Grand Hotel** 江陽グランドホテル 2-3-1 Honcho, ☎(0222)62-6311. A French *fin de siècle* interior in—Sendai? Yes, and not to be believed. Look at the lobby and decide for yourself about the rooms. Singles from ¥7,000, twins from ¥15,000.

4 **Tokyo Dai-ichi Hotel Sendai** 東京第一ホテル仙台 2-3-18 Chuo, ☎(0222)62-1355. Another business hotel, one of a chain, without any pretensions. Handy to shopping areas and the tourist spots. Singles from ¥5,800, twins from ¥12,000.

5 **Sendai Tokyu Hotel** 仙台東急ホテル 2-9-25 Ichibancho, ☎(0222)62-2411. Another chain member, but a notch above the usual business hotel in both facilities *and* prices. New, with the usual Japanese-Las Vegas-style flash. Singles from ¥9,500, twins from ¥10,500.

6 **Sendai Pacific Hotel** 仙台パシフィックホテル 1-3-12 Chuo, ☎(0222)63-6611. Practically on top of Sendai Station, so you can leap out of bed and be on a train to the area's seashore and mountains in a jiffy. Singles from ¥5,500, twins from ¥9,000.

7 **Sendai Washington Hotel** 仙台ワシントンホテル 2-3-1 Omachi, ☎(0222)22-2111. Another chain product, right on pretty Aoba Dori, handy for Nishi Park and Aobayama. Singles from ¥6,458, twins from ¥13,029.

SENDAI EATS AND DRINKS

8 **Matsuribayashi** 祭囃子 大町2-7-7 ☎(0222)64-3205
Edo-style cooking characteristic of northeastern Japan. The portions are a bit larger, the flavor stronger, with very salty *miso* soup and pickles. Better call in advance for a seat. This cozy little place a couple of blocks north of the Washington Hotel packs them in. English menu. ¥3,500–¥6,000 courses; 5–10:15 P.M.; closed Sun., holidays.

9 **Restaurant Rheingold** レストラン ラインゴールド 一番町4-2-4 ☎(0222)25-8691
The name and atmosphere—beam ceilings, red brick walls, lantern lights—lead you to believe this is a German restaurant, but the menu puts you back on the track: just more "Western-style" food. The usual spaghetti, hamburger patty, and pilaf dishes. In the evening, fish, pork, or beef courses with bread or rice, salad, and coffee for between ¥1,500 and ¥6,000. 11 A.M.–9 P.M.

10 **Noix** ノア 八幡3-9-13 ☎(0222)22-1111
A lovely room with white stucco walls, brick floors, white linen, fresh flowers, and a garden outside the front door. Spaghetti, curry rice, or pilaf dishes for lunch; cakes and coffee in the afternoon; steaks from ¥4,500 in the evening. Features the cuisine of one European country for a couple of days each month in special courses at ¥6,500. Handy place for lunch after visiting Osaki Hachiman Shrine. Lunch, ¥2,000–¥3,000; 11:30 A.M.–9 P.M. Reservations a good idea.

11 **Kurumaya** 車屋 国分町2-5-17 ☎(0222)65-1131
This Japanese restaurant, easily spotted as it has a waterwheel outside its door, is right on Kokubuncho Dori behind Hotel Rich and features inexpensive sukiyaki and *shabu shabu* from ¥2,500. 5:30–10 P.M.

12 **Peter Pan** ピーターパン 国分町2-6-1 ☎(0222)64-1742
Another third-floor room off Kokubuncho Dori. "Rock and Tea Since 1972" says the sign. Coffee or booze and recorded rock music. 2–10 P.M.

13 **Count** カウント 一番町4-5-42 ☎(0222)63-0238
The recorded jazz here practically blows the roof off this end-of-an-alley room, off the street running south from the side of Mitsukoshi department store. Owner has a huge collection of Count Basie records, hence the name. Noon–11 P.M.; closed second and third Mon.

14 **Viva Mexico** ビバ・メヒコ 国分町2 ゴロク三番館ビル ☎(0222)63-7806
A drinking spot with Mexican snacks such as tacos, enchiladas, and

chili rellenos. In the Goroku Building just behind Hotel Rich on the
fourth floor. 5 P.M.–2 A.M.

SENDAI SHOPPING

What to buy after *kokeshi*? The craft shops have other folk art from the
Tohoku area. Sendai chests (*tansu*) are considered the best in Japan,
and you can see the new ones in department stores. The old ones are
becoming scarce. *Hira* cloth wallets, made from a kind of hemp, wear
forever. The local lacquerware, deep red and durable even in dry
climates, is called *tamamushi-nuri*. Typical ceramics include *Tsutsumi-
yaki*, with a creamy underglaze plus an overglaze in a different color,
from Miyagi Prefecture; *Soma-Koma-yaki*, easy to recognize with its
prancing horse patterns, from Fukushima Prefecture; and *Hirashimizu-
yaki*, much prized for its simple tan-and-brown-spotted surfaces, from
Yamagata Prefecture.

15 **Shimanuki** しまぬき 一番町3
A wide assortment of *kokeshi*, plus other Tohoku folk art in two locations: in the Chuo Dori shopping mall near Fujisaki department store
and in the basement of S-Pal attached to Sendai Station. 9:30 A.M.–
7:30 P.M.; closed second and fourth Thurs.

16 **Ganguan Kokeshiya** 玩具庵こけし屋 国分町1-6-3
Kokeshi exclusively, and lots to pick from. Just off Kokubuncho Dori
across from "Cake and Tea Kenzo," a block south of Hotel Rich.
8 A.M.–6:30 P.M.

17 **Kogensha** 光原社 一番町1-4-10
Quality folk art from all over Japan, plus a few other Asian countries.
Two blocks south of Aoba Dori on Kokubuncho Dori. 10 A.M.–
6:30 P.M.; closed fifteenth of each month.

18 **Craft Corner** クラフトコーナー 中央2-4-8
More folk art, but some trendy, modern crafts here as well. On Chuo
Dori shopping mall behind Daiei department store. 10:15 A.M.–
6:45 P.M.; closed Thurs.

SAPPORO

札 幌

THE ORIENTAL KANSAS CITY

You notice the difference not long after you leave Chitose Airport. What Hokkaido has that Japan's other islands don't is space. Also, it has a climate like that of the northern United States or Central Europe, with vegetation to match: elm trees instead of bamboo; corn, potatoes, and dairy cows in dry fields instead of rice paddies. To an American, all this looks vaguely familiar. Maybe you're in Iowa or Vermont.

Hokkaido is Japan's last frontier. The Ainu, the island's earlier dwellers who once lived by hunting and fishing, have, like the American Indians, been all but driven out by their conquerors. What remains of them, especially around the tourist centers, is a pretty sorry sight.

The Japanese, mostly second, third, and fourth sons from Honshu's northern provinces, only began migrating to Hokkaido in any numbers during the past century. Matsumae, one of the Tokugawas' generals, set up a fortress in the port town of the same name in the early seventeenth century. Hakodate, along with four other ports, was opened to foreigners after Commodore Matthew Perry barged in to demand that Japan be opened to trade in 1853. The government moved to Sapporo in 1871, and the city has taken the lead on the island ever since.

Sapporo is an attractive city of about 1.3 million, and thanks to the influence of American advisers early in its history, it's an easy city in which to get around. The streets are laid out in the familiar grid pattern. A sparkling new subway with automated ticket turnstiles can whisk you across town either north–south or east–west over two lines which intersect at Odori, a handsome park running through the city from east to west.

Since the Winter Olympics of 1972, which brought a large number of new Western-style hotels and department stores, Sapporo has a streamlined, modern look, especially in the business district near Sapporo Station—a "Little Tokyo," the residents say. But throughout the city there are surviving Victorian frame buildings right out of a New England landscape.

Sapporo Agricultural College, now part of Hokkaido University, was founded by an American, Dr. William S. Clark, during a year's stay in Japan at the invitation of the Japanese government in 1876. His memory is much revered by the locals, and his students were so impressed by his Christian influence that they went with him on horseback as far as Shimamatsu, twenty-four kilometers south of the city, when he left the college to return to the United States. His last words, "Boys, be ambitious," are plastered all over town. A bust of Clark, also the college's first dean, is just inside the main entrance to **Hokkaido University**, which occupies Japan's largest campus and is about a ten-minute walk northwest of Sapporo Station. A must stop for young Japanese romantics is the university's "**Poplar Walk**," a dirt road lined with poplar trees next to the agriculture experimental station.

Sapporo's symbol is the **Clock Tower Building**, once the military exercise hall for the college. The white frame building with a clock tower over its main entrance is now overpowered by the nineteen-story city hall across the street.

The nearby **Old Hokkaido Prefectural Government Building**, a red-brick, many-gabled example of Victoriana, looms over two lotus ponds set in a small park crowded with munching office workers during the noon hour.

One block west is the handsome **Hokkaido University Botanical Garden** (¥360; Apr. 29–Sept. 30, 9 A.M.–4 P.M.; Oct. 1–Nov. 3, 9 A.M.–3:30 P.M.; closed Mon.), a wide expanse of lawns, old trees, azaleas, and rose gardens. The **Hoppo Minzoku Shiryoshitsu** holds a collection of Ainu handicrafts gathered by Dr. John Batchelor, an English minister who lived in Hokkaido.

Nearly 2 million visitors ignore the chill each year during the first weekend in February when Sapporo and many other cities in Hokkaido hold their **snow festivals**. In Sapporo the event takes place at two locations: Odori Park and Makomanai, a Self-Defense Forces base just in front of Jietai-mae Station on the Nanboku Subway Line. Tons of snow are brought in from the nearby mountains to build gigantic snow sculptures with a variety of themes, including Japanese fairy tales, world-famous landmarks, and cartoon characters. Hotel space is always tight, and the interested book well in advance. If you don't like crowds, come a couple of days before the actual start. The sculptures are usually completed by then.

Sapporo's **shopping district** stretches from Sapporo Station to Susukino along the wide, tree-lined Sapporo Eki-mae Dori. The merchandise is no different from what you see in Tokyo, except for the souvenir shops well stocked with grotesque Ainu-style wood carvings—lurking bears with salmon in their mouths being the most popular theme. There is also some rustic local pottery and an abundance of white chocolate made with milk from Hokkaido's prolific cows.

Stretching underneath Sapporo Eki-mae Dori between the Odori and Susukino subway stations is **Pole Town**, an underground shopping arcade providing relief during the city's nippy winters.

One of Sapporo's nicest features is its accessibility to the great outdoors. An eight-minute subway ride to Maruyama Park Sta-

Odori Park

Sapporo Bier Garten

tion will bring you to **Maruyama Park**, a virgin forest covering a perfectly round mountain. You can climb it by following a trail that starts behind the Shinto shrine at the base. There is also a zoo and a baseball stadium.

The city's closest real mountain is **Mt. Moiwa**, just a twenty-five-minute bus ride from Sapporo Station. You can reach the 531-meter summit by a cable car to an observation platform about halfway up, then by foot the rest of the way. If it's clear you can see Mts. Teine, Eniwa, and Tarumae to the west, Ishikari Bay to the north, and the lofty Daisetsu mountains in the center of Hokkaido to the east.

Nakajima Park is just south of the business district, between two rivers with a lake, another Victorian gingerbread building now used as a wedding hall, and a teahouse—one of the few hints of anything traditionally Japanese in the whole city.

Sapporo is less than an hour from some of the best skiing in all Japan, a fact made known to the world during the Winter Olympics. The **Teine Olympia Ski Grounds**, site of the alpine, bobsled, and toboggan events, is just forty-five minutes by bus. There is good skiing even closer at Mt. Moiwa and Mt. Arai, the latter being the tamest of the slopes.

Susukino is considered one of the liveliest nightlife quarters in all Japan outside Tokyo, and no man heads for Sapporo from Honshu without being ribbed by his buddies about the neighborhood's pleasures. Some 3,000 bars, cabarets, and striptease joints are crammed into this area, and the action goes on well into the early-morning hours. A tradition is to wind up the evening with a bowl of Sapporo's own *ramen*, a great bowl of Chinese-style noodles with the sauce of your choice.

Having traveled this far off the beaten tourist track on Honshu, you'll no doubt want to sample some of Hokkaido's scenic attractions, which to most people are the prime reason for going there. Lakes, smoking volcanoes, deep gorges, and rugged coastlines may be seen in the three national parks.

Shikotsu-Toya National Park between Sapporo and Hakodate is easiest to reach for the short-time visitor. A recommended route for an overall view of the park's sights is a trip by Donan or Jotetsu bus from the terminal beside Sapporo Station to **Toyako Onsen** (¥2,550), a lakeside spa at the foot of a very active volcano named Mt. Usu. The town, like most on this island, is grim, but if you cast your eyes across the lake to Naka-noshima, a mountain in its center, and beyond to Mt. Yotei, you'll be enchanted.

Another hour-and-thirty-minute Donan bus ride from Toyako will bring you to **Noboribetsu** (¥1,340), a spa famous for the variety of its mineral waters and the fact that it's one of the few places where men and women still bathe together. But don't over-anticipate. At the **Daiichi Takimoto Hotel**'s giant terraced bath (¥2,000; 7 A.M.–5 P.M.), where everyone gathers, bathing etiquette is meticulously maintained. One must keep one's little towel in its proper place—grandmas and grandpas excepted as they always are in Japan. The town itself is as unattractive as Toyako, but the gorge in which it sits is spectacularly covered

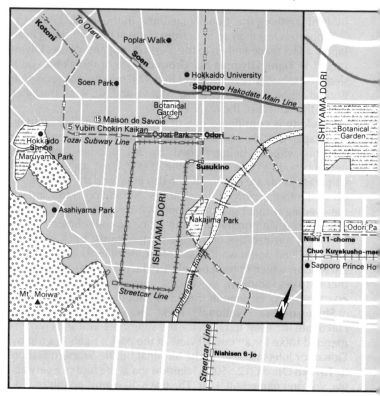

with a variety of trees. A ten-minute ride by cable car (¥1,900) will bring you to the top of Mt. Kuma, where the cable car developers have built concrete pits for 180 (count them) very smelly bears and a few thatched Ainu huts for some tourist-conscious Ainu. Incidentally, there is also a nice view of the Pacific and mountain-locked Lake Kuttara below. From Noboribetsu there are buses back to Sapporo, with a stop at Chitose Airport for those returning to Honshu.

Daisetsuzan, in Hokkaido's center, is the most spectacular of the three national parks, and the largest in Japan, encompassing five peaks over 6,500 feet. It can be reached within one hour and thirty minutes from Sapporo by express train to Asahikawa (¥3,400), then by bus (¥1,750) or hired car for another hour and

fifty minutes to **Sounkyo Onsen**, a spa in a deep canyon which serves as a gateway to the park.

Farther east, and a journey requiring several days to do it justice, is **Akan National Park**. It's not as high as Daisetsuzan, but it's equally rugged and mostly unspoiled, with dense forests and three major lakes, Kutcharo being the largest mountain lake in the country. Lake Akan boasts the *marimo*, small balls of duckweed which float on the lake's surface and which are found at only two other lakes in the world (one in Switzerland, and one on the Siberian Island of Sakhalin). The most interesting gateway to the park is **Bihoro**, a dirt-street-and-clapboard town reminiscent of the American West. North of Bihoro is **Abashiri**, a small port town open to the Okhotsk Sea with good beaches, camp sites, a botanical garden, a fine collection of Ainu artifacts in its museum, and a prison built like a European castle for the country's most dangerous criminals. The Ainu in and around Akan are still living by hunting and fishing, unlike their brothers at **Shiraoi**, which is more frequented by tourists.

If you come by train from Tokyo to Hokkaido, you'll stop first at **Hakodate**, the island's third city. Built on hills overlooking the Tsugaru Straits, it's considered one of Japan's three most beautiful cities by night (along with Kobe and Nagasaki). A cable car up **Mt. Hakodate** offers the best view. Adding to the old-fashioned Western flavor of the town is the **Japan Orthodox Resurrection Church**, a Byzantine-style edifice, the original of which was founded by a Russian prelate in 1862; and **Goryokaku**, a massive Western-style star-shaped sandstone fort built for the island's defense in 1855. At this spot the Tokugawa forces held out against the new Meiji government in 1868.

SAPPORO SLEEPING

[1] **Rich Hotel** リッチホテル Kita-Ichijo, Nishi 3-chome, Chuo-ku, ☎(011) 231-7891. Handy location in the center of town and two minutes by foot from the JAL office. Singles from ¥6,100, twins from ¥11,700.

[2] **Hotel Sun Flower Sapporo** ホテルサンフラワー札幌 Minami-Gojo, Nishi 3-chome, Chuo-ku, ☎(011)512-5533. Smack in the heart of swinging Susukino. Singles ¥6,400, twins ¥12,300.

[3] **Tokyu Inn** 東急イン Minami-Shijo, Nishi 5-chome, Chuo-ku, ☎(011) 531-0109. Also in Susukino. Singles ¥7,500, twins ¥13,700.

4 **Sapporo Washington Hotel** 札幌ワシントンホテル Kita-Shijo, Nishi 4-chome, Chuo-ku, ☎(011)251-3211. Just beside Sapporo Station. Singles from ¥7,350, twins from ¥14,690.

5 **Yubin Chokin Kaikan** 郵便貯金会館 Minami-Ichijo, Nishi 26-chome, Chuo-ku, ☎(011)642-4321. Three minutes from Maruyama Koen subway station. Singles ¥4,370, twins ¥8,470.

SAPPORO EATS AND DRINKS

6 **Sapporo Bier Garten** 札幌ビール園 ☎(011)742-1531
Somebody wisely insisted on not tearing down Sapporo Beer's original brewery. It's been fixed up like a German beer hall inside with a roaring fire for those cold winter nights, and an outdoor garden for summer guzzling. Sapporo Beer, Japan's best and the city's most famous product, never tasted better. On draught, of course. You can order a variety of snacks such as the island's own potatoes or corn. The specialty is Genghis Khan barbecue. You grill New Zealand lamb, plus a variety of vegetables, on a gas-fired grill at your table. Ask for the King Viking special—all the beer you can drink and all the Genghis Khan you can eat during a two-hour period, for ¥2,700. If you prefer seafood, always excellent on Hokkaido, ask for *dosankoyaki*—salmon, crab, and scallops, also grilled at the table (¥1,500). It's wise to make reservations to avoid a possible long wait. It's a short taxi ride from Sapporo Station. Just tell the driver ''*Biiru-en*.'' Free buses leave every thirty minutes between 6:30 and 9 P.M. from the ''Garten'' to Gobankan department store, a block from Sapporo Station. 11:30 A.M.–9 P.M.

7 **Hyosetsu-no-mon** 氷雪の門 中央区南5条西2 ☎(011)521-3046
Hokkaido's own king crab served 30 different ways is what draws the crowds to this locally famous place. Folk dances 6–8 P.M.

8 **Ezogoten** えぞ御殿 中央区南3条西6 ☎(011)241-8451
More crabs, buttered clams, squid, and buttered potatoes served amid Hokkaido farm implements. 5–11 P.M.

9 **Ramen Ryuho** ラーメン龍鳳 中央区北1条西3 (011)222-3486
There are over 300 *ramen* noodle restaurants in this city, but this one packs them in for its noodles in a *miso* sauce (*miso ramen*). From ¥550; 11 A.M.–10 P.M.; Sun., holidays, 11 A.M.–6 P.M.

10 **Ajino Sanpei** 味の三平 中央区南1条西3 大丸藤井ビル ☎(011)231-0377
This place claims to have created *miso ramen* way back in 1963. They also started the novelty of adding bean sprouts to the ingredients. 11 A.M.–7 P.M.; closed Mon.

11 **Silo** サイロ 中央区南5条西3 北専会館 ☎(011)531-5857
Ishikari nabe, a winter fish stew made with Hokkaido salmon, is the chief attraction, or try their roasted venison (*Ezo-shika*) or buttered corn (*tomorokoshi*) on a stick. 5–11 P.M.; closed Sun.

12 **Irohanihoheto** いろはにほへと 中央区南5条西4 ☎(011)521-1682
One of Susukino's most popular drinking spots for young people. Hokkaido snacks with the drinks. 5 P.M.–12:30 A.M.; Sat. till 3 A.M.

13 **Tokachi Wine Restaurant** ワインレストラン 十勝 大通西5 ☎(011)231-9360
Tokachi wine from Hokkaido may be Japan's most famous wine. The Tokachi area's own beef is also served. 11 A.M.–9 P.M., closed Sun. and holidays.

14 **Ikoi** 憩 中央区南5条西5 ☎(011)521-0918
Fishnets, pilot wheels, and a buoy or two dispel any doubt about what's offered here—broiled fish from the island's waters. 6–11:30 P.M.; closed Sun.

15 **Restaurant Maison de Savoie** レストラン メゾン・ド・サボア 中央区北1条西15 ☎(011)643-5580
T. Ohara, the owner, offers a tasty ¥2,500 French lunch of several courses, and the vegetables come from his own garden in the country. Warm, homey atmosphere with red-brick walls and modern lithographs. 12–10 P.M.; closed Mon.

16 **Sushi-Dokoro Narita** 鮨処成田 中央区大通西4 ☎(011)251-8878
Businessmen and office ladies crowd up to the counter during lunch and dinner hours for the always-fresh and inexpensive *sushi* served here. 11 A.M.–9 P.M.; closed Sun.

SAPPORO SHOPPING

17 **Seibansha** 青盤舎 中央区南7条西4
The city's best folkcraft shop, with lots of Hokkaido's local pottery, plus items from all over Japan. 10 A.M.–8 P.M.; closed Sun.

18 **Hokkaido Boeki Bussan Shinkokai** 北海道貿易物産振興会 中央区北1条西経済センタービル
All of the island's famous products on display—Ainu carvings, semi-precious stone jewelry, sealskin accessories, smoked fish, white chocolate, and dairy products. Closed Sun.

19 **Kato Butsusankan** 加藤物産館 中央区北4条西4
One of the city's biggest souvenir shops right in front of Sapporo Station.

20 **Hokkaido Mingei Center** 北海道民芸センター 中央区南2条西6
More of those gruesome bear carvings, plus a coffee shop in the basement. In Tanukikoji (Racoon Alley), a covered arcade which draws the city's students.

HELPFUL READING

A History of Japan by George Sansom; Charles E. Tuttle Co., Inc., Tokyo, 1963. The most readable history of this fascinating country. Comes in a paperback, three-volume set.

Everyday Life in Traditional Japan by Charles J. Dunn; Charles E. Tuttle Co., Inc., Tokyo, 1969. An interesting look at the lives of the four classes during the Tokugawa era.

Kyoto: A Contemplative Guide by Gouverneur Mosher; Charles E. Tuttle Co., Inc., Tokyo, 1964. Thoughtful musings about Kyoto's best.

Kanazawa: The Other Side of Japan by Ruth Stevens; Society to Introduce Kanazawa to the World, 1979. A rare thing—details in English on a Japanese provincial city. A must, if you spend any time in Kanazawa.

Roberts' Guide to Japanese Museums by Laurance P. Roberts; Kodansha International Ltd., Tokyo, 1978. Practically every museum in Japan is included, with explanations on how to find them.

Foot-loose in Tokyo by Jean Pearce; Weatherhill, Tokyo, 1976. Walking tours of the neighborhoods around every station on the Yamanote Line that circles Tokyo. Lots of fun.

Eating Cheap in Japan by Kimiko Nagasawa and Camy Condon; Shufunotomo Co., Ltd., Tokyo, 1972. As essential as your stomach, if you are eating outside the big hotels.

Earth'n'Fire by Amaury Saint-Gilles; Shufunotomo Co., Ltd., Tokyo, 1978. Japan's ceramics, kiln by kiln, from Kyushu to Hokkaido.

Kites, Crackers, and Craftsmen by Camy Condon and Kimiko Nagasawa; Shufunotomo Co., Ltd., Tokyo, 1974. Listings of 50 shops in Tokyo where things are still made by hand.

What's Japanese about Japan by John Condon and Keisuke Kurata; Shufunotomo Co., Ltd., Tokyo, 1974. An enlightening attempt to explain the rituals of Japanese life.

Japan: A Travel Survival Kit by Ian McQueen; Lonely Planet Publications, Victoria, Australia, 1981. Practical information on many out-of-the-way spots.

In and Around Sendai by Margaret Garner, James Vardaman, and Ruth Vergin; Keyaki no Machi Co., Ltd., Sendai, 1982. Informative and thorough. Covers the city as well as Matsushima, Hiraizumi, and Narugo.

The Narrow Road to the Deep North and Other Travel Sketches by Basho, translated by Nobuyuki Yuasa; Penguin Books, Harmondsworth, England, 1966. One of those pocket-size Penguin Classics.

Exploring Tohoku: A Guide to Japan's Back Country by Jan Brown with Yoko S. Kmetz; Weatherhill, Tokyo, 1982. At last a thorough guidebook in English about this rustic area.

A Guide to the Gardens of Kyoto by Marc Treib and Ron Herman; Shufunotomo Co., Ltd., Tokyo, 1980. For lovers of landscape and/or Zen aesthetics. Very thorough.

Tokyo Access by Richard Saul Wurman; Access Press, Ltd., Los Angeles, 1984. Well-designed guide for the design- and fashion-conscious.

212

Tokyo, Now and Then by Paul Waley; Weatherhill, Tokyo, 1984. Historical minutiae well written—and fun.

Discovering Shitamachi by Sumiko Enbutsu; Shitamachi Times, Ltd., 1984. Shitamachi, Tokyo's old downtown districts, deciphered for foreign comprehension.

SUBWAYS IN TOKYO

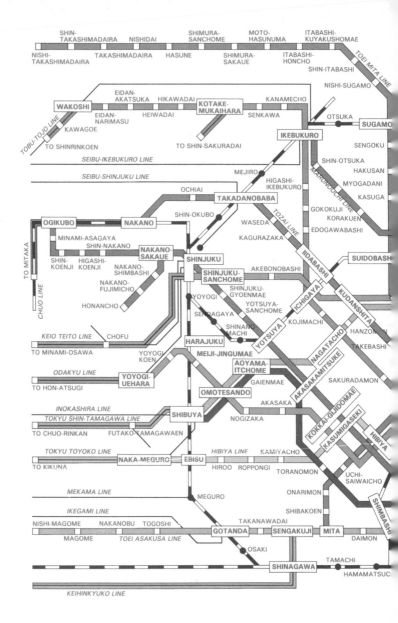